# Economics, Science and Technology

Dr Steven Payson is a Senior Science Resources Analyst with the US National Science Foundation (NSF), where he has been since 1994. He had previously worked as an Agricultural Economist for the US Department of Agriculture for three years, a Research Associate for the Inter-American Development Bank for four years, and a consultant for ICF, Incorporated for five years. Dr Payson has also been a Lecturer of Economics at Marymount University (Virginia) since 1997, and had previously taught economics at three other universities. He received a BA in Mathematics and Bio-Psychology from Wesleyan University (Connecticut) in 1979, an MSc in Economics from the London School of Economics in 1982, and a PhD in Economics from Columbia University in 1991. Since 1998, Dr Payson has served on the Advisory Board of the journal *Technological Forecasting and Social Change*. His previous writings include *Quality Measurement in Economics: New Perspectives on the Evolution of Goods and Services* (Edward Elgar, 1994), *National Patterns of R&D Resources* (NSF, 1999), and *US Corporate R&D* (with Carl Shepherd, NSF and the US Department of Commerce/Office of Technology Policy, 1999).

# Economics, Science and Technology

Steven Payson

**Edward Elgar**
Cheltenham, UK • Northampton, MA, USA

Published by
Edward Elgar Publishing Limited
Glensanda House
Montpellier Parade
Cheltenham
Glos GL50 1UA
UK

Edward Elgar Publishing, Inc.
136 West Street
Suite 202
Northampton
Massachusetts 01060
USA

A catalog record for this book
is available from the British Library

**Library of Congress Cataloging in Publication Data**

Payson, Steven, 1957–
   Economics, science and technology / Steven Payson
   Includes bibliographical references and index
      1. Economics.  2. Science and industry.  3. Technological
   innovations. I. Title.
   HB171.5.P34 2000
   330—dc21                                                     99–086197

ISBN 1 85898 672 9

Printed in the United Kingdom at the University Press, Cambridge

To Vyviahn, Mikhail, Shirley, Emanuel, and Faith

Anyone who writes a book, however gloomy its message may be, is necessarily an optimist. If the pessimists really believed what they were saying there would be no point in saying it.

*Joan Robinson (1970)*

# Contents

# List of Figures

# List of Tables

# Acknowledgments

I am indebted to the friends and colleagues who have encouraged me to take on this work and who have offered me valuable advice along the way. I owe a great deal to the late Professor Kelvin Lancaster, who supported me in many of the areas of research that led to this book. I appreciate the advice and reviews offered to me by Mary Burke, David Colander, Anne Houghton, John Jankowski, Alvin Mayes, Francis McFaul, Richard Nelson, and Larry Rausch, and I especially appreciate the thorough help I received from Harold Linstone, Carl Shepherd, and Mike Weiss. Finally, I want to thank my loving and understanding wife, Vyviahn, and my children, Mikhail, Shirley, Emanuel, and Faith for tolerating all of the time I spent away from them to finish this work.

Though most of the book contains original material, some of it contains revised sections of earlier publications. Certain pieces of Chapters 1–3 contain material that I had previously written for an article in the *Journal of Post Keynesian Economics*, entitled, 'Regardless of Philosophy, Economics Will Not Be a Science Until it is *Based* on Science'. Those pieces have been reprinted with permission from ME Sharpe, Inc., Publisher, Armonk, NY 10504.

Chapters 7 and 8 include revised sections from three previous publications: (1) Pages 96–102 from my earlier book, *Quality Measurement in Economics: New Perspectives on the Evolution of Goods and Services* (Aldershot, UK: Edward Elgar Publishing Company, 1994); (2) 'Product Evolution and the Classification of Business Interest in Scientific Advances,' *Knowledge and Policy: The International Journal of Knowledge Transfer and Utilization*, Winter 1997, 9(4), pp. 3–26; and (3) 'Quality Improvement Versus Cost Reduction: A Broader Perspective on Evolutionary Economic Change', *Technology Analysis & Strategic Management*, 1998, 10(1), pp. 69–88.

Finally, Chapter 9 is a revised version of an earlier article, 'The Difficulty of Measuring Capital, Revisited: Does Science Offer an Alternative?', *Technological Forecasting and Social Change*, 1997, 56, pp. 131–54. I appreciate permission to reprint these writings here.

# Preface

This book provides an interdisciplinary, futuristic, and critical approach to major issues involving economic thought, natural science, and technological change. It is committed to an understanding of true causal relationships, and to providing ideas that are useful for determining future areas of research, better methods of collecting and classifying data, and more effective policy decisions. I wrote this book for a wide audience of teachers, practitioners, scholars, policy analysts, and anyone else who might have a general interest in the interrelationships between economics, science, and technology. For example, I wrote it for methodological economists probing into whether economics is truly a science, microeconomists studying technological change, political analysts examining science and technology policy, industry strategists investigating patterns of technological change, scientists and engineers wondering about the economic returns to research and development, and futurists hypothesizing about upcoming technological advances.

Given such a diversity of topics, a reasonable skeptic might wonder whether a book of this kind contains 'a little of everything', and perhaps, therefore, 'a lot of nothing'. That suspicion will prove to be false. In writing this book I have taken the integration of ideas very seriously. However, it is also true that I could not thoroughly cover all of the important interrelationships that exist between economics, science and technology – there are just too many of them. In particular, I have not included many topics about science and technology that are peripheral to standard economic thought, like research program management or public policy debates on research funding. My omission of these topics is not meant to suggest that they are any less important than the topics I do cover. Their omission is simply a reflection of my interest in focusing on problems in mainstream economics, as well as my desire to write a 300 page, rather than a 600 page, volume.

As many economists already know, most economics books today, especially on topics like technological change, comprise collections of individual papers that originated as contributions for workshopshops 'invited' by organizations with vested interests in their sponsorship. These papers, which are often disjoint or even conflicting, then get renamed as chapters, and bound together in a single volume, with only the introduction and conclusion of the book devoted to making sense of the whole picture. Readers will find that my book is extremely different in this respect. It contains a single body of coordinated ideas, from a single author – the way most economics books used to be written many years ago, before the modern era of the invited conference paper.

Furthermore, unlike nearly every modern economics book on technological change (or at least every one that I know of), my book has not been sponsored by, or 'rubber-stamped' by, any institution or society. That is, no organization paid for the research and writing that led to the creation of this book. Likewise, my book has no political constituency, or scholarly constituency (other than the economics profession as a whole), and thus owes no one any favors. Instead, it reflects a free and unconstrained flow of ideas, which I present in the hope of improving economics and the economics profession. I see those improvements as occurring through enhancements in information, reasoning, and the profession's commitment to useful discovery.

Because of the absence of any institutional backing, and its candor about fallacies in existing research methods, my book is very likely to make some enemies. My purpose is not to make enemies, though my purpose is not to make friends either. My purpose is to move economic science forward, and in any such movement I believe 'traction' has always required some degree of 'friction'. I therefore criticize whenever criticism is appropriate and useful, and I do not downplay that criticism with polite qualifiers about how 'I happen to think this way' but 'it's OK if other people look at it the other way'. As will be obvious, I wrote this book for serious questioners and decision makers who are most interested in the truthfulness and usefulness of arguments.

Likewise, I refer to, but do not necessarily 'pay homage' to, the latest shipments of economic models and policy-oriented buzzwords that have recently appeared in economics literature. Nonconformists within the economics profession may find my lack of enthusiasm for many of these models and buzzwords to be refreshing; conformists within the economics profession may find that lack of enthusiasm to be insubordinate, egocentric, and egotistical. On this charge, I will ask only for a fair hearing, in which the evidence I provide and the reasonableness of my arguments can be allowed to speak for themselves.

PART I


A Scientific Critique of Economic Discourse

# 1. Economics of Science versus Science of Economics

## INTRODUCTION

In most of economics, 'science' is rarely discussed. When it is, it is usually in reference to the science 'enterprise', that is, the money society spends on science research and education, rather than the concept of science as a method of inquiry. In this book, however, 'science' will refer to the latter. Among economists, only historians of economic thought have discussed the method of scientific inquiry on any regular basis, primarily addressing the age-old question of whether economics is a science or an art. Unfortunately, the history of economic thought, especially in the last few decades, has become removed from most of economic discourse and in fact is no longer required material for the acquisition of most advanced degrees in economics. As a result, whether economics is a science or not has become a topic of interest only to historians of economic thought, who are relatively few in number, and who, unfortunately, have limited influence on the profession.

'Technological change', in contrast, receives a great deal more attention in economics. It pervades many areas of economic inquiry, such as growth theory, productivity analysis, industrial organization, and third-world development. It also represents a subfield of economic thought in its own right. As a concept, 'technological change' has two separate interpretations in economic discussions. Its most common interpretation is that it is, metaphorically, a 'black box', or more precisely, an 'unexplained residual' in an economic analysis. Here, economists acknowledge that *something* is going on, we just do not know what it is – we know only its effects in terms of improved products and processes. When this interpretation is used, as in economic 'growth theory', economists likewise do not usually attempt to understand what is occurring at a scientific, engineering, or organizational level. It is enough to acknowledge and measure the effect, and study it only as a component of all of the other economic forces, like capital accumulation, that account for economic change. In itself, there is nothing inherently wrong or unscientific about this approach, *if* our research goal is distinct from the goal of understanding the process of technological change itself. For example, economists modeling economic growth in the macro-economy need not know the details of how technological change takes place, no more than a physician prescribing a medication needs to know the physiology that makes it work.

If our goal is to understand the process of technical change itself, however, then we must have a very different perspective, and move beyond the 'black box' interpretation. Actually, this is old news – Nathan Rosenberg, for instance, expressed this basic idea in the titles of books he had written on technological change (*Inside the Black Box* and *Exploring the Black Box*). This book will likewise adopt the goal of understanding technological change as a phenomenon in itself. 'Technological change' in this sense is a very real, *scientific* phenomenon, existing in actual time and space, as opposed to a theoretical construct defined according to economic modeling assumptions. To carry out this goal, I have argued throughout that an interdisciplinary approach is essential. That is, our approach must transcend categories of knowledge that have usually been isolated within separate subfields of economics, natural science, and engineering.

A small number of economists have, in fact, done excellent work in understanding the relationships among science, technology, and economic change. Those economists, however, have long remained a very small minority within the economics profession. As a result, they, and their findings, have been relegated to specific, relatively isolated subfields within the profession, rather than being integrated into the general core of economic discourse. This isolation has occurred not because the majority of economists genuinely disagree with their findings, but rather because the proper, scientific study of technological change by economists has been severely constrained by: (1) our lack of interest, which follows, in part, from our limited backgrounds in science and engineering; (2) the absence of appropriate conceptual constructs within the discipline to adequately address the topic; and (3) the fact that the process of technological change itself contradicts many of the implicit assumptions that commonly underlie traditional economic discourse. All of these factors will be discussed at length throughout this book.

In spite of the limited coverage of technological change in economic thought, the importance of technological change as a component of economic growth is already widely accepted. Such acceptance follows from three aspects of recent history. (1) The end of the cold war eliminated one of the central roles of economic thought as a means of advocacy for capitalism, thereby diminishing the indirect demand for certain areas of economic inquiry like those focusing on the 'stability of market equilibria'. (2) The general success of macroeconomic and political policies to raise income levels, and to control phenomena like inflation, business-cycle fluctuation, and government debt (at least in the United States and Western Europe) has left economists with less to argue about and less to study. Thus, in looking for more to do, economists are tending to address other long-run strategies for growth, where technological change is emerging as a central theme in policy discussions. (3) Science and engineering have recently passed extremely important milestones, especially in information and communication technologies, suggesting possibilities for dramatic economic progress. These milestones will be addressed in the latter chapters of this book.

Among economists there is widespread agreement that science and technology do have major implications for economic growth, but there is no agreement as to whether science and technology could ever be well understood in economics. Some economists would argue that the inner workings of scientific discovery and technological change are simply too far removed from the purview of economic discourse. In some sense I agree with this outlook, but would offer, as a partial solution, that the field of economics itself be expanded, so that economists can become capable of better understanding technological change.

Other economists may question the extent to which *any* area of inquiry could understand new directions taken by science and technology. This pessimism is analogous to the pessimism economists have often expressed with regard to understanding any phenomenon in which changes are dominated by random influences and automatic adjustments for expectations. For example, we have often argued that if anyone could know beforehand how the stock market will change, then he or she could trade on the market to gain financially from that knowledge. Such trading would change the market itself, until eventually no more gains from advanced knowledge could be made, leaving the market in an unknowable state. Thus, in an environment in which people are continually conducting research on how they could make more money, any knowledge older than instantaneous becomes accounted for, rendering it impossible for a newcomer to the analysis to make profitable predictions over significant amounts of time. The same type of argument is sometimes made regarding advances in science and technology. Moreover, the very concept of prior knowledge of new scientific discoveries and inventions is itself a *non sequitur*.

However, the distinction between what is knowable and unknowable, while crystal clear in mathematics and some branches of philosophy, is often extremely fuzzy in real life. Many experts make a good living from predicting change in the stock market by being able to obtain and interpret new information, and likewise the success of scientists and engineers in their own research is often due, in part, to their superior understanding of future change in their own areas of interest. Investment in research and development, of course, does not just happen, but is based on prior knowledge and understanding of scientific and technological change. Surely, analysis of scientific and technological change cannot be an exact science. The relevant question is whether such analysis can be performed better in economics. In this book I will argue that it can.

In large part, the problem lies not only in the subject matter, but in the researchers. When it comes to understanding technological change, the economics profession faces a Catch-22 situation. The fragmentation of the profession into isolated, and often self-serving, subgroups has made it difficult for technological change economists to expand their influence on the profession, and to discover new areas of inquiry. As a result, economists who are not directly involved with the study of technological change are often left with the impression that the area of inquiry is only as important as the fraction of the profession that it currently employs.

Another important constraint on the economic study of technological change is the absence of useful economic data that could be used to study it – what Zvi Griliches, in his 1994 presidential address to the American Economic Association referred to as the 'data constraint'. This constraint ties in quite strongly with the previously-mentioned third obstacle to improved discourse: the fact that technological change often contradicts the implicit assumptions that underlie traditional economic analysis. All of these issues will be discussed in detail throughout this book.

## TABOOS THIS BOOK WILL VIOLATE

This book will violate certain taboos that commonly exist in economic discourse, which are listed below. Four motivations exist for their violation, which are: (1) to identify problems in the sociology of the profession that have bearing on the ideas presented in this book; (2) to clarify misconceptions about economic concepts and economic methodology; (3) to facilitate the broad perspective adopted throughout the book; and (4) to move quickly past matters of style, so that the book can focus on more substantive issues.

### The Bias Against Simple Ideas

As many of us know, economic studies tend to be as mathematical as possible, leaving out concepts that are simple to understand, even if those concepts could have significant bearing on our findings. This problem occurs for a variety of reasons, one of which, for instance, is the fact that most economic discourse is carried out in the form of articles in technical journals, where style and space constraints dictate against 'stating the obvious' regardless of how important the obvious may be. The most common example of this problem with regard to the economic topics covered in this book is the tendency for studies of technological change to carry out complex econometric analyses of industrial data, and to discuss only the econometric findings. In many cases, the greatest source of error in these analyses lies in the inaccuracy, ambiguity, and sometimes even irrelevance, of the data that are used, due to arbitrariness and often simple sloppiness in the way those data have been defined and categorized. The idea that our data may be inaccurate (or worse), causing our findings to be simply wrong, is a rather unimpressive, plebeian idea, and therefore we do not often bring it to the fore in scholarly literature. In this book, I will discuss problems of this kind, extensively in some cases, because I believe the attention given to a problem should be based on how much that problem prevents useful results, regardless of whether that problem is simple to understand.

## New Kinds of Data

I have explored new types of data in this book. For example, I collected data on the incidence of articles in business journals about different types of scientific and technological advances. Besides introducing new data, I discuss the comparative benefits and costs of utilizing those data. Unfortunately, in economic analyses of technological change, explorations into new types of data, especially industrial data, are rare. Moreover, when such new data represent alternatives to standard statistics, they are sometimes seen as a slight against the standard statistics that well-established institutions compile. Needless to say, no slight is intended – I am only trying to expand the possibilities for additional data, not to replace existing measures. Unfortunately, it has been difficult to explain what may be beneficial about new types of data, without explaining some of the limitations in existing data.

## Sociology of the Profession

Economists specializing in history of economic thought dabble much more in philosophy than in natural science, and are likely to disagree with my approach. In fact, some may be shocked at the absence of any discussion of the history of ideas on the philosophy of science. For example, in this book I do not discuss 'positivism', 'anti-positivism', or 'modernism'. I do not talk about the writings of Kuhn, Lakatos, and Popper, or about many of the methodological concepts, like 'falsification', that are often associated with those writings. Rather, I focus on scientific practice (including scientific knowledge itself), behavior, and sociology.

Occasional books, like this one, written on economic methodology but which address behavioral and sociological factors, might appear, to some naive readers, as being less intellectually sophisticated as books on economic methodology that specifically address the philosophy of science. The former do tend to be easier to read than the latter. Nevertheless, the validity, as scholarly discourse, of the sociology of science is widely recognized, even by those who write about the philosophy of science. For instance, Clive Beed, in his 1991 article 'Philosophy of Science and Contemporary Economics', remarks:

> The sociology and anthropology of science is now an active field of study . . . coexisting uneasily with the study of the philosophy of science. . . . The extensive literature in the sociology of science is mainly a post-1970s development . . . However, studies in the sociology of science soon began to threaten the philosophy of science. In investigating the actual practices of scientists, sociology of science examined the nontechnical, nonlogical, and nonrational aspects of scientific work, elements that it believed had been ignored by philosophy of science. As such, sociology of science can be viewed as an alternative conceptualization of scientific activity to philosophy of science, and may even be supplanting it. (p. 472)

Several economists like David Colander[1] have addressed concerns regarding the sociology of the economics profession, and how it often has negative effects on the usefulness of economic discourse. However, it is rare to find mention of sociological problems in economic articles and books written on topics other than sociology itself (like technological change). I agree that it is poor style, and not very convincing, to criticize people's opinions about particular economic issues by referring to whatever sociological motivations may underlie their opinions, as opposed to directly addressing what might be right or wrong in their arguments. However, in the economics profession, sociological factors are often deep rooted, and have substantial bearing on people's perspectives. In my opinion, to neglect those sociological factors in some cases would be unscientific, as it would be neglecting a real phenomenon that has substantial causal influence over the ideas being expressed.

**Dismissal of Subfields**

The prevailing attitude among most, though certainly not all, economists, when reconciling differences between schools of thought, is 'live and let live' or 'I'm OK – You're OK' There are a variety of reasons for this, such as economics being a field of study that attracts more than an average proportion of conformists and supporters of the *status quo*. There is also a degree of silent conspiracy, whereby economists of conflicting subfields, who restrain from strongly criticizing each other, benefit mutually from not exposing negative aspects of each other's subfields to the rest of the world. Furthermore, economic culture often blends with political and diplomatic culture, in which being nice is often as important, culturally, as being smart.

Our behavior in this regard has been unscientific, and definitely inefficient in terms of the economic utilization of human resources. I believe that criticism, when it is carried out in a logical manner, is an essential component of progress in scientific thought, and always has been. To suppress it may allow us to lead peaceful, complacent lives. However, such supression would carry the cost of slower, if not stagnant, progress in useful thought, and the cost of associated missed opportunities for correct social decision making. It follows that our commitment to scientific progress requires a commitment to constructive criticism in otherwise apathetic settings.

Furthermore, there is generally a fixed sum of economists and economic literature. Therefore, when a subfield of economics does not contribute much to actual progress, it draws valuable human and financial resources away from the other subfields that are, in fact, contributing. It follows that we should require subfields to defend their very existence. As economists, we, and many prominent members of our community like Milton Friedman, have upheld the view that capitalism is efficient because it gives people 'the right to fail' – we, equally well, should be held to our own standard.

## ECONOMICS AND THE SCIENTIFIC METHOD

The first published concerns over scientific methodology in economics had been traced by Mark Blaug[2] to Nassau William Senior's[3] *Introductory Lecture on Political Economy* in 1827. Alfred Eichner[4], in his book *Why Economics is not yet a Science*, attributes the first major work on the question of whether economics is a science to Thorstein Veblen's[5] essay, 'Why is Economics Not an Evolutionary Science'. In that book, Professor Eichner points out that over eighty years had passed with the question of economics as science still hanging over economists. Since then, Professor Eichner too has passed on, and his book on economics as science is quickly being forgotten. Yet, the proliferation of scholarly treatises on the topic continues to proceed, undaunted, in a business-as-usual fashion. The philosophical and sociological factors that account for the absence of science in economics have already been discussed and analyzed *ad nauseam*, and any thorough review of this vast body of literature would take up an encyclopedia, authored by dozens of scholars who have devoted their lives to the topic. Nevertheless, while economics continues to be unscientific in many respects, the art of writing about the problem has remained a lucrative activity for many academic scholars. Like Oscar Wilde's[6] character Dorian Gray, economists who espouse the concept of 'economic science' have continued to appear young and attractive to economics students and the public, while, like Dorian Gray's portrait, the historical literature continues to age and be hidden from observers.

The question of economics as science will soon be 200 years old by the above description, and as the philosophical literature rots in the attics of libraries, the fundamental flaws of much of economic thought continue to linger on in perpetuity.

As suggested, methodological criticism of economics, solely for the sake of supporting the reading and writing pastimes of methodological economists, implies a waste of resources. Time has demonstrated that philosophical discourse on the scientific validity of economic practices has had a very limited beneficial effect on the profession. The reason, from a plebeian perspective, is simply that 'talk is cheap'. In order to change the profession for the better, I have come to believe (having been in the profession for some time) that stronger action is required. Such action should involve serious recommendations that many economists would not like to hear. For example, I recommend that economic research that is basically of no value, but exists primarily to serve the interests of the individuals who perform it, should be objectively identified by other economists who know enough about the topic to make such judgments. Efforts should then be made at the public policy level to ensure such research is not publically supported. Unlike talk, funding priorities are *not* cheap.

In actuality, as many scientists have observed, for any scholar to know and understand science, or to be a 'good scientist', requires little knowledge of the philosophy of science. Ronald Giere[7] remarks, 'The shortcomings of both the philosophy and the sociology of science stem from the fact that, in being true to their disciplinary backgrounds, both philosophers and sociologists of science have failed their subject matter – science.' Isaac Newton, of course, was a brilliant scientist who lived long before most writings on the philosophy of science. The *practice* of science is reliant upon a certain frame of mind – a commitment to learning about the causality of phenomena. If this were not the case, then professorial scientists would be expected to require students of science to study the philosophy of science, which is hardly the case.

Along these lines, Stephan Fuchs[8] also writes:

> Nothing mysterious is revealed to happen in science once we open the black box of scientific rationality which philosophy has kept firmly closed as the sacred taboo of modernity. Inside the black box, we find mundane reasoners making sense, not rational reasoners discovering objective reality; we meet ordinary social actors engaged in everyday conversations, not quasi philosophers following the rules of scientific method; we observe competitive owners of intellectual property fighting over credits and priority claims, not polite and disinterested participants in rational discourse committed to the collective search for truth.

The discussions that follow will not suggest that science is, by any means, a glorious solution to all of the methodological problems that economics faces. However, the lack of scientific *practice* in economics may be identified as one of the weakest links in the chain of ideas that make up economic discourse. Consequently, I believe the practice of science itself, as opposed to the study of its philosophy, history, or sociology is the direction that we must take.

## ECONOMICS, LIKE SCIENCE, SHOULD BE INTERDISCIPLINARY

One byproduct of scientists' commitment to understanding reality is their willingness to pursue interdisciplinary study when reality suggests they should. In contrast, because economists tend to have little or no training in the natural sciences, and often little training in other social sciences, they often undervalue interdisciplinary scholarship. This problem does not appear to exist in other social sciences to the same extent.

As an example, a comparison could be made between the orientations of economics and psychology. Here, the frequent excuse that economists are limited by having to study human behavior would have no bearing on the comparison, since psychology is, by definition in fact, committed to the study of human behavior. In psychology one of the most difficult areas for a researcher to be scientific is abnormal psychology, in which, for example, Jung and Freud have contributed theory that is quite difficult to verify with empirical observation. Nevertheless, even in abnormal psychology, a strong commitment toward science exists. For instance, in a typical introductory text on the subject, Robert White and Norman Watt[9] discuss paresis, a mental disorder that results from the contraction of syphilis. Because the cause of the disease had been discovered, and a treatment found, White and Watt uphold this advancement of human knowledge with great admiration:

> This is the kind of story of which medical science is rightly proud. Careful observation, patient research to which hundreds of workers contributed, the constant development of more refined techniques which carried the investigation forward in unexpected ways, led at last to the discovery of underlying causes and thus to the possibility of prevention and treatment.

As many know, most of abnormal psychology has not been as successful. Yet, Professors White and Watt do not provide excuses about how enigmatic human behavior is, or how important or 'useful' approximation and simplification are. Quite the contrary, they emphasize the need for interdisciplinary study and the need for understanding, in spite of complexity:

> Increasing one's knowledge means not just storing new facts; there must be a growth of sensitivity, and increase of perceptiveness, that makes it possible to reach intimate terms with the subject under study. . . . Because the field includes disorders that are

> somatogenic, in whole or in part, he [the student of abnormal psychology] must perceive these problems with the eye of a biologist. Because it includes a wide range of psychogenic phenomena, . . . he must [view] . . . things with the eye of an experimental psychologist. . . . Because disordered personal behavior occurs in a social setting . . . he must be able to assume the outlook of a sociologist. (1973, p. 43)

In sharp contrast, one might find an introductory economics text that reads as follows:

> For example, we may consider demand and supply behavior. Here one group of economic agents determines how much they wish to demand of some good as a function of its price. This determination of demand is presumably the result of some underlying maximization, *or at least can be modeled as such.*[10] (my own italicizing)

It is not unusual for a student of psychology to be asked to see a particular problem through the eyes of a biologist, and indeed undergraduate psychology majors are required to take biology courses given the fact that biology underlies many psychological phenomena. By the same token, biology majors are required to study chemistry, and chemistry majors, physics. Economics majors, like physics majors, must learn mathematics. But mathematics does not 'underlie' economic phenomena as much as it simply characterizes, or describes, economic phenomena. Human and institutional behavior underlie economic phenomena, and these involve psychology, sociology, political science, and business studies. Furthermore, when it comes to understanding production in economics, all of the natural sciences and engineering fields come into play.

## WHEN SCHOLARSHIP CONFLICTS WITH PROGRESS

In discussions on economic science, confusion often exists over the relative importance of the history of ideas. The history and sociology of the economics profession has generated an emphasis on what economics has been, in contrast to what economics should be. Even discussions on what economics should be has been dominated by syntheses over what the 'great economists' have said economics should be, as opposed to what others, for example, professionals outside the field and the authors of the works themselves, think economics should be. The *curse of scholarship* on economics has been the requirement that those who seek to address what economics should be are usually expected to address the enormous baggage of what economics has been, and what others have said economics should be. This leaves little room for a comparison between economics and other sciences. Anyone wishing to write a technical journal article that compares economics to other sciences must first be an expert on two fields: the history of thought in economics and the philosophy of science, and only then add something on another field of science. Expertise is simply stretched too thin, not only for the author of such an article, but for the reviewers, who are likely to know little about other fields of science themselves.

Moreover, the task of addressing what economics should be cannot be done without identifying areas of economics that should not have been. This raises again the idea that there can be little traction without friction, but in the sociology of the economics profession, friction has traditionally imposed a high cost on its producer. Nevertheless, from an evolutionary perspective, the more economics drifts into its own separate reality, the greater the costs will be to pull it back out.

Confusion also exists over the distinction between (1) the justification for a science being unique, and (2) the idea that, as a unique science, economics has the privilege of being as separate and distinct from other sciences as economists' hearts desire. The justification for any science to be distinct is rather simple: it may be distinct if the phenomena it studies have their own characteristics, or patterns of behavior, that cannot be easily understood in terms of more elementary phenomena of other sciences, or larger aggregates of other sciences. Chemistry is distinct from biology and physics because atoms and molecules have distinct characteristics and behavioral patterns that cannot be easily understood in terms of subatomic particles, on the one hand, or living cells on the other. Nevertheless, the interconnections between biology, chemistry and physics are extremely important aspects of science in their own right. Any contradiction between any of these fields, e.g., a disease observed by biologists that appears to have no chemical basis, would never be discarded by scientists on the basis of each field having its own perspective. Quite the contrary, such a contradiction, more often than not, serves as a rallying cry for greater levels of interdisciplinary research, precisely because both scientists want to exploit a new opportunity for discovery.

The case for economics as a separate science is strong,[11] but the tendency of most of economics to be isolated from other sciences is suggestive of a contradiction of the fundamental notion of a single objective reality, and, thus, a contradiction of science itself. For these reasons, natural science must be studied within economics, by economists (especially those examining technological change), and not looked upon by economists as a peripheral area of interest. If economists knew more about science and engineering, they would be better equipped to understand current processes of technological change, and be better able to address important policy issues involving new technologies. Examples of this problem will appear throughout this book. In essence, as economists we are often unscientific, not because our philosophy differs from the philosophy of science, but because our behavior differs from scientific behavior. The next chapter will explore this perspective in greater detail.


# IS A FOCUS ON BEHAVIOR LEGITIMATE?

A scientist, who by definition is interested in true causal relations, would likely be suspicious about the idea of differences in human behavior being the true cause of the differences between economics and natural science. He or she might reason as follows: human behavior is primarily reactive to the conditions under which human beings are exposed. Therefore, the ultimate *cause* of differences between the fields must be inherent aspects of what makes those fields different to begin with, which is their subject matter, as opposed to any inherent differences in the individuals who happen to take up those fields.

This naive view, of course, neglects the flip-side of the debate – the idea that the subject matter of a field is, itself, a function of the behavior of the researchers within that field. It is conceivable, and in fact will be argued throughout this book, that a circular situation exists: Fundamental problems and limitations in the subject matter of economics induces fundamental problems and limitations in our behavior as economists, and our behavioral problems, in turn, prevent the correction of problems in subject matter. Yet, whether we can ultimately blame our problems in economic discourse on aspects of the initial subject matter, or on aspects of our initial behavior, is truly unimportant. With regard to the cliché analogy of *The Emperor's New Clothes*, it is not relevant whether one claims the emperor was naked *because* of the 'subject matter' of his actually having no clothes, or because of his, and his kingdom's, *'behavioral'* inabilities to recognize and/or act upon the fact that he was naked. Such philosophical distinctions are precisely that – philosophical distinctions – they are not solutions to any of the problems at hand. In terms of solutions, I believe both changes in behavior and changes in subject matter are simultaneously necessary for the system to break out of its perpetual dilemma. Consequently, in this book, the behavior of economists, and the subject matter of economics, will each be discussed as the two major causal factors that prevent economics from being more scientific.

As an example of why behavioral or sociological issues should not be dismissed, Stephan Fuchs, a sociologist, wrote the following about the differences between social science and natural science in an article entitled, 'A Sociological Theory of Scientific Change':

> There can be little doubt . . . that the social sciences . . . differ from more mature fields. The dominant philosophical explanation for this is that there are some deep

ontological differences between things natural and things social, and that two different methodologies are required to study them. Silent natural objects and their immutable laws can be explained by strong and nomothetic natural sciences, while interpreting people who interpret themselves requires a softer and idiographic approach. From a sociological perspective, however, the difference is not in the nature of the things studied, but in the structures of the groups and organizations doing the studying. . . . The . . . social sciences . . . are . . . "soft" fields not because they study people who are more complex than quarks or solar neutrinos, but because they have fewer, weaker, and more dispersed resources than most of the natural sciences. In current sociology, for example, there are a great number of fairly independent and autonomuous schools and perspectives. . . . These are sustained by separate organizations . . . that often control their own means of scientific production and communication, i.e., journals, newsletters, and meetings.[12]

As discussed in the next two chapters and in other parts of this book, this problem of isolation, and, to some extent, self-servitude, is one of the key behavioral factors  that precludes economics from being more scientific. Other key sociological factors are discussed as well.

## NOTES

1. See, for example, Colander 1989.
2. Blaug 1992, p. 51.
3. Senior 1827.
4. Eichner 1983.
5. Veblen 1898.
6. Wilde 1891.
7. Giere 1988, p. 5.
8. Fuchs 1992, p. 45.
9. White and Watt 1973, p. 16.
10. Varian 1984, pp. 3-4.
11. See, for example, Hausman 1992.
12. Fuchs 1993, pp. 945-46.

# 2. The Difference in Behavior Between Economists and Scientists

## INTRODUCTION

The philosophical writings on whether economics is a science appear to be based on the false assumption that economists could be taught to think like scientists, if only they study what philosophers of science have prescribed. For a true scientist, proper thinking is something that one expects to do for a lifetime. Therefore, in natural science itself, science educators take a much different approach from that of philosophers. They have generally realized that what their students, or new scientists, need most is a simple understanding of basic guidelines. These are guidelines that they will maintain in their long-term memories and always put into practice throughout their careers. What they do not need are detailed philosophical and axiomatic rules. If such rules were required for their courses, they would likely soon forgot them once they regurgitate them on the final examination.

For instance, David Keeports and Dean Morier[1] provide an undergraduate course at Mills College, in which they explain to students simple examples of the scientific method, by contrasting science with 'pseudo science'. In one such example, they remark, 'let's hypothesize that the Earth is flat. From this hypothesis we might then correctly predict that some portion of the Earth's surface, such as a particular field in Kansas, should be flat, and that all people on Earth should feel like they stand upright.' Consequently, they emphasize, 'A failure to acknowledge the possibility of a false hypothesis leading to true predictions through sound reasoning lies at the heart of pseudoscientific belief.' That is, even though a particular premise may lead to true conclusions, it may be false, nevertheless. In economics, this perspective coincides with Milton Friedman's F-twist perspective, in which Professor Friedman[2] argues in favor of a hypothesis for which '[d]espite the apparent falsity of the "assumptions" . . . it has great plausibility because of the conformity of its implications with observations.' But, of course, the difference between these perspectives lies in their conclusions: The perspective of science teachers is that the Earth is not flat; therefore the hypothesis is wrong. The fact that the Earth's surface can be usefully approximated as flat is certainly clear in the minds of science teachers and students – they realize that whenever they use a road map. What is truly being taught to the science class is the ultimate wrongness and unacceptableness of the flat-Earth hypothesis. In essence, what is entering and remaining in the long-term memory of the science student is a sense of commitment and an emphatic distaste for hypotheses that ignore the most accurate view of reality.

Although Professors Keeports and Morier hold specific classes on the scientific method, methodological issues in the natural sciences are something that is generally accepted as an integral part of doing science. For economists, on the other hand, methodology has become a specialized subfield, of concern only to the few of us who choose to publish in that area. In the culture of natural science, methodological issues are like donning clothes in the morning – everyone is expected to have a reasonable level of competence. Among practicing scientists, methodological competence is rooted not in thick layers of philosophical scholarship, but often in thin layers of what, one might dare call, common sense. Education alone may not be sufficient to provide that level of competence, which is why actual experience at scientific investigation is often regarded as an essential aspect of a scientist's training. Along these lines, Derek Hodson[3] writes:

> Though necessary, conceptual knowledge and knowledge about procedures that scientists can adopt, and have adopted in particular circumstances in the past, are insufficient in themselves to enable a student to engage successfully in scientific inquiry. That ability is developed only through experience. In other words, one can only learn to do science, and one can only experience science as a mode of inquiry, by doing science.

As yet another example of the cultural differences between the natural science and economics professions, I recall a question once raised in a chemistry class. The professor had just gone over an elaborate equation that interrelated the pressure of a gas with its volume, temperature, and chemical properties. He had discussed various aspects of the equation, and then asked the class a trick question: suppose you were conducting an experiment; you had a certain quantity of gas in a container, and you needed to know its precise pressure. What would you do? The first responses by students in the class involved utilizing the equation just discussed, but the professor responded negatively. When the class of approximately 100 students was stumped, the professor stated the correct answer: the best thing to do would be to measure the pressure directly with a pressure meter. The point he was making was that direct measurement is the best, most reliable source of objective knowledge, while the application of theory would be second-best, and used only when direct measurement was not possible or not reliable. The class of potential natural scientists was embarrassed at having not been able to see through the trick question, and would not be likely to fall for it again. Coincidentally, the same chemical equations discussed in that chemistry lecture can be found as examples for economists to emulate in a book about the economics of technological change by Devendra Sahal.[4] However, the trick question, which could be just as easily applied to economic models, does not seem to be observed in economics classes.

## SCIENCE IS MORE THAN MATHEMATICS

Many economists, unfortunately, think that 'science' is mathematics. For example, the epitomic introduction to modern economics was Paul Samuelson's famous book in 1947 called *Foundations of Economic Analysis*. That book begins with a quotation by J. Willard Gibbs: 'Mathematics is a Language.' In effect, the 'foundations' of modern economics had been firmly rooted in the glorification and admiration of a different field of study. An outgrowth of this obsession with math is the notion of economics as a 'formal' or 'axiomatic' science.[5] For instance, in 1990 an economist named Bernt Stigum's wrote a volume containing over one thousand pages, entitled *Toward a Formal Science of Economics: The Axiomatic Method in Economics and Econometrics*. That huge book is purely theoretical, containing no reported empirical observations of any kind. It is ironic that the main effect of *Toward a Formal Science of Economics* was the movement of economics away from *actual* science. In contrast to Professor Stigum's perspective on the topic, formal science in economics is a substitute, not a complement, for actual science. In support of his formalist approach, he remarks, 'Most of all formalism in science is required for the purpose of confronting theories with data.'[6] That is certainly true, but the magnitude of formalism currently in existence in economics has the exact opposite purpose and effect – it allows us to promote our careers *by avoiding* the confrontation between theories and data. True: formalism is necessary for scientific discourse, but at present, 'less is more'.

Mathematics is, without a doubt, the only subject close to science that economists, as a group, study extensively, and it is often the only subject close to science that economists study at all. It is, therefore, quite understandable that economists' impression of 'good science' is confused with 'good mathematics'. One of the key factors that makes mathematics interesting to mathematicians is 'mathematical elegance'. I am defining the concept here to mean a situation that arises in which one would normally expect considerable complexity and weak connections among certain concepts under consideration, when there is, in fact, a surprising degree of simplicity and strong connections among those concepts. The observed (or reasoned) simplicity and connectedness of those concepts is intriguing, conveying one of two impressions: (1) a circumstantial coincidence among the phenomena being studied, or (2) a fundamental interrelationship among those phenomena that has thus far been overlooked. It is, of course, this second category of mathematical elegance that conveys the accomplishment of increased knowledge of the topic being studied.

In science, on the other hand, people often construct mathematical models to describe and understand real phenomena. The elegance of the model must always be weighted against its accuracy at depicting reality. Elegance is neither necessary nor sufficient for a good scientific model, though, all else being equal, elegance is certainly preferred (as in accordance with Occam's Razor). Therefore, if a student is trained in mathematics alone, and then approaches social science, he is likely to have a bias toward overemphasizing elegance over accuracy, which is seen quite often in economics.

In physics, for example, there is an important distinction between fundamental and circumstantial elegance. Fundamental elegance is found in the fundamental equations of physics such as Maxwell's equations and $E=Mc^2$. One could write, for instance, the equation for the displacement of a cannon ball fired from a cannon, based on the assumption of a constant initial horizontal component of velocity until it hits the ground. Maximization of the horizontal distance traversed by the cannon ball, assuming it is subject to the gravitational pull of the Earth, with respect to the angle of trajectory, yields the finding that the cannon ball will go farthest when it is shot up at a 45-degree angle. The 45-degree solution to such a problem is mathematically quite elegant, since 45 degrees is precisely halfway between 0 and 90 degrees, which are the obvious lower and upper bounds for the problem. However, except for it serving as an illustrative example of basic mechanics, this mathematically elegant solution in physics is not given any attention. It is recognized as circumstantial elegance – a product of the mathematical circumstances of the problem – not something that is very useful in explaining causal interrelationships among physical phenomena. In economic models, circumstantial elegance plays a much greater role for the reasons mentioned above, plus the well-known fact, of course, that economics does not have the benefit of physical absolutes (that is, there is no $E=Mc^2$ in economics).

## TAKE CHESS FOR EXAMPLE

Part of the problem in distinguishing between circumstantial and fundamental elegance lies in identifying the goals of the analysis. This point can be illustrated using the game of chess as an example, which provides a conveniently simple context in which to explore these concepts. Because chess is so well-defined, the distinction between circumstantial and fundamental elegance can be easily illustrated, even to someone who does not know how the game is played.

Among some people who play chess, there is an additional pastime of solving 'chess problems', in which a certain situation is set up on the chessboard in terms of the location of pieces, and a player tries to solve a stated problem. For instance, if the problem requires, 'black to move and win', then the player tries to figure out the correct sequence of moves that will always guarantee a win for the person playing black, regardless of what the person playing white does. All chess problems are elegant, in that their solutions are initially unexpected, but mathematically optimal in terms of the way the game is played.

There are two general kinds of chess problems, which are analogous to mathematical models in any field of science or social science. The first is problems that illustrate a unique coincidence in the set up of pieces, whose solution is extremely counterintuitive, and thus enjoyable to some chess enthusiasts for the surprise that it conveys. Many problems of this kind require only two correct moves to win, where the best strategy for solving them is often to guess the first move as the one that appears to be the most counter-intuitive. Problems of this kind are seen as amusing, but chess players generally recognize that there is little or nothing to be learned from them in terms of improving their knowledge of the game. The second type of problem exploits a fundamental theme in the nature of chess itself, and chess players often do learn something from such problems, though they are also entertained by their mathematical elegance.

The ability of chess players to distinguish between the first type of circumstantial chess problem and the second type of fundamental chess problem follows from their overall understanding the game. For example, there is a circumstantial chess problem that 'proves' that a rook is better than a queen (Figure 2.1). However, the situation associated with the proof is so incredibly rare, that it would probably never show up, not even once, in an entire lifetime of chess playing. Thus, if a chess player presented this problem to a group of other players, and then seriously argued that a rook is better than a queen, his argument would be shot down instantly on the grounds that the circumstances of the problem presented were too special. In equivalent language, the assumptions underlying the model that a castle is better than a queen are unrealistic. Here, intuition about the game, alone, would render this conclusion. Even if intuition were disallowed, for the sake of rigorous and objective peer review for instance, the inapplicability of the assumptions could be proven mathematically (given the mathematical nature of the game).

Examples in economic theory analogous to the above chess problem are not difficult to find. The right assumptions, and the right model, can prove just about anything. For example, an article in the *Journal of Political Economy*

Note: If Black now moves to get a queen, then White forces a stalemate with a check. However, Black wins with a rook, given the king's ability to pivot between the C-7 and B-6 positions after White moves to A-5.

*Figure 2.1 A rook is better than a queen.*

(one of the most prestigious economic journals) by Colin Camerer, George Loewenstein, and Martin Weber (1989) illustrates 'the curse of knowledge' which states, 'more information is not always better'. Their argument proceeds as follows:

> Call the random variable being forecast X. . . . Forecasts of X depend on the information set available to the forecaster . . . sets $I_0$ and $I_1$, where $I_0$ is a subset of $I_1$. . . . Denote the optimal forecast of X given . . . $I_0$ by $E(X|I_0)$. . . . An agent with $I_1$ who forecasts the forecast of an agent with . . . $I_0$ is estimating $E[E(X|I_0)|I_1]$. . . . When the curse of knowledge occurs, the forecaster with . . . $I_1$ *overestimates* the scope of $I_0$ . . . $E[E(X|I_0)|I_1]$ is *not* equal to $E(X|I_0)$, but somewhere between $E(X|I_0)$ and $E(X|I_1)$.

In short, given the assumptions specified, a forecaster with more information is worse off than one with less information.

Now let us briefly step into a fantasy world that is hybrid between the game of chess and world as we know it. Suppose, in this Alice in Wonderland setting, the rooks of the chess set formed a trade association. That association issued grants to prominent economists to perform scholarly research on the possibility that rooks might be more powerful chess pieces than queens. Opposing groups questioned their assumptions, but the research, being mathematically elegant, was able to be published in leading journals. In the end, the idea that castles are sometimes better than queens was accepted as defensible by the economics profession as a whole. This scenario leads us into the next section.

## ELEGANCE AS ADVOCACY

In 1985, when I was in graduate school in economics at Columbia University, apartheid in South Africa was alive and strong. As on many other campuses, there was a hunger strike at Columbia, and in our case a building was partially occupied by student protesters for several days in order to persuade the university to divest in South Africa. Shortly thereafter, a prominent professor in our department, who specialized in development economics and international trade, came up with an economic model which demonstrated that apartheid was economically inefficient. He spent a lecture presenting and explaining the equations of the model, which some students found motivating. His reasons for developing the model were clear. In fact, a central, underlying theme of the lecture was that if you know enough about economic theory you can use it to promote a cause.

Among many of us it is common to view the theoretical economic model as a tool for advocacy, rather than as a means for understanding objective reality. This is the case even in empirical studies, although the particular position being advocated does occasionally run into difficulty if the data object too strongly. The profession has become so accustomed to this practice, that some some of us who use models in this way do so with a clear conscience, as if theory were simply an alternative language through which advocacy could be expressed. As many economists know, writings by Deirdre (formerly Donald) McCloskey, in particular, about 'the rhetoric of economics' have tended to support this perspective.[7] Indeed, the professor described above, and the students who attended his lecture, seemed to view the model as his contribution to the cause, analogous to painting banners or writing letters to political leaders. Moreover, there is a common perception of an abstract democratic process occurring within the economics profession, in which the position that receives the most support in terms of published economic models wins the 'economists' popular vote'.

I will not insult anyone's intelligence by discussing why such behavior is unscientific. On the other hand, I am reminded of a routine once performed by the American comedian Alan Sherman, entitled, 'how it came to be that I got fat'. Sherman explained that, when he had been a boy during World War II, his mother had always insisted that he finish his plate, because – she would say – 'people are starving in Europe'. So – as he explained – he did finish his plate, as often as he possibly could, because somehow he had been convinced that in doing so he would somehow prevent massive starvation. He had realized only too late how wrong he had been, concluding 'the people in Europe *kept* starving – while *I got FAT*'.

Our creation of theoretical, circumstantial elegance as a tool for advocacy is a reflection of our intellectual recreance. Apartheid, of course, was wrong for ethical reasons. As such, we should address it on ethical grounds. By polluting the arena of public debate with irrelevant, mathematical elegance, we accomplish nothing for society, in spite of the fact that we 'mean well'. We also discredit the importance of ethics itself, for the sake of our own illegitimate participation in the debate as supposed experts. In turn, by indirectly diminishing the relative importance of ethics in public debate, we could easily hurt, in the long run, the very causes they have been trying to support. Finally, like the 'boy who cried "wolf"', we make it more difficult to convince the public in the future when we may actually have something important to say.

Ethics, however, is rarely the basis for economic advocacy. It is more frequently observed that advocacy relates to economic principles themselves. As a result, there is often confusion and chaos as to the true value of any economic theory being developed. As a case in point, the dramatic growth of the Rational Expectations school of thought in the 1980s, and the enormous amount of economic literature that it generated, involved the creation of theory that was highly mathematical, while the inherent theme of the approach was quite basic. That theme, of individuals and organizations adjusting their expectations on the basis of observable patterns, was almost always in reference to price movements, and was essentially no different from the monetarists' (Milton Friedman in particular) theme of inflation expectations. Thus, the growing popularity of the Rational Expectations school in the 1980s was due, in large part, to the growing popularity of the view that inflation must be brought under control, even at the price of increased unemployment. Rational Expectations theory, in effect, served as advocacy for tough controls over inflation, when, in fact, the models used did not address that broad issue *per se*, but were primarily exercises in mathematical derivation.[8] Conversely, once inflation had been brought under control for some time, we became less interested in rational expectations.

Again, through lack of experience with, and/or sometimes lack of appreciation for, scientific perspectives, economists as a group have been complacent about the use of mathematical elegance as advocacy. Concern over inflation, if it were addressed scientifically, would be focused on the actual costs of inflation to society. More attention could have been given, for example, to the additional search costs that consumers face when prices are less stable, and the additional resources used by firms in information acquisition and strategy development. Such direct attention to the issue has rarely been done at an applied, empirical level, though it could have provided compelling evidence for the support of strong controls on inflation. Thus, genuine debate over the magnitude of societal losses due to inflation hardly ever surfaced. Statistically, one might expect the most popular opinion to win in any case, since that opinion would likely be associated with the greatest share of economic literature. However, what is obviously missing from such a 'democratic process' is reasoned decision making, and the exchange of ideas that would be pertinent to the issue at hand. In short, in spite of impressive mathematics and occasionally some data, what is blatantly absent from our 'model-popularity contest' is the practice of science.

## SCIENCE IN THE ECONOMIST'S 'MIND SET'

Because of the sheer importance of natural science as a causal factor of economic change, economists should have at least some familiarity with the subject and with other social sciences. This does not mean we need more years of education, because we can easily afford less mere memorization of existing mathematical models, which now accounts for nearly all of our graduate-level education. With regard to data analysis, in addition to understanding what our data actually mean, those of us who learn about other areas of science may develop a better understanding of what our data should be *designed* to mean. Measures of welfare and human conditions, for instance, could benefit greatly from consideration of medical and sociological factors, as has often been mentioned, for example, by Amartya Sen, who won the Nobel Prize in economics in 1998.[9] Some would argue that the moral philosophies and 'social welfare functions' of economists are what determine our inclination to accept GDP per capita as the variable of consensus for the measurement of well-being. Another, simpler explanation could be offered: we, like many others, tend to avoid areas of inquiry for which we have little or no training. If economists were better educated on the medical and sociological characteristics of nations, then we would tend to examine the conditions of nations according to those other variables.

Economists often use measures that cannot be connected to physical entities, but instead are tautologically defined, and consequently cannot be applied in any empirical test. While this has often been criticized on epistemological grounds by advocates of science in economics,[10] such criticisms have, again, often fallen on deaf ears, perhaps for lack of an appreciation among economists for the physical rather than the metaphysical. If we were concerned about understanding the underlying causal factors associated with those measures, then we would make greater efforts to avoid, or at least rely less upon, tautological constructs.

Along these lines, the famous argument by Milton Friedman about the 'impossibility of testing a theory by its assumptions' in his 1953 *Essays in Positive Economics*[11] would not receive the same acceptance among those economists who are familiar with natural science. For example, Professor Friedman (who also won the Nobel Prize in economics, in 1976) claimed that a physicist might use the formula for the speed of a falling object in a vacuum for approximating the speed of a falling object when it is not in a vacuum. Dr Friedman used this comparison to argue in support of economists' habit of using simplifying assumptions. What Dr Friedman ignored in his comparison, however, was that certainly a physicist might make such an assumption, but only if that physicist had good reason to believe that air resistance, in the experiment being conducted, was negligible. Otherwise, the physicist would include air resistance, which does receive ample attention in his field. Consequently, economists who understand something about natural science would know that Friedman's supposition is false: air resistance is not 'assumed away' in physics for reasons of convenience in the same way that important factors are often assumed away in economic models.

As another example, in public economics an important debate has been underway for some time over the usefulness of contingent valuation (CV) analysis. CV analysis is a particular kind of analysis, which is often highly sophisticated, regarding survey results about what consumers say they would be 'willing to pay' for a nonmarketable good, like clean air. The main objection that some of us have expressed about CV is what Peter Diamond in 1993, and many others, have called a 'warm glow' factor. The term 'warm glow' reflects the idea that respondents to survey questionnaires about willingness-to-pay often express the answers that make them feel good about themselves as they are answering, but may not reflect what they themselves would actually do in a real situation. For example, when asked on the phone if they would pay $10 of their own money to support environmental protection, they may say yes, but if someone actually knocked on their door to collect the money, they would send him away. The 'warm glow' factor described by Professor Diamond is presented as merely a heuristic of the tongue-and-cheek variety, and not as a legitimate objection, in itself, to the CV survey methodology. Instead, in virtually all economic critiques of CV, mathematical properties of observed preferences dominate over the warm glow factor. The reason for the focus on mathematics is that economists are simply well trained in mathematics, and very poorly trained in human psychology. Had neuropsychologists been in charge of investigating the validity of CV, they might rename the 'warm glow' effect to a 'positive self-reflection response', which they might be able to monitor and measure with an electroencephalogram. Of course, as economists, we should not be expected to read electroencephalograms. Nevertheless, we could learn to acknowledge and perhaps even measure, rather than belittle, factors outside our own sphere of understanding (like the 'warm glow feeling'), and regard such factors as legitimate considerations in the shaping of public policy.

# THE FAILURE OF METHODOLOGICAL WRITINGS

As mentioned in the previous chapter, the study of the methodology and epistemology of economics, and its relationship to the philosophy of science, may be interesting to read and write about, but it has often failed as a means of actually making economic research and economic discourse more scientific. One could even argue that it may have had a *negative* effect on the degree of science in economics, because it has created a different problem of its own – preoccupation with philosophy rather than science. Again, the practice of science itself relies very little on philosophy, as evidenced by the fact that many scientists know little about the philosophy of science, but go on to achieve great scientific accomplishments. Furthermore, scientists, as a group, are not very interested in philosophy. As a neuropsychologist might put it, scientists tend to be 'left-brained', making them more mathematically oriented than verbally oriented. Therefore, if the philosophy of science, being a predominantly verbal field, were required in economics programs, the effort might actually backfire by making economics seem less interesting to potential scientists, and more interesting to potential rhetoricians and literary scholars.

Thus, the problem is not only that we do not know how to behave as scientists, but also, we simply do not know enough about science itself. This is not a function of an inherent lack of applicability of science to economics. Science is extremely applicable to economics in a wide variety of ways, as already suggested, and as will be demonstrated throughout the remainder of this book. The only explanation for science not being used very much in economics is that most of us today are simply carrying out the only functions that we have ever learned to perform: high-powered mathematics, neoclassical synthesis, and 'scholarship' in the game of getting published.[12]

If we knew more about Earth science, then environmental and resource economics would be more relevant and useful. If we learned more psychology, consumer economics and labor economics would be more applicable. With more physics, chemistry, biology, and engineering, the study of technological change might help shape industrial policies with greater efficacy. Scientists studying the interrelationships among intelligence, education, and motor skills could make great strides in the development of useful theories about the labor market. Those studying robotics, nanotechnology, telecommunications, and artificial intelligence could map out the technological directions that mankind is heading. Those studying sensory perception might better understand certain long-run trends in consumer products like virtual-reality entertainment.

The first steps to negating economists' ignorance of science would be for economics departments to encourage interdisciplinary research, and perhaps even offer interdisciplinary degrees in economics and other subjects. At present, public economics, environmental economics, natural resource economics, health economics, and some programs in agricultural economics and economic development are taking this direction. If it is science that we want, then we should *just do science*, not philosophy.

## MISCONDUCT VERSUS BAD ETIQUETTE

How can one tell, without knowing much about the subject matter, what makes one research topic more important that another? Many academic departments, research-funding organizations, and individual researchers themselves, believe the relative importance of a research topic is reflected by the relative number of citations that are made to it in the literature. However, perhaps a better indicator of importance is how often ideas on a topic are stolen, or how hard researchers must work to prevent their ideas on a topic from being stolen. In his book, *The Subjective Side of Science*, Ian Mitroff, a noted sociologist of science, wrote:

> In science, statistical significance is one measure of the importance of a work. Perhaps the sociological test of the real significance of a scientist's work is whether it is worth stealing. There has long been an unwritten (but not unspoken) rule of science: Do not divulge what you are up to until you are 99 percent sure that you have beaten the competition in the race to print.[13]

In fields like medical research, where many researchers often study the same topic, and where a path-breaking discovery would be remote, but highly rewarded should it actually happen, scientific misconduct – that is, one scientist stealing another's work – is widely recognized as a critical issue. In fact, such 'misconduct in science' is often the subject of technical articles, workshops, books, law suits, and criminal prosecutions. In particular, leading journals in the natural sciences, such as *Science* published by the American Association for the Advancement of Science, not only report frequently on issues regarding scientific misconduct, but often organize workshops and discussion groups about it.[14]

For economists in the United States, there is no single journal that would be comparable to the journal, *Science*, or the British journal *Nature*. Rather, a combination of economic journals would be comparable: *American Economic Review, Journal of Economic Perspectives,* and the *Journal of Economic Literature*, all published by the American Economic Association (AEA). These journals are among the most influential in the American economics profession in terms of prestige, and in terms of the qualifications economists seek for tenure and grant awards.[15]

The three AEA journals appear to have never contained a single article on misconduct in economics. One reason for the absence of such discussions in economics may simply be cultural. These journals, and the majority of their readership, tend to be followers of the 'party line', at least in comparison to their counterparts in the natural sciences.

For example, in 1992 an article by Daniel Hamermesh appeared in the *Journal of Economic Perspectives,* entitled 'The Young Economist's Guide to Professional Etiquette'. The article does make a brief passing reference to 'plagiarism', but in the context of proper etiquette, as opposed to ethical or legal standards. Specifically, in words of advice to new authors of economics papers, Hamermesh writes:

> If you have borrowed heavily and fairly generally from someone else's work, be sure to include a statement to that effect in the footnote or elsewhere in the paper. A journal editor asked one department chair about a young colleague whom a referee accused of wholesale plagiarism. The young man had not plagiarized; but the problem would have been avoided (and the paper perhaps not summarily rejected) if he had noted his intellectual debt.[16]

This prescription, and the article more generally, suggests that success in economics is as much about our accommodating colleagues as it is about our making important discoveries. Thus, etiquette, while rarely mentioned in natural science, is important in economics because of the inherent social process through which our work as economists is recognized. Social processes also demand amicability, hence another reason for little mention of misconduct in economics – it sounds harsh in an environment where we are generally trying hard to make friends. As Professor Hamermesh advises new job applicants at the end of his article, 'First do not be hostile. People pay attention to correct and interesting ideas they read or hear. Hostility only reduces the attention your ideas receive by concentrating listeners on your style instead of your substance.'

As for the theft of other's findings, however, that happens much less in economics than in natural science, due to the fact that recognition in economics is more socially based. A typical example of misconduct in natural science might be as follows: a molecular biologist finds out about the results of another molecular biologist's experiment, runs the same experiment himself, and attempts to publish the results first, claiming the experiment was his own original idea. In contrast, suppose an unknown economist finds out about an economic model that another, prominent economist is developing for a paper. The model is likely to be an extension of the prominent economist's previous work, for which he may have already received a research grant. Moreover, depending on the topic being studied, the prominent economist may already be known to be pursuing that line of research by the 10 to 20 prominent economists in the world within the same research niche.

With so much sociological baggage, if not cronyism, associated with the economic model being studied, the thief would be caught instantly unless he, too, belonged to the same niche of 10 to 20 prominent economists (which would probably account for most of the thefts in economics that are, in fact, successful). A nonprominent thief, however, would be caught in the effort to have the work published, as it would need to be peer reviewed by the prominent group to begin with, and perhaps even by the very person from whom the work was stolen.

Conversely, in natural science, a prominent but unethical scientist who is a journal referee may reject a research paper by a young scientist who performed a pivotal experiment, in order to perform the same experiment himself and take credit for it. Economic models surely do not have the same pivotal effect – their popularity, again, is largely based on institutional and social factors that can be peripheral to the model itself. Thus, an economic model from a young economist that might be pivotal in a perfect world could easily be ignored by the prominent niche. This is why apprenticeship is typically a crucial first stage of an economist's career, in which his first new ideas are generally published as extensions of previously-established old ideas that are already widely accepted by the niche.

Unfortunately, it follows that there is less theft in economic discourse, because, effectively, there is less interest in genuine discovery as an end in itself. In short, there is less theft because there is less to steal. For instance, one might imagine how incredibly valuable an issue of the British science journal *Nature* would be today if that issue had magically appeared from 50 years into the future. An issue of the *Economic Journal* that came from 50 years into the future would not, needless to say, generate the same level of interest.

## ECONOMICS AS A MUTUAL ADMIRATION SOCIETY

We tend to have great adoration of, and pay great homage to, our most famous scholars – more so, perhaps, than any other area of human inquiry, with the exception of religion. It is one of the most deep-rooted and fundamental problems that faces our profession, and one of the greatest obstacles to economics becoming a true science. I provide below some qualitative and heuristic examples.

Long after PhD economists complete their dissertation, they continue to be associated with their dissertation advisor. People will remark, for example, 'there goes Dr Y, who had studied under Dr X'. The implication, especially if Drs X and Y teach at prominent universities, is that Dr Y is carrying out the legacy of Dr X. In other words, Dr Y is the 'heir apparent' to the line of inquiry previously pursued by Dr X. This concept of 'student as heir apparent' is not simply cultural, but integrally related to research funding and research recognition, making it quite similar to the concept of 'heir apparent' to an estate. For example, some of us might reason as follows: Dr X, known for his great work on the X-model, has been getting too old to continue, so the research grant should now be given to Dr Y.

People familiar with scientific research may wonder how this process is any different from the way it is done in any of the other sciences, or in the other social sciences or humanities for that matter. The difference exists in two respects: fragmentation and rigidity. The subfields of economics are fragmented into many small, and generally self-contained (that is, rigid) parts, each dominated by a handful of heirs apparent. As such, these subfields are subject, over time, to adverse 'inbreeding' effects[17], where researchers often feel more obliged to pay proper homage to their predecessors (through expansion of their predecessors' economic models) than to compete among themselves to discover something new about the world. As they pile their predecessors' work higher and deeper, they will come to expect the same treatment of their own work from the graduate students who they will later advise.[18]

In both the written and oral presentation of economic ideas, economists frequently associate a concept, an argument, or an entire economic model to the famous economist who developed it. In science, in general, this practice of attaching a name to a discovery, termed 'eponymy' (Stephan 1996) is not uncommon. In economics, however, eponymy is taken to new heights; when a famous name can be attributed to a statement, no further justification is required, even if other prominent economists would disagree with that statement. The cultural environment that lends itself to such habits of presentation, based on admiration, often dominates over scientific validity in determining the popularity of alternative economic theories. Admittedly, this would not happen if our field were more committed to the discovery of objective truth.

For example, Albert Einstein, probably the most famous scientist who ever lived, was not only referred to as the most intelligent person in the world, but generally seen as a kind, loving man who devoted much of his time to the promotion of world peace. In sharp contrast, Werner Heisenberg was a despicable Nazi sympathizer who tried unsuccessfully to provide Hitler with the atom bomb. Einstein's disagreement with the Heisenberg Uncertainty Principle is well known, of course, as it was responsible for Einstein's famous remark, 'God does not play dice with the universe'. Nevertheless, the Heisenberg Uncertainty Principle has come to be generally accepted in modern physics, in spite of Einstein's protest, Einstein's popularity, and the disdain people have had for Heisenberg as a person. This could only have happened because physics is a science.

In the economics profession, I have found admiration to be pervasive. I know of no other profession associated with a field of science or social science in which one finds the selling of 'trading cards' – analogous to baseball cards – with pictures and 'stats' of prominent individuals in that field. As many of us know, the Economics Club at the University of Michigan-Flint sells 29 such cards (at last count), at $6.00 each, at economic conferences and through the Internet. These cards have continued to be sold for at least a decade.

I once met an economist who was just beginning a temporary administrative position in the US government while on sabbatical from her university. I asked her what area of economics she focuses on, and she answered my question, not by specifying an area of inquiry, but by telling me that, for over 20 years, she had collaborated with a particular, highly-prominent economist. This is not an uncommon response. In general, when one of us meets another, the question frequently arises as to where we had graduated. Once that information is conveyed, the next question commonly asked is 'who was your advisor' – not 'what was your area of specialization'. In other words, economists often associate themselves more with their personal affiliations in the profession than with the subject matter that they investigate. Again, this does not happen in science to the same extent – when astronomers talk to each other about their work, the conversation is usually about telescopes, comets, the age of the universe, and so on, but usually not about former astronomy professors they had when they were students.

## PEER REVIEW

Any discussion of peer review in natural science versus peer review in economics would tend to mirror the above discussion on misconduct. Natural scientists pay a great deal of attention to peer-review issues, in articles, workshops, and books, while economists in general avoid discussing it publicly, and some may even view such a discussion as poor etiquette.[19] In recent history, there appears to have been only two articles in AEA-published journals on the topic of peer review. The most recent of these, 'Fact and Myths about Refereeing', was published in 1994 in the *Journal of Economic Perspectives*, precisely two years after the same journal's article on etiquette. As if the world were not small enough, that article was written by Daniel Hamermesh, who had also written the one two years earlier on etiquette.

As many American economists already know, all of the articles in the *Journal of Economic Perspectives* are invited by the editors and advisory board – there is no peer-reviewed competition for their publication. Thus,

Professor Hamermesh is, effectively, the AEA spokesperson on both etiquette and the efficacy of peer review – a combination that some may view as potentially troublesome. The thrust of his article on peer review was on why refereeing takes so long – an important issue no doubt, but not as important as whether journals are unbiased or scientifically valid in their publication decisions. The closest the article comes to those greater concerns is in a section on 'Are referees assigned fairly?', which measures the extent to which authors with fewer citations are assigned to referees with fewer citations.

In contrast, one aspect of the peer review process in economics that can be heralded as scientific, and in fact admirable, is the seriousness of several economics journals with regard to the issue of 'blind review'. Two types of blind review exist: (1) where authors are not told who the referees are, or 'single-blind' review, and (2) where neither the authors nor the referees know who each other are, or 'double-blind' review. In the only other recent AEA-published article mentioned above on peer review, which appeared in *American Economic Review* – itself a peer-reviewed journal – Blank (1991) reported the results of a truly-scientific experiment. The experiment tested whether there is a difference between double-blind and single-blind reviewing, and found that there is such a difference, that is, 'acceptance rates are lower and referees are more critical when the reviewer is unaware of the author's identity' (p. 1041). While the study was enlightening, it acknowledged that, in most cases, referees can actually identify authors from the text they submit, even when they are not told their identity by the journal editor. Again, this is a reflection of the sociological character of success in economics, which is largely independent of the particular peer review rules that a journal might establish.

Peer review in economics is heavily self-regulated; unlike peer review issues in science, external organizations (like the news media and legal systems) are rarely, if ever, involved. As suggested above, the absence of other organizations' involvement is primarily a result of a lack of public interest in economic studies, plus the fact that the stakes are low in comparison to natural science. Nonetheless, self-regulation in peer review is not a comforting thought. As Charles McCutchen has remarked, 'Self-regulation of any profession runs afoul of collective self-interest and pack loyalty. When disciplinary committees operate in secret, these influences have full rein.'[20]

## BUT PEOPLE ARE PEOPLE, AREN'T THEY?

Critics of criticism are always quick to argue that no one group, like economists, should be singled out as deviating from good science practice – such problems exist in all fields of science and social science. Indeed, an enormous amount of literature exists on the sociology of science, documenting countless cases of scientists, in the natural sciences, acting cliquish, childish and petty and appearing to have little or no interest in proper methods of inquiry. Thus, in conversations among scientists or social scientists, when one person says 'economists are not scientific' such a remark is often followed by, 'but neither are scientists'. Regardless of any arguments I might make to the contrary, some critics of this book will be sure to write that I have unfairly juxtaposed *real* economists against *ideal* scientists, or real economics against an *ideal* science. Real science and real scientists, some might argue, have the same problems that real economics and real economists have.

That argument, however, is false. It will typically be made by two types of individuals: individuals with a strong background in economics, and little or no background in natural science; or the opposite: individuals with a strong background in natural science, but little or no background in economics (in which case they may be willing to give economists the benefit of the doubt). From my experience, people with backgrounds in both, like those who attend conferences on science and technology policy, are the strongest critics of economics.

The fact that more literature exists on the problems of natural science methods than on the problems of economic methods is probably not due to the presence of more problems in natural science, but to the greater concerns natural scientists have, to begin with, with employing proper methods. As a case in point, most of the literature on the methodological problems in natural science involve cases of scientists supporting the wrong theories in spite of scientific evidence,[21] while most of the literature on methodological problems in economics involve cases of economists generating theories that have little scientific relevance in general. That is, as economists, we often do not have the luxury that natural scientists have of needing to decide whether one theory should replace another — rather, we more often need to decide whether the theories we already have are valid enough to be upheld.

Yet, it has long been a stylized fact that social science is inherently 'fuzzier' than natural science, and therefore, events in social science are more difficult to predict than events in natural-science. For instance, John Casti, in his book, *Searching for Certainty: What Scientists Can Know about the Future*, wrote:

> It is in those areas of the natural sciences least susceptible to human influence that we have the best 'programs' for prediction and explanation. As we move away from hard physics and astronomy and into the Jell-O-like realm of biology, our capabilities for prediction and explanation begin to deteriorate. And by the time we reach the almost totally gaseous state of economics and other social sciences, there's far more "social" than "science" in our capacity to say what's next and why.[22]

I think this perspective, however, is overly simplistic, and to some extent, anachronistic. An important distinction must be made between the complexity and difficulty of a field and the validity of the methods used to investigate it. A freshman, introductory textbook on astronomy certainly describes more predictable phenomena than an introductory textbook on biology, which in turn describes much more predictable phenomena than an introductory textbook on economics. On the other hand, graduate work in economics on trends in international exchange rates, for instance, involves more predicable and reliable phenomena than biological research on the AIDS virus, which, in turn, involves more predictable phenomena than graduate-level research on the cutting edge of particle physics or astronomical research on the search for extraterrestrial life. In modern times, many economic phenomena, like exchange rates, do not even involve humans very much – they are economic variables whose fluctuations have largely been entrusted to computer programs. Yes, humans wrote the programs, but they did it based on data and mathematical principles, not based on urges from human hormones or other fuzzy influences. Other factors in the economy, like the growing importance of computers, are functions of science and engineering discoveries themselves, and therefore, in the aggregate, they have no more to do with humans than the computer science that underlies those changes. Yes, humanity still plays a role: the economic demand for wine, for example, exceeds the demand for grape juice, surely because of factors associated with humanity. But, even then, much of those aspects of humanity can be understood in terms of biology or neuroscience. Indeed, when we stop and look at the big picture, and at the frontiers of economics and science, economics may be seen as existing in a much more 'deterministic universe' than many areas of science and engineering. Our excuses may work well on undergraduates, who, in their undergraduate courses, see fuzzy topics of economics juxtaposed to rock-solid, and 'proven', principles of physics, chemistry, biology and geoscience. On the graduate level, however, when the rock-solid sciences also come to look fuzzy, our excuses for economics no longer hold.

Astronomical research looking into the possibilities of life on other planets certainly does not involve more predicable phenomena than most economic variables. Yet, for the reasons outlined in this book, that astronomical research is likely to be more scientific. Our main problems in economics lie primarily in our methods of inquiry, *not* in the difficulty of our subject matter.

## NOTES

1. Keeports and Morier, 1994, p. 47.
2. Friedman, 1953, p. 20.
3. Hodson, 1993, p. 125.
4. Sahal, 1981, pp. 6-9.

5. See, for example, Clower 1989.

6. Stigum 1990, p. 16.

7. See, for example, McCloskey 1985.

8. For an interesting and useful discussion of the Rational Expectations' rise to fame in the economics community, and its associated political connotations, see Miller and Neff 1997.

9. See, for example, Sen 1993.

10. See, for example, Eichner's (1983) discussion of the variable, capital (pp. 213–14), which is also discussed in Chapter 9.

11. See Friedman 1953, pp. 18-20.

12. See, for example, Colander 1991.

13. Mitroff 1974, p. 76.

14. See, for example, Bloom 1995 and Science 1995.

15. See, for example, the report by Arora and Gambardella in 1996, on NSF support for research in economics, which gives 'impact scores' of, for example, 100 for the *Journal of Economic Literature*, 59 for *Journal of Political Economy*, 34 for *American Economic Review*, 15 for *Economic Journal*, 8 for *Economic Inquiry*, 4 for *Applied Economics*, 2 for *Journal of Development Economics*, 1 for *Journal of Post Keynesian Economics*, and 1 for the *Eastern Economic Journal*.

16. Hamermesh 1992, p. 171.

17. Some economists do recognize the inbreeding problem, and take positive steps against it. For example, after completing my dissertation in 1991 I was hired by the Economic Research Service (ERS) of the US Department of Agriculture, even though my dissertation had almost nothing to do with agriculture, and I had not taken a single course in agricultural economics. The division director who hired me had explained that he and others at ERS did not restrict the agency to only agricultural economists, because they wanted to avoid 'inbreeding'. Having been raised and educated in an urban environment, it was my first encounter with the term 'inbreeding' in this context, which is surely something that would tend to be used by agricultural economists. I have used the term here as a substitute for the more common, though less palatable, term – 'incestuous relationships' (whose offensiveness, of course, may be traced to the adverse consequences of inbreeding).

18. This is not always the case, of course – my own dissertation advisors allowed me considerable latitude to explore my topic in my own way, guided by broad, established principles of scientific inquiry. As one might hypothesize from the style of this book, the way I ended up with such advisors did not happen by chance alone, although I was still lucky in a general sense.

19. Notable exceptions to this remark would be Colander and Coats 1989, Eichner 1983, and Mayer 1993.

20. McCutchen 1991, p. 34.

21. See, for example, Mitroff 1974.

22. Casti, p. 408.

# 3. Measurement in Economics Must be Taken More Seriously

## MEASUREMENT IN SCIENCE VERSUS MEASUREMENT IN ECONOMICS

In science, measurement is never taken for granted – it is always questioned. When I think of measurement in science, I am reminded of how I had been taught in chemistry-laboratory classes to properly measure a liquid in a glass tube. There is usually a slight ambiguity as to where the liquid ends, since it usually forms a crescent, or 'meniscus', at the top, due to its adhesion to the glass. We were instructed in chemistry to always measure the quantity of a liquid from the bottom of the 'meniscus', thereby eliminating some measurement uncertainty with regard to fractions of a drop. In science, of course, accuracy in measurement is crucial. Tiny perturbations in a star's orbit around the galaxy may be seen as strong evidence of its possession of a planet. This is hardly the case in economics. In economics small disturbances in a measured economic variable could be due to any number of unimportant circumstances, from the idiosyncracies of individual corporate leaders, to changes in a survey's design. Surely, it is fair to say that measurement accuracy is generally more important in natural science than in social science, because of the relatively more reliable behavior of physical phenomena in comparison to social phenomena. Nonetheless, this does not mean that measurement issues in social science are not important and need not be addressed. In economics, the lack of interest in measurement issues, especially within the most influential professional circles, is one of our profession's greatest faults.

As Professor Thomas Mayer notes in his 1993 book, *Truth versus Precision in Economics*, the acquisition of 'numbers' by economists is carried out by a separate, and often less respected, sector of the economics community. The economists who apply those numbers for testing theoretical economic models rarely question how the numbers were obtained, and thus, rarely know what the numbers ultimately mean. Conversely, those who compile the initial data may be fully aware of the data's advantages and limitations, but may not be aware of the models that will be used to test those data, and thus they may underestimate, and under-report, the importance of those limitations. Consequently, empirical model-testing in economics is often *scientifically invalid*. As Jerry Ravetz wrote a 1995 article entitled, 'Economics as an elite folk science: the suppression of uncertainty':

> [O]ne can speak of a new and significant sort of pseudo-science of our times, one defined not by its cosmology (as astrology or numerology) but by its methodology. I call this a "GIGO-science," referring to the American acronym, "Garbage In, Garbage Out" which defines the limits of possible improvement of input data by a computer program. I have defined such a science as one where uncertainties in inputs must be systematically suppressed, lest the outputs become indeterminate. (p. 172)

The following factors describe how we have allowed this problem to occur in economics:

**Simple Ignorance**

Sometimes we simply do not know about sources of error in the data we use. This situation can occur, for example, in time series data, when accounting methods change at a point in time in the series, but the importance of that change is underemphasized (or not reported) in the original documents containing the data. It also occurs when data do not coincide with a well-defined physical concept, like hours of labor, but with more abstract concepts like purchasing power parities among foreign currencies. In the latter case, because the measurement is abstract, more knowledge is required to understand how the numbers are actually obtained. Researchers who use the data may simply not have the information needed to acquire that knowledge, or may simply be too disinterested in the topic to seek that information.

Simple ignorance applies not only to the meanings of economic variables, or their measurement biases, but also to their variance (or 'measurement error'). We sometimes make strong conclusions about findings that are largely due to chance, rather than some fundamental aspect of the economic system. In theory, this should not happen because we are only supposed to report on findings that are 'statistically significant', for example, with less than a 5 or 1 percent likelihood of occurring by chance alone. With modern econometric software, however, we can run tens or hundreds of different econometric experiments at an enormously rapid rate, for example, one per minute. With a decent size database, it often does not take very long to run enough independent tests to acquire statistically significant findings. Once statistical significance is aquired, as long as the economic model has some precedence in the literature, and we can 'tell a good story about it', our statistically significant findings can be published. As the saying goes, 'If you keep torturing the data long enough, it will eventually cave in and say "OK – I give up – I'll tell you anything you want to know"'.

## Conspiracy of Ignorance

We may be aware of major flaws in the data we use, but may use the data in any case, because it will enable us to publish papers and thereby advance in our profession. The question remains why such papers, based on data known to be erroneous, survive the review process. To this question, I offer the following answers:

1. Because we are frequently highly-specialized, our very livelihood may greatly depend on having access to data on a small number of specific variables. Consequently, the reviewers of our papers, being experts in exactly the same subfield, and thus, 'being in the same boat', are usually empathetic to the problem of having to rely on bad data. Such reviewers, often responsible for the same actions, tend to require only that authors qualify their conclusions as being limited by 'imperfections' in the data. In general, qualifications of, or even apologies for, known problems often carries considerable weight in economic discourse.
2. Along with this camaraderie among members of the same subfield, a fairness factor arises as well – the idea that, if one member of the group were allowed to publish using the data in a similar model, then another member of the group should be given the same right. A similar fairness factor arises in the competition among subfields – if economists in one subfield who use equally questionable data are able to publish, then economists in other subfields should be allowed to do the same.
3. Specific data often come from a single source, for example, a particular governmental agency or international organization. Often, those who use those data in testing economic models have exclusive rights to them, or at least have access to them before anyone else does. When the recipient organization is not within the same organization, it may have to compete for the favored status that it enjoys. Not only may that favored status be jeopardized by the recipient's criticism of the data, or reduced utilization of the data, but that favored status, to begin with, may derive from the recipient's presentation of the data in a favorable light.
4. When the supplier and recipient are within the same organization, even greater incentives may exist for 'not making waves' about the inadequacy of the data. In theory, the recipient, as a final user of the data, should be given some power over how the data are initially compiled. However, in actuality, the individuals in charge of data gathering frequently have more power in an organization than those who perform the analyses. The reason

is circumstantial: large data collection is relatively expensive, while analysis of the data once it is collected is relatively inexpensive, and authority in an organization is usually correlated with the cost of the operations managed. That is, people who analyze the data tend to be specialized experts who spend a good proportion of their time reading new books and journal articles, while those in charge of contracting-out data collection are often high-level managers in their organization. Given these circumstances, the organizational culture often does not allow analysts much opportunity to scrutinize the process of data collection.

5. As economists, we have tended to be very accepting of the idea that, if one does the best one can, with what one has, then that is all that is required. This outlook, however, can be inconsistent with the more scientific view that research must meet pre-established standards of competence and reliability, and if not, that research should be discarded, in spite of the fact that it might be the best one could do with what one has.

While the solutions to the problems mentioned thus far may appear to be straightforward, the remaining problem of 'intrinsic ignorance' could prove to be much more troublesome.

**Intrinsic Ignorance**

Suppose a researcher had a barrel of apples, and was performing a study that used as input the quantity of apples it contained. If the barrel provided a label that said, 'this barrel contains approximately 100 apples', when in actuality it contained 95, then the mistake of using 100 as the measured amount would constitute 'simple ignorance' as defined above. If the researcher knows, however, that the label probably exaggerates the number of apples, but he decides to use 100 anyway, because he does not want to criticize the manufacturer, then that would constitute a 'conspiracy of ignorance', as also defined above. Now suppose the label provides additional information, that is, 'this barrel contains approximately 100 apples, the weight of the product is 13.34 kilograms'. In other words, the weight of the contents of the barrel was measured precisely, while the number 100 was roughly approximated and probably subject to significant 'rounding error'. In this case, the researcher would probably be better off to use 13.34 kilograms as the measure of apples for his study. If he chooses not to, however, simply because he does not really understand kilograms very well, and studies like his have always used the number of apples rather than kilograms, then this kind of ignorance could be referred to as 'intrinsic ignorance'.

In more concrete terms, I define 'intrinsic ignorance in measurement' as occurring when economists fail to sort out important differences in measurement between the true physical nature of the phenomenon being studied and circumstantial aspects of how data on that phenomenon have been defined and collected. Examples of this problem are provided in the remainder of this chapter. As these examples imply, the problem is pervasive throughout economic discourse, especially whenever real data are used as inputs for economic models. One special case of intrinsic ignorance is in the economic measurement of physical capital, which I considered to be a large enough problem to be discussed in a separate chapter – Chapter 9.

## EXAMPLE 1: TECHNOLOGICAL CHANGE AND 'HIGH–TECH' INDUSTRIES

Economic studies of technological change have varied a great deal in terms of the questions they raise and the methods they use to answer them. These questions, whether empirical or theoretical, start with certain 'elemental units of analysis' – the smallest pieces of the puzzle they are trying to solve. For example, the elemental units of chemistry, are called, by no coincidence, 'elements'. Those elements are 'well behaved' in terms of consistent scientific properties, unless there is some disturbance in the homogeneity of atoms. When such elements then cease to be well behaved the science of general chemistry, itself, becomes less applicable, and quantum mechanics must be introduced to explain such things as isotopes and the splitting of atoms.

Thus, the strength of any science depends, in large part, on the extent to which its elemental units behave consistently. The fact that an oxygen atom is the same today as it has been throughout history has enabled scientists to research, and thereby come to understand, its properties. However, when the elemental unit changes physically, as the split atom studied in nuclear physics, or the species studied in biological evolution, then 'good science' demands that such change, itself, be the main object of study. It is not enough, for example, to study the evolution of species by measuring the quantities of various organisms over time, because doing so would not explain why such change has occurred. It is necessary, rather, for theory to be tied to causality, for example, in the case of biological evolution, that beneficial 'traits' be identified, leading to an understanding of *why* organisms have evolved in the directions they have. Here, the concept 'traits' becomes a new elemental unit of the analysis that explains changes in species, while species, itself in this context, has lost its homogeneity, and is no longer elemental.

Technological change is widely recognized by economists as an evolutionary process,[1] but the study of technological change often suffers from the absence of elementary units that provide useful information about causality. As argued in the subsequent chapter, industries are often categorized on the basis of superficial and archaic descriptions, that have only historical precedence in data recording as their primary justification. Technological change is usually then measured in terms of the incidence, among these categories, of nominal events like patents and innovations. Such events are rarely measured in terms of their economic or scientific importance.

As always, we are left with data that tell a story. It is often an interesting, mathematical story, or a story that lends itself to the exploration of new methods in econometrics. Nonetheless, it is a story that explains little about the practical significance of the effects measured, or why such effects really occurred.

The problem, in most cases, does not reflect a deliberate or conscious effort on our part to ignore questions of causality in our work. Rather, in large part we are victims of circumstance ourselves, in having to rely on whatever data are available, or affordable to acquire. In short, the problem is a lack of data that reflect causal relationships, or, in reference to the above discussion, the absence of adequate information about meaningful, elemental units of analysis. As mentioned above, this problem exists in the definition, measurement, and classification of data used in economic analysis of technological change. In turn, the problem leads to economic models which, like the data they examine, do not offer good causal explanations for economic change.

Most technological change economists would dispute the accusation that they ignore causality. Superficially we do not, but our explanations of how and/or why technological change occurs are generally quite weak, and might more accurately be called descriptions of associated events rather than true causal explanations. Such descriptions, including work I have done myself, usually take the form of anecdotes, heuristics, restatements of the obvious, tautological exercises in thought, references to observations by others, and combinations thereof.

One example of our superficial explanation of technological change would be our analysis of 'high-tech industries'. High-tech industries are usually defined to be certain industrial sectors, according to a standard industrial classification system, for which there is a high ratio of R&D expenditures to total sales.[2] This definition, in itself, is flawed for a variety of reasons. The denominator (sales, or revenue) is invalid because the true amount of economic activity carried out by firms would best be characterized by their 'value added', not their revenue, where value added is revenue minus the cost of materials purchased from other firms. (The brokering of financial assets, for instance, generates enormous revenues but relatively little value added.) In productivity analysis, in fact, and in standard national accounting of each sector's contribution to the gross domestic product (GDP), value added, rather than sales, is properly used by the US Bureau of Economic Analysis as a measure of each sector's economic 'output'. (If sales were used, then economic activity would be 'double counted' whenever materials are purchased by other manufacturers.) Thus, the R&D/value added ratio would be a much more meaningful measure of a firm's relative commitment to R&D.

It follows that the R&D/sales ratio is biased against industries that lie further downstream in the production process. For example, computer chip manufacturers and computer manufacturers might have similar R&D/value added ratios, but chip manufacturers will have higher R&D/sales ratios because their raw materials include the chips – and thus the sales – of chip manufacturers. The sales of computer manufacturers therefore overstates their relative economic contribution, and their R&D to sales ratio understates the relative tendency to conduct R&D.

Futhermore, within each major sector examined, for which a single measure of R&D/sales is taken, there is often substantial variance in the R&D/sales ratios among the subsectors within that sector, as well as substantial variance in R&D/sales among the individual firms within each particular subsector.[3] Such variance implies that the R&D/sales ratios for major sectors may be circumstantial, depending on arbitrary aspects of how subsectors had been aggregated into sectors. (The arbitrariness of existing industrial classifications is discussed in Example 4 below, and is discussed again, more extensively, in Chapters 7 and 8.) For example, Professor Kirsty Hughes, in a 1988 article on 'the interpretation and measurement of R&D intensity,' writes:

> If there is a distribution of R&D intensities [R&D/sales] across firms within an industry, then industry studies are likely to be misleading in a number of ways. For example, estimating a relationship between R&D intensity and export performance, or productivity growth, based on an industry R&D intensity is likely to produce a biased estimate of the coefficent – whether this is a positive or negative bias will depend on the underlying distribution. (p. 302)

In spite of these problems, however, sectors defined as 'high-tech industries' by virtue of their relatively high R&D/sales ratios (or similar measures) are used by economists as a basis for comparing nations in terms of 'technological development'. They are also used in export/import analysis of 'high-tech trade flows' from which major policy implications are sometimes drawn.[4] Given the above observations, one might well ask why the measure is used, if it is so flawed. Its widespread use, in spite of its questionable validity, is attributable to intrinsic ignorance, as defined above. More precisely, two factors are at work here: (1) such data are readily available because R&D levels and sales levels are part of the publically-distributed standard accounts of corporations, while value added is not; (2) those of us most inclined to use R&D/sales ratios in our research do so because there is already a precedent for doing so, while the distinction between revenue and value added, or the variance of R&D/sales among the firms within each sector, are simply not topics of interest.[5]

## EXAMPLE 2: AGRICULTURAL MEASURES

In agricultural economics, studies on consumer demand for food have used pounds as the unit to quantify food, which is a scientifically invalid measure of its useful quantity, since the weight of food is so heavily dependent on water content (as well as the content of other substances that offer little in terms of nutrition). In measuring the consumption of fruits and vegetables, for instance, a study might equate one pound of watermelon with one pound of avocado, even though an avocado has approximately four times as many calories per pound.  Consequently, a two pound per capita increase in watermelon consumption, combined with a one pound decline in avocado consumption, would render, according to agricultural economists, a measured *increase* in overall consumption of fruits and vegetables. This is unscientific, to say the least, especially if consumers tend to drink more water when eating an avocado than when eating a watermelon. Yet, high-powered econometric techniques, reflecting graduate-level mathematics, are often applied to numbers like these.  This serves as a typical example supporting Thomas Mayer's principle of the 'strongest link'[6] – economists have a tendency to keep building up the 'strongest link' in the chain of ideas that justify a model, while the greatest limitations in the model, in terms of its truthfulness and usefulness, may be largely ignored.

From a scientific perspective, of course, a pound of food, by definition, experiences the same gravitational pull as a pound of lead, but the level of nutrition it offers could vary enormously. Often medical studies are conducted that ask, suppose a person replaces his consumption of food X with food Y; what would be the medical effects?  If the subjects are allowed to choose the quantity of food they wish to consume (reflecting a real-life situation) then there is little question that any hypothesis explored by these researchers on the effect of the substitution will be based on the assumption that people who eat N calories of X will switch to eating N calories of Y.  Calorie information on food products is generally well known and easily available, and, of course, any data on prices per pound could then be easily converted to prices per calorie consumed.

Yet, in 1976 George Ladd and Veraphol Suvannunt wrote a seminal study in agricultural economics that used the price per pound of food as the dependent variable.  The independent variables included calories, water, air per pound, and other factors.  Calories per pound were found to be significantly related to price per pound, with a coefficient of 0.02 cents per calorie, while water and air were not significant. Dummy variables for distinguishing vegetables from meats, and so on, were not used. Thus, owing to intellectual isolation and some impressive econometrics (at the time the study was published), these agricultural economists were able to receive considerable recognition for work that largely ignored basic principles of food consumption – basic principles, in fact, that life scientists had already known for centuries. At present, their study has remained highly regarded in the field of agricultural economics, to the degree that anyone doing hedonic price studies of food products would be expected to cite it.[7]

Another example of the same problem can be seen in the way that agricultural economists have tended to measure pesticides – again in pounds. Several studies have been done using 'pounds of active ingredient' of pesticide applied per acre as the dependent variable of the analysis, which is then treated as a function of the characteristics of the pesticide. Suppose, for example, that pesticide X is twice as potent per pound as pesticide Y, and potency is a characteristic of pesticides. Of course, farmers will tend to use N pounds of pesticide Y per acre and N/2 pounds of pesticide X per acre. Yet, sophisticated Box–Cox hedonic regression techniques have been used for cross sectional analyses of different pesticides, with pounds as the quantities used in the analysis. Of course, these studies have found a significant, negative statistical relationship between the 'quantity' of pesticide applied per acre and its potency. A much more meaningful dependent variable would have been the number of applications of a pesticide, where an application is the physical quantity that is supposed to be applied to an acre according to the instructions issued by the company. This alternative dependent variable would at least explain how inclined farmers are to apply different pesticides, as opposed to a meaningless dependent variable (pounds) that provides some obscure mixture of information about farmers' inclination to apply a pesticide combined with the circumstantial chemical properties of a pesticide.[8] The fact that pounds (or price per pound) was used as the unit of measure appears to have simply been a circumstantial consequence of prices being initially provided in pounds, plus the fact that 'price per pound' is a variable with a strong historical precedence in agricultural economics.

## EXAMPLE 3: MEASURING THE ECONOMIC RETURNS TO R&D

A key factor in economic studies has been the effect of R&D on 'productivity'. Productivity has different meanings, depending on the particular question being asked. The most common definition is the amount of a good or service, or 'output', that can be produced with a certain number of workers. For example, productivity is said to rise in the United States when the total output per worker rises. More detailed analysis of productivity recognizes other 'inputs' into the production process besides labor, such as capital and materials. For instance, if the amounts of inputs remain the same in a factory but the existing machinery is adjusted to render greater output, the 'productivity of capital' is said to rise. In economic studies of technical change, a concept called 'total factor productivity' is often used. This represents the productivity that can be associated with *all* of the inputs involved in production. In many cases, total factor productivity is preferable for looking at the effects of technical change, because separating out productivities among inputs is often difficult or ambiguous. The traditional method for analyzing productivity in economics has been to use a 'production function' to interrelate the quantity of output produced with quantities of inputs utilized – primarily capital and labor. Labor is measured in terms of full-time-equivalent employees per year, and capital in terms of how much the equipment and facilities would cost if they were rented for a year. Productivity is said to increase when more output can be produced with the same amounts of inputs. When observed changes in productivity can be associated with R&D activities, the *value* of those productivity changes is considered a *return* on R&D investment.

Studies in this area range from examinations of a specific innovation and the particular effects that it had to examinations of aggregate estimates of productivity growth for an entire economy as a result of R&D performed. Such studies focus on particular types of research such as fundamental research, academic, government supported, and private; and types of economic effects, such as cost reduction and quality improvement to the organization performing the research, and spillover effects that benefit those who did not pay for the research.

In 1980, Nestor Terleckyj divided the effects of private R&D into two groups: '(1) direct increases in productivity of industries conducting the privately financed R&D, and (2) indirect increases in productivity of industries purchasing capital and intermediate inputs from the industries conducting the privately financed R&D.'[9] He found the latter effect to be greater, on average, across all industries. In another study in 1982, David Levy and Nestor Terleckyj examined government–financed R&D and observed that it had the effect of stimulating additional private R&D expenditure. Similar complementarity between government and private R&D was observed again by Professors Dennis Leyden and Albert Link in 1991.

In spite of the abundance of studies on this topic (many came before and after those mentioned), in reality, economic analysis of R&D investment has progressed very little since the mid-1960s. Magnitudes of these returns have varied enormously, from negative returns to positive returns of over 100 percent per year. Furthermore, in all such studies, the measurement of returns has required strong, simplifying assumptions.

For example, a survey article by Ishaq Nadiri in 1993 examined 63 studies in this area published by prominent economists, mostly in reference to the United States, but also in reference to Japan, Canada, France, and Germany. Looking at the results of these studies, he concluded that R&D activity renders, on average, a 20 to 30 percent annual return on investments. He also found that R&D renders a much greater return to society overall, from 20 to 100 percent, with an average of approximately 50 percent.

These figures for the aggregate effects of R&D have been consistent with the high returns often found in the analysis of individual innovations. For example, Edward Mansfield in 1994 examined three studies of sets of specific innovations, which reported social rates of return of 56, 70, and 99 percent. Likewise, work by Erik Brynjolfsson and others found the returns from information technology to be quite high, exceeding 80 percent per year from 1987 to 1991.[10] And, if that sounds high, Manuel Trajtenberg in 1990 found the social rate of return from innovations in a particular type of medical equipment (CT scanners) to be as high as 270 percent per year.

These high rates of return have led others to take the analysis one step further, and argue that the social 'optimal' amount of R&D investment should be much larger. In 1997, Charles Jones and John Williams, for instance, remarked, 'Using a conservative estimate of the rate of return to R&D of about 30 percent, optimal R&D investment is at least four times larger than actual investment.'[11]

The enormous variance in the results of these studies reflect inherent problems in the data used and ambiguities as to how to interpret those data. A typical analysis of these effects is provided, for instance, by Ishaq Nadiri in 1980, in which the logarithm of the following equation is estimated econometrically:

$$Q_t = A K_t^{\alpha_1} L_t^{\alpha_2} R_t^{\alpha_3} e^{\rho t}$$

where $Q$ is economic output, $A$ is a constant, $K$ is capital, $L$ is labor, $R$ is research and development, and $\rho$ is 'the rate of exogenous technical change' (p. 377). Simple ordinary-least-square regressions in this case, using cross-section time series data (for different industries in different years) simply do not work because of peculiarities in the data. Professor Nadiri explains:

> [W]e encountered estimation problems due to the high multi-collinearity among the variables. The pairwise correlations among $K$, $L$, $R$ and $t$ often were about 0.90. A consequence of the high degrees of multi-collinearity among these variables is to make some of the variables look statistically insignificant when in fact they should be

significant on theoretical grounds. . . . The coefficients of employment, *L*, in each case were very large – above one, and the signs of the coefficients of *K* and *R* were sometimes negative and their magnitudes turned out to be statistically insignificant, and the fit of the equation was generally poor.[12]

In addition, several economists have noted basic, conceptual problems in the theory associated with estimations of this kind. For example, Richard Nelson, in an important article on the validity of such methods, concludes:

> The family of models developed in this article all point to cross industry differences in technological opportunity as the key to the positive cross sectional relationship between R&D intensity and total factor productivity growth. Strong technological opportunity naturally induces high R&D intensity. Within these models one cannot argue that industries marked by low total factor productivity could significantly increase the latter if they increased the former, because steady-state total factor productivity growth in an industry is invariant to R&D intensity.
>
> Nor can the estimated cross sectional coefficient on R&D intensity be interpreted as measuring the private (or social) rate of return on R&D. There are serious flaws in the logic that have led some to that interpretation. Economists interested in measuring the rate of return on R&D must look to other means.[13]

In 1994, Zvi Griliches' presidential address to the American Economic Association on 'Productivity, R&D, and the Data Constraint' examined data on different industries from 1958 to 1989 and provided evidence that industrial productivity increases with increased R&D expenditure as a proportion of sales volume. He noted that the computer industry is a major 'outlier' in the data, having both the highest productivity growth and the highest ratio of R&D to sales. With computers left out of the data, according to his analysis, the relationship between R&D and productivity is not as strong, though it is still significant.

It is quite amazing, however, that so many studies have been done, and continue to be done, that find R&D to be a statistically-significant, contributing factor to productivity growth, but few, if any, of these studies address which industrial sectors, or which fields of science, appear to have higher rates of return than others. There is something very wrong here: if the ability to measure rates of return is, indeed, valid, then why would it not be used to provide useful information on which types of activities have higher returns than others? One would think that such information would be invaluable for the strategic decision making of both private and public institutions that fund research. The answer to this question is two-fold:

1. Such studies, in fact, have questionable validity, as evidenced alone by the incredible variance in their results, and evidenced again by the testimony of other experts in the same field. When one study, for instance, comes up with a 0 percent return, and the other with a 100 percent return, it is surely

unscientific to conclude that the return is somewhere around 50 percent. (If a professor is thought by some to be teaching at New York University, and thought by others to be teaching at University of California/Los Angeles, then it would not be safe to conclude that he teaches at the University of Kansas.)

2. The conclusion that R&D has high returns, on average, is politically palatable. The conclusion that sector X has high returns, and sector Y does not, would not be popular among those individuals whose livelihoods, and political constituencies, depend on sector Y.

Economic studies on the 'returns to R&D' have been carried out continually, and frequently, for more than four decades, beginning with Zvi Griliches' original work on the effects of research on 'hybrid corn' (maize), published in 1958. This proliferation of studies has occurred in spite of the enormous variance in results, strong criticisms by colleagues, suspicious disinterest in comparisons among industrial sectors or fields of study, and the absence of genuine progress in more than two decades. Given this list, it would be reasonable for us to question whether further research in this area should be endorsed without greater scrutiny.

## EXAMPLE 4: SCIENTIFIC VERSUS SUPERFICIAL CLASSIFICATION OF DATA

A cultural tendency exists among economists to accept, rather than question, the current methods of defining and classifying economic data. Conversely, researchers who actually obtain and develop economic data often do so with little or no interest in epistemological issues that might pertain to how the data are analyzed. The processes under which economic data are compiled by statistical agencies occur in an atmosphere of common service to the general public. As a case in point, the very idea that a 'conceptual framework' should form the basis of data classification is looked upon as an *option*, rather than a scientific imperative. For example, in 1993 Jack Triplett offered the following opinion with regard to standard industrial classification (SIC):

> In response to user concerns about the SIC, the US Bureau of the Census sponsored the International Conference on the Classification of economic activities . . . Public responses indicate substantial support for examining economic concepts for classifications, though also some reservations. Of the respondents who favor a conceptual framework for economic classifications, some favor a supply-based system and some a demand-based system. Respondents also have substantial concerns about costs and feasibility, as well as about potential disruptions that any new system would produce in time series.[14]

In other words, the context for classification has been to find the one classification that pleases the greatest number of customers, most of whom have little or no interest in answering fundamental questions about causal relationships among economic phenomena. At present, there appears to be little if any official interest in having more than one economic classification system for the purpose of answering different types of economic questions. As Dr Triplett has argued, 'Multiple classification systems might increase costs, create confidentiality problems, and lead to potential confusion among users.'[15]

Furthermore, the fear of 'confusing users' points directly to a difference in mind-sets between scientists and economists.[16] In biology, for example, three types of classifications of organisms are used, each existing to serve a different role within the context of scientific inquiry: numerical phenetics (based on the similarity of features), cladistic classification (based on genealogy), and evolutionary classification (based on inferred evolutionary history).[17] The taxonomy of organisms and comparisons among these classification methods is a complex topic in biology, with sophisticated methods and definitions, and ongoing debates in technical papers on the preferability of alternative classification methodologies. Thus, one would hardly expect biologists to drop two of their three classifications for the sake of reducing confusion among nontechnical readers.

It is true that a nontechnical clientele may be confused by more than one classification scheme, especially if they are used to only one existing for some time. On the other hand, economic studies that we present to the public are often highly sophisticated, and often much more confusing than any multiple classication scheme could be. As I argue in Chapter 7, there are other, more deeply-rooted problems that preclude our development of better systems of classifying industrial data.

## EXAMPLE 5: METHODS AND DATA USED IN 'EXPERIMENTAL ECONOMICS'

Experimental economics has grown in the last couple of decades into a substantial subfield of economics. It is perhaps the easiest subfield of economics to define, because it is not associated with any particular aspect of the economic system, but is based simply on how information is gathered – through 'laboratory experiments' with human subjects. These experiments typically involve groups of people, usually students, who are paid to participate in an organized game (like an auction) in a controlled setting (such as a classroom). Their actions, for example, the bids they make in an auction, provide a wealth of data for economists to analyze in econometric models.

The ability to use data that are not provided by official sources can be an important advantage to researchers, especially if they are studying a sensitive area in which official statistics may not exist. Moreover, the data can be as specific to any topic as they like, since the experiment can be created to test any hypothesis. However, as Daniel Friedman and Shyam Sunder remark, two important concerns arise: (1) 'Do the data permit correct causal inferences?' and (2) 'Can we generalize our inferences from laboratory to field?'[18] The second of these might candidly be reworded as: does the behavior of students paid to play a game for an hour in a classroom accurately reflect the behavior of economic agents in general, spending their own money, in the real world?

Before examining the issue of the participants of experiments, it should be noted at the outset that there is something fundamentally unscientific about the very concept of 'experimental economics' itself. The fact that many of us appear to be oblivious to this problem in the concept serves as evidence that we often do not have a good sense of the true meaning of science.

The problem is one of basic logic. One first needs to ask, why should a single subfield of economics be categorized as 'experimental economics'? In all the rest of science, an experiment is viewed as a method of investigation, not a topic of study in itself. The fields and subfields of science are divided among the types of phenomena they address, not among alternative methods of studying those phenomena. One might occasionally encounter a term like 'experimental biology', which distinguishes it from biology carried out in field studies, but that would not be an actual subfield of biology. No one takes a course in 'experimental biology', but in cell biology, molecular biology, and so on. Experimental economics, on the other hand, is a separate, unique course in economics.

Furthermore, the distinction given to 'experimental economics' as a separate subfield makes it quite explicit that other areas of economics conduct very few experiments. The question then becomes, in what areas of economics are those experimental-economics experiments actually conducted, that is, what are the categories of economic phenomena being studied through those experiments? Given that there are at least two such categories, for example, game theory and consumer demand theory, then why would it not be more consistent and logical to let these categories of study include the experiments conducted on their behalf? In other words, why is a study that runs an experiment about consumer demand not classified as a 'consumer demand' study, instead of an 'experimental economics' study? Experiments in botany, in contrast, would still be part of 'botany' – not 'experimental biology' as a concept distinct from botany.

The isolation of experimental economics from other subfields – subfields that such experiments are supposedly designed to study – suggests that the methods of experimentation, themselves, are somehow more important than the results those experiments provide. This situation, in itself, is inherently unscientific – it is a clear case of the cart pulling the horse.

There appear to be three general motives behind experimental economics studies, which, from worst to best, are: (1) propaganda for the public's perceived credibility of economic discourse, (2) methodological discussion for within the subfield itself, and (3) genuine scientific discovery. Each of these is discussed below.

In no other subfield of economics does there appear to be greater pride in the methods used than in experimental economics. Some experimental economists continually espouse how their work compares with the best work ever done in any of the social or natural sciences. For example, in 1982, Vernon Smith, one of the 'founding fathers' of experimental economics, writes:

> The pricing system – How is order produced from freedom of choice? – is a scientific mystery as deep, fundamental, and inspiring as that of the expanding universe or the forces that bind matter. For to understand it is to understand something about how the human species got from hunter-gathering through the agricultural and industrial revolutions to a state of affluence that allows us to ask questions about the expanding universe, the weak and strong forces that bind particles, and the nature of the pricing system itself.[19]

In some respects, experimental economics is seen, most often by experimental economists themselves, as the first line of defense against the criticism that economics is not a science. In truth, such a defense is not a matter of pride as much as it is a matter of money. When organizations must justify their support for economic research, it is desirable for such research to be seen as having everything that any other type of scientific research has, like experiments.

Moreover, experimental economists appear to believe that they represent the 'scientists' among economists, as reflected by the fact that their main international organization goes by the broad name of the 'Economic Science Association' rather than 'Experimental Economics Association'. The Economic Science Association's restriction in scope to only experimental economics is evident from its journal being named *Experimental Economics*, and its mandate, which states that the association exists to promote 'controlled experiments as a means for understanding economic behavior'. Apparently, no other significant association or society of economists goes by the name of 'economic science' or by any other terminology expressing the same concept.

It is ironic that experimental economists often defend economics as a science to funding institutions, to the press, and to their students, using their own work as examples, but, indirectly, through their own self-proclaimed status, they effectively criticize the rest of economics as being unscientific. If experimental economists truly believed that other subfields were also scientific, then how could they have established an 'economic science association' that would have only experimental economists as its members? Conversely, if other subfields were as scientific as the experimental economists, why would members of those other fields not protest experimental economists' pronounced, exclusive entitlement to 'scientific economics'. The only explanation for the current status of the Economic Science Association is that most economists simply do not care whether they are viewed as scientists or not – that is why the experimental economists can lay claim to the concept of 'economic science' without our resistence.

Perhaps what is most disturbing about this entire situation is that, if experimental economists truly believed that their framework was the only scientific one, one would think that they would be critical of the methods used by others. Scientists, as a rule, are, and have historically been, outspokenly critical of unscientific or pseudoscientific methods employed by others. Such criticism comes with the territory of being committed to science and scientific methods. Their complacency, therefore, calls into question their true commitment to science.

Since the early 1980s, experimental economics has grown widely, due, in part, to the image factors mentioned above. In 1993, John Hey and Graham Loomes identify the following major categories of work in this area: methodological concerns (how best to conduct experiments), preference reversals (inconsistencies in preferences – discussed further below), willingness to pay and willingness to accept (for example, how much someone would pay to give up a property right he already possesses, vs. how much he would pay to acquire that property right), expected utility and generalizations, games, bargaining, auctions, public goods, and markets.

Another reason for this growth is that studies in experimental economics have been relatively cheap and easy to produce. Suppose, for example, one wanted to study the effects of different types of rules on the final outcomes of auctions (a typical topic for an experimental economics study). One could research where auctions with different rules are actually taking place, obtain permission to attend them and record information about them, travel to them, process the data acquired, and struggle to interpret the results by attempting to distinguish the separate effects of alternative auction rules from the other differential aspects of the auctions. A much cheaper and easier approach, however, especially for someone who is already teaching at a university, is to conduct an experiment. That is, simply gather a group of student subjects in a classroom (their salaries as experimental participants would be minimal), give them a little money to bid with, and run a few 'controlled experiments' involving auctions with different rules. If the results obtained are too difficult to interpret, one could simply make a few procedural changes and try it again.

The greatest limitation in such methods is that they may reflect intrinsic ignorance (as discussed above) regarding the measurement of experimental observations.[20] In particular, Professors Friedman and Sunder in their book, *Experimental Methods: A Primer for Economists*:

> Some economists question the . . . validity of laboratory data and feel that such data . . . is not representative of the real world. For example, [a] . . . referee of a paper on laboratory asset markets discounted the . . . work on the grounds that "experienced traders used to dealing with large sums of money [may not] use the same heuristics, etc., exhibited by rather naive students who may or may not take this seriously."[21]

Unfortunately, Professors Friedman and Sunder's own response to this criticism is rhetorical in nature, and appears to be written to a plebeian audience, or an audience with little background in scientific methods. They write:

> Experimentalists in other disciplines have encountered similar skepticism. Galileo's critics did not believe that motion of pendulums . . . on inclined planes had any relation to planetary motion in the celestial sphere. More recently, some people question whether substances found to be toxic in large doses in laboratory rats will harm human beings exposed to small doses over long periods of time.
>
> Deductive logic does not provide the basis to reject such skepticism. From the mere fact that you have observed the sun rise every morning for twenty years you can't really deduce the proposition that it will rise again tomorrow morning. Yet people do make the leap of faith that the sun will rise. This is *induction*. (p. 15)

The reliability of the sun rising in the morning, however, or even the commonality among mammalian illnesses, involve fairly reasonable assumptions. The assumed similarity between the behavior of professional stockbrokers on the market floor, and the behavior of undergraduate students paid to play a game for an hour in a classroom, however, is much more questionable.

Nevertheless, Daniel Friedman and Shyam Sunder dictate convenient epistemological rules for evaluating the validity of economic experiments, under the authority of 'parallelism'. They write, 'According to parallelism, it should be *presumed* that results carry over to the world outside the laboratory. An honest skeptic then has the burden of stating what is different about the outside world that might change results observed in the laboratory."[22] These are very strong words. They imply that critics of an economic experiment who do not, themselves, bear the burden of proof for their criticism are, in some sense, 'dishonest', and can rightfully be ignored by the experimental economists being criticized. This posture on the part of some experimental economists provides good pep talk for colleagues, though, obviously, it may not be as convincing to other economists or observers outside the profession.

In actuality, and borrowing some of Dr Friedman and Dr Sunder's words, evidence is, in fact, easy to find of economic experiments being different from the 'outside world' in ways 'that might change results observed in the laboratory'. Indeed, such evidence can be found in the results of economic experiments themselves. For example, consider again the remark by an anonymous referee that Friedman and Sunder objected to in the above quotation. That remark was in reference to laboratory asset markets, and expressed the idea that 'experienced traders used to dealing with large sums of money' would bid differently from 'naive students who may or may not take this seriously'. One key aspect of trading on financial assets is the uncertainty of asset prices – in effect, such trading represents a form of gambling. If students are shown to exhibit a very different type of gambling behavior from that of financial traders, then, according to Friedman and Sunder's parallelism rules, this should represent an 'honest' criticism of the experiment on laboratory asset markets.

In gambling experiments, students and other subjects have been shown to exhibit 'preference reversal' – an inconsistency of preferences among alternative gambling options. An example of preference reversal is provided by Professor Tversky in which students are given two types of bets, $H$ and $L$. Bet $H$ offers a 28/36 (or 77.8 percent) chance of winning $10, and bet $L$ a 3/36 (or 8.3 percent) chance of winning $100. Preference reversal is then explained as follows: 'When offered a choice between the two options, most subjects choose the $H$ bet over the $L$ bet. However, when asked to state their lowest selling price, the majority state a higher price for the $L$ bet than for the $H$ bet.'[23] Dr. Tversky describes this phenomenon as 'the overpricing of long shots', which he interprets as 'an effect of scale compatibility: because the prices and payoffs are expressed in the same units, payoffs are weighted more heavily in pricing than in choice.'[24]   Much has been written on such preference reversals in highly technical contexts, involving axioms, philosophical issues, and so on. At the risk of appearing amateurish, in the discussion below I opt to address the topic from a simpler and more direct perspective.

Such preference reversals, of the magnitude suggested above, would be easily observed among students having fun as subjects of an economic experiment. It would not be observed among professional financial analysts in the trading of financial assets. Indeed, if traders on Wall Street tended to overprice long shots, there would be a great deal of easy money to be made by selling long-shot stocks for more secure stocks. Thus, the experimental results acquired using non-professional experimental subjects would be unreliable measures of real-world events. In particular, unlike students bidding freely on the basis of intuition, professional traders would likely handle the $H$ and $L$ bets described above as simple, mathematical exercises. They would find the expected value of $H$ to be $7.78, and the expected value of $L$ to be $8.33.

They would only buy *H* or *L* if the price were lower than its expected value, and sell if the price were higher.

In 1992 Daniel Hausman examined preference reversals in a broader context. He devoted a chapter of his book, *The Inexact and Separate Science of Economics*, to the topic, in which he argued that, although preference reversals are measured by economists, they are taken most seriously by psychologists. According to his thorough review of the topic, economists have made great efforts to dismiss it or 'explain it away' in order to preserve the sanctity of economists' mathematical theories of consumer preferences. Such dismissal of the issue would also, as suggested in the above discussion, give greater credibility to the use of students in asset market experiments. This tendency for economists to largely ignore preference reversal leads Professor Hausman to conclude:

> The general complaisance with which most economists continue to regard the claims of economic theory and their unwillingness to take seriously relevant psychological hypotheses is hard to defend. The attractions of a separate science run deep, but there is no justification for insisting on such a structure, and doing so creates unreasonable barriers to theoretical and empirical progress.[25]

Professors Friedman and Sunder do suggest on page 16 of their book that, when the experimental economist is criticized along the lines that experimental subjects are not representative of professional traders, 'The appropriate response is to conduct experiments with . . . more experienced (or professional) traders.' Yet, on the next page they remark with regard to experiments in general, 'Among the more important do's and don'ts: . . . Find subjects whose opportunity costs are low . . . Undergraduate students are usually a good bet.'[26]

There has long been a coexistence of numerous experimental studies on preference reversal, and numerous other experimental studies on hypothetical financial markets with students pretending to be traders. This coexistence is a *non sequitur*. As suggested by Professor Hausman, it is a reflection of complacency among experimental economists toward each other's work. For example, the more general criticism that subjects with experience in asset trading behave differently from those with no experience has been used as the rationale for more experiments to test this idea,[27] but apparently has never been used to criticize other studies for the inexperienced subjects they used in their experiments.

In conclusion, experimental economists, as a group, have done well to look out for each other, in spite of the findings of their own experiments. This may be how a subfield of economics expands, but, as Hausman also suggests, it is not how a science progresses. At present, the rich supply of cheap, undergraduate subjects for economic experiments is not likely to be challenged within the experimental economics subfield. Because virtually all experimental economists have used student subjects, it appears that no one is willing to 'throw the first stone' at any experimental economist who appears to be drawing unjustifiable conclusions. At the same time, economic researchers, even with the best funding, can rarely afford to hire subjects who are professional financial traders. Thus, in spite of the absence of published criticism in this area, the empirical findings of many such studies are highly suspect.

## OTHER EXAMPLES

One incredibly simple example of intrinsic ignorance is in the manner in which we have classified generic drugs when constructing price indexes. Generics are chemically equivalent to their corresponding original brands, but chemical equivalency does not appear to have been important in the eyes of the economists who compile economic statistics. Since generics have different names, they are treated as different products, which renders an extremely different interpretation of economic events than if they were treated as the same product. In 1994 Zvi Griliches summarized problem as follows:

> (I) Generics are introduced at roughly half the price of the original brand. (ii) The brand price, however, does not decline . . . with the ex-monopolist depreciating optimally her original position and with generics gaining between half and three-quarters of the market . . . (iii) But because generic versions are treated as separate commodities . . . the price index does not fall, and since the value of shipments declines as the market shifts to generics . . . so does measured "output" in this industry and the associated productivity measures.

In other words, while the introduction of generics is, for all practical purposes, a cost reduction that benefits many consumers, it is interpreted by economists as an output and productivity reduction, simply because of economists' intrinsic ignorance of the physical nature of what we have been measuring.

As technology and income levels advance, products and services become more sophisticated, and they embody greater levels of scientific and engineering achievements. When typical goods, for example, are horses and loaves of bread, one does not need to understand very much about science or engineering to monitor a nation's economy. When typical goods become televisions sets and automobiles, the problem becomes more difficult. When they then become computers and laser surgery operations, we, as economists, should do our homework and study precisely what it is that we are measuring.

As another example of intrinsic ignorance regarding measurement, Jerry Ravetz examines monetarists' employment of the 'Fisher Equation', $MV \equiv$

*PT,* and points out that the equation contains variables that have rather fuzzy meanings, in which measured quantities would necessarily be interdependent (for example, the price level, itself, *P*, is defined in terms of indices that are constructed on the basis of weighted transactions, *T*). From this problem in measurement and definition, Professor Ravetz goes on to suggest that the economists' knowledge of the philosophy of science may have actually contributed to this breach of basic scientific principles, 'Perhaps the economists were the victims of the doctrines they learned from the philosophy of science, which concentrated on abstract problems of validation of theories while ignoring the principles of measurement.'[28]

## NOTES

1. See, for example, Nelson and Winter 1982.
2. In many cases, high-tech sectors are defined by an area of technology, for example, 'biotechnology', 'aerospace', and so on, but those areas, to begin with, were chosen on the basis of the R&D/sales ratio or a similar measure like the ratio of scientists and engineers to total employees. For additional background on the definition of high-tech industries and how they are determined, see Graves 1989, and Rausch and Bond 1999.
3. For data on R&D/sales ratios for sectors, subsectors, and individual firms, see, for example, Shepherd and Payson 1999a, 1999b.
4. See, for example, Callan et al 1997.
5. For additional analyses questioning the common uses of R&D intensity and 'high-tech' characterizations in economic discourse on technological change, see, respectively, Nelson 1988 and Baldwin and Gellatly 1998.
6. Mayer 1993.
7. Several other studies, like Nelson (1991) make the same basic error by attempting to quantify food according to 'quality attributes' by way of highly elaborate modeling that is rooted in historical, microeconomic theory on utility maximization. The quality adjustments being considered basically ask: how many pounds of food Y have the same 'quality' as one pound of food X? Juxtaposed to such high-powered theory is empirical work on quality adjustments based on ideas like: boneless poultry contains more meat per pound than bone-in poultry. Again, graduate-level mathematics and economic theory are used in combination with simplistic ideas on measuring quantities of food. The simplest and most scientific approach, but the one that would have trouble being published, would be to count food in calories, and use price paid per calorie as a scientific measure of quality.
8. More precisely, the dependent variable in the econometric analysis is price per pound, when it should be price per application. Beach and Carlson (1993) correctly use price (or 'expenditure') per application in their analysis, while Carlson and Hubbell (1993) use price per pound. However, even in the Beach/Carlson paper other variables are used on a per pound basis. For example, they have as one variable, 'toxicity' defined as the 'amount of product required to kill half a sample of rats' (milligrams of pesticide/Kg of body weight). However, with the single application as the elementary unit of analysis, the only toxicity measure that would make sense is the fraction of the pesticide application that 'would be required to kill half a sample of rats'. For example, if one application of pesticide X involves 10 kilograms of an active ingredient (per acre of land), and pesticide Y involves 5 kilograms, but both chemicals had the same toxicity in milligrams/Kg, then the toxicity factor would be unchanged according in the Beach/Carlson model. In reality, pesticide X would be twice as toxic as pesticide Y *per application*, which *should* make an important difference to the farmer and farm workers being exposed, and thus affect farmers' demand for the product.

9.  Terleckjy 1980, p. 376.
10. Their findings were summarized in Magnet 1994.
11. Jones and Williams 1997, p. i.
12. Nadiri 1980, p. 377.
13. Nelson 1988.
14. Triplett 1993, pp. 45 and 49.
15. Triplett 1993, p. 48.
16. I had expressed these ideas earlier, in Payson 1997a.
17. Mayr 1988.
18. Friedman and Sunder 1994, p. 5.
19. Smith 1982, p. 952.
20. For this reason this section on experimental economics was placed in this chapter on measurement issues, though it could have equally well been located in the previous chapter, given the behavioral factors just mentioned.
21. Friedman and Sunder 1994, p. 15.
22. Friedman and Sunder 1994, p. 16.
23. Tversky et. al 1990, p. 204.
24. Tversky et. al 1990, p. 214.
25. Hausman 1992, p. 244.
26. Friedman and Sunder 1994, pp. 16-17.
27. See, for example, Camerer 1987.
28. Ravetz 1995, p. 174.

PART II

Economic Literature on Scientific Advancement,
Technological Change and Related Topics

# 4. Science as a Public Good

## R&D IS NOT JUST ANOTHER TYPE OF INVESTMENT

In a competitive market system the economic value or worth of a product or endeavor can often be estimated by the amount that the market is willing to pay for it. In the case of scientific research, for example, the value of that research may first be approximated by the total funds that investors are willing to contribute to it. A simple theory would suggest the following: if investors thought that R&D efforts had greater payoffs than the costs of such efforts, then their demand for R&D would be greater than its supply. Consequently, they would 'bid-up' the amount of money spent on R&D, by increasing the level of R&D efforts and by paying higher prices for ownership of the companies carrying out R&D projects. R&D would thereby command greater funds and become more expensive, until it reached a point at which the expected return would be no greater than its cost, that is, demand would equal supply, and R&D would be worth precisely what investors would be willing to pay for it. Conversely, if investors first thought that R&D was less worthwhile than the amount they were paying for it, they would reduce and 'bid-down' R&D activities, until the same market equilibrium was reached.

This model of the value of scientific research may be useful in certain contexts, but it has long been regarded by economists as overly simplistic and misleading in terms of offering a useful explanation of the economic importance of scientific research. Because basic research is often published in scientific journals and shared among colleagues, it cannot be 'owned' the way someone might own a patent. As a result, basic research is generally not profitable to the scientists and institutions that conduct it. Nevertheless, the spillovers, or ripple effects, of basic research have often yielded high returns to subsequent applied research, or have had positive effects for the consumers of final goods or services that rely on the new technology. Consequently, the overall net benefits of basic research to private investors and to society overall may be quite high, even when such returns cannot be captured by the individuals and institutions that first perform the basic research. Therefore, the social benefits of research exceed the private benefits, and the true value of the research to society as a whole is usually greater than the return to private investors. From a historical perspective, these 'spillover effects' of technological change could be seen as the single, best explanation for the success of market systems at improving the overall quality of life.[1]

In addition, the benefits of any specific type of research are simply not known until after the research is performed. Investors can only guess or speculate about such benefits, and therefore the amount that they are willing to pay for a particular research project may not be closely related to what that project will actually yield. Because investors, in general, tend to prefer less risk over more risk, investment in R&D would be less attractive to them than low-risk investments like savings bonds, even if they think that R&D will yield the same return on average across all possible investments. This risk-adverse behavior implies that individual investors would spend less on R&D than they would if they knew, beforehand, what the return to R&D would be.

One might argue that, as a general rule, the more basic the research, the broader the possibilities are for future benefits, but the longer society will have to wait for them. Therefore, societies locked into short-term planning, or which 'discount' the future, may tend to undervalue basic research and overvalue applied research.[2] Basic research, on the other hand could be overvalued as well. For example, if only basic research were conducted, then that research would likely suffer, because much of the scientific equipment and applied knowledge that might go into that basic research could depend on applied research. (For instance, see the example provided below on how basic research on functional brain mapping has relied on applied development of scanning devices.)

It follows that basic research must rely on public support, or support from industrial alliances that could pool together funds for basic research.[3] Because basic research very often generates knowledge that cuts across industrial categories, there may be more sharing of new knowledge when basic research is publicly supported. That is, public support of basic research generates new knowledge that could be freely accessed by any firm that is willing and able to profit from it. For this reason there traditionally has been widespread consensus on the important role of government funding of basic research.


## WHAT IS MEANT BY A PUBLIC GOOD

In news stories about public policy, the words 'public good' are often mentioned by journalists, which could represent a social objective, for example, the 'the park was built for the public good' or a description of an existing entity, for instance, 'Johnson Park is a public good'. The second case is the one that will be examined in this discussion. In theory, every good (or service) can be identified as either a 'public' or 'private' good. However, the term as it is used in common language is quite ambiguous. Someone who reads, 'Johnson Park is a public good', in the newspaper might conclude: (1) the park is open to the public, (2) it was funded through public support, (3) it exists for the good of the public, or (4) any combination thereof.

In economics, however, 'public good' is a technical term with a precise definition. Specifically, a good or service is said to be a 'public good' if it meets the following criteria:

1. *Nonexludability.* A person cannot be prevented from enjoying the benefits of the good or service, even if he does not pay for it.
2. *Nonrivalrous consumption.* Anyone's consumption of the good or service does not, in any way, diminish anyone else's consumption (except at extreme levels in which there are crowding effects).[4]

The classic example in the economic literature of a public good is a lighthouse, because people who do not pay for a lighthouse service may still benefit from it, and when they see a lighthouse they do not diminish the ability of others to see it.[5]

Given this definition, strong arguments have been made that 'basic research' in science and engineering is a public good. Basic research, as it is measured in the United States according to official statistics, is defined as follows:

> Within the federal, university, and nonprofit sectors, basic research is defined as research directed toward increases in knowledge or understanding of the fundamental aspects of phenomena and of observable facts without specific application toward processes or products in mind. For the industry sector, basic research projects are defined as "original investigations for the advancement of scientific knowledge ... which do not have specific commercial objectives, although they may be in fields of present or potential interest to the reporting company."[6]

When such fundamental knowledge is acquired, the information is generally published in scientific journals, presented in public hearings, then written about in textbooks and taught in standard classes. The dissemination of such knowledge easily meet the above criteria for a public good.

Like other public goods, because basic knowledge cannot be easily restricted, it cannot be charged to customers, and is thus not very profitable in a market economy. Consequently, economic arguments have long existed for governmental funding of basic research, and for governmental funding of applied research devoted to development of other public goods like national defense.

The remainder of this chapter will provide five examples of science and engineering advances that meet the criteria of being either public goods themselves, or serving the purpose of enhancing other public goods. These examples will serve a variety of purposes, namely:

1. They will show how scientific and engineering research is, in fact, a public good.
2. They will demonstrate the complex relationships that often exist between economic objectives and scientific and engineering research. As a result, they will lend support to the idea that economists need a rather broad perspective on the nature of research in order to understand the true effect it has on economic progress.
3. They will illustrate the interdisciplinary nature of research, and thus the inherent difficulty one faces in trying to categorize different types of research into industrial categories (a topic addressed throughout this book).
4. They will provide useful information about the nature of science and engineering achievement itself, which, as argued in previous chapters, is something many economists should know more about.

## EXAMPLE 1: FUNCTIONAL BRAIN IMAGING

Fundamental discoveries in physics, combined with dramatic achievements in computer science and electrical engineering, have rendered medical imaging devices far superior to their predecessor, the X-ray machine. The techniques associated with these devices have evolved from X-ray computed tomography (CT) developed in the 1970s, to positron emission tomography (PET) of the 1980s, and to magnetic resonance imaging (MRI) of the 1990s. Electrical recording techniques have also made great strides in terms of accuracy and reliability, in areas such as electroencephalography (EEG) and magnetoencephalography (MEG), which measure electrical and magnetic fields. These advances have had profound effects on modern medical practice, especially in diagnosis. However, the benefits of this area of technology extend beyond the practice of medicine. Neuroscientists, for example, have adopted the new technology to develop a greater understanding of how the human brain works, that is, how it processes sensory perception, thoughts, muscle control, and other neural functions. In essence, they have learned how to produce images of the brain that vary according to the functions the brain is performing – hence the term, 'functional brain imaging'.

The basic method of experimentation in this area is to monitor subjects first in an inactive 'control state', and then again in a 'task state' in which they perform a simple action, such as reading a word. Functional PET and MRI scans highlight neural activity, which is widespread throughout the brain in both the control state and task state. From these two states, two pictures of brain activity emerge. The difference between the two pictures reveals the neural activity that is attributable to the specific task. For statistical accuracy, this same experiment is performed repeatedly with the same subject and same task, allowing averages to be taken of the observed differences between the control and task states.[7]

Functional PET uses a radioactive isotope of oxygen (oxygen 15) in water, which has no deleterious effects, to trace blood flow. The effect must be observed in less than 10 minutes, beyond such time the radioactivity of the water almost completely decays. Changes in blood flow attributable to the task being investigated can thereby be observed using the subtraction method just mentioned. In effect, the neuroscientist can use functional PET to develop evidence on the physical locations of various mental activities in the brain. As a result, the brain ceases to be the black box that it once was, and is rediscovered as a physical entity with its own unique and ordered topography.

Functional MRI has several advantages over functional PET: it has superior spacial resolution, being able to display parts as small as 1 or 2 millimeters; it is 'nonintrusive,' i.e., it does not require the subject to induce any substance to make the imaging work, and it does not expose the subject to radiation. Furthermore, it detects flows of oxygen, rather than blood, which tells scientists more about how the brain is functioning in relation to the subject's assigned task. Finally, with the right equipment, functional MRI can be used to monitor a subject's neural activity in continuous, real time. That is, it can display neurological events as they actually unfold.[8]

While functional PET and MRI reveal chemical processes taking place in the brain, they do not reveal information exchanges among parts of the brain, which occur much more quickly. These information exchanges are electrochemical, and as such require electrical recording techniques in order to be detected. Two existing techniques that measure these information exchanges are EEG and MEG, which have undergone substantial improvements in resolution. On the other hand, EEG and MEG cannot boast the same degree of resolution as functional MRI, and unlike functional MRI and PET their resolution worsens the deeper into the brain they attempt to image. Nevertheless, while PET, MRI, EEG, and MEG techniques have their own sets of advantages and limitations, the simultaneous application of combinations of these technologies may be of great benefit in neuroscientists' efforts to understand brain activities.[9]

The potential benefits in understanding better how the brain functions could be enormous. As an example, any understanding of the brain that would enable the correction or partial alleviation of learning disabilities would be greatly welcomed. Approximately 120,000 additional students per year in the United States are labeled as 'learning disabled', for whom competency in reading or math falls short of what would be expected according to their IQ scores.[10] Approximately 2.3 million schoolchildren in the United States are diagnosed with learning disorders. Of these, 80 percent are identified as dyslexic. In the mid 1990s, public schools in the United States spent approximately $8,000 per year on each learning-disabled student, compared to $5,500 for each ordinary student. Consequently, learning disabilities among public school students cost society billions of dollars.[11] Of course, learning disabilities among adult Americans involve other disadvantages for both them and the rest of society.

While functional brain imaging has not led to any solution for learning disabilities, it has recently increased scientists' ability to understand the physical processes associated with learning disabilities. As always, it is through more knowledge that scientists hope to find solutions. Using functional PET and MRI, neuroscientists at Learning Disability Research Centers (LDRCs) have made discoveries about the thalamus, a double-egg-shaped structure located deep within the brain, that may account for many instances of learning disability. More precisely, they have found differences in the levels of thalamus activity between ordinary and learning-disabled subjects. One study found 'subjects who scored on the bottom 10 percent of the population on a standard reading test had less activity in the left thalamus'.[12] This involvement of the thalamus is consistent with the known roles of the thalamus as an intermediary processor of information between sensory input and the cerebral cortex, and as a provider of rapid and precise timekeeping. Researchers have identified another area of importance, a portion of the prefrontal cortex, which is a crucial component of speech–sound processing.[13] As these studies progress, more may become known about the actual physical factors associated with learning disabilities, bringing science that much closer to possible solutions.

Several factors associated with the social and economic effects of functional brain imaging can be identified. There is a strong connection between engineering know-how, in the development of imaging technology, and basic knowledge. The engineering technology used in functional brain imaging is not only applied to medical services, but is recycled right back into research for the sake of advancing knowledge in the neurosciences. The connection between basic knowledge and the development of human skills is strong as well, because in this case, the knowledge is about human skills.

Initially, the market system does not seem involved in the process, or at least not in the research on functional brain imaging, which is funded largely by government and academia. However, the development of the imaging technology could be attributed to commercial aspects of medical advances. While the cost for MRI, PET, and MEG equipment was, in the mid 1990s, typically between $2 million and $4 million per machine,[14] the development cost to a company would not have been financially justified unless many units could have been sold. Again, imaging equipment was originally created through the development of new services, and innovation in the production of existing goods (allowing the equipment to be produced more cheaply). In essence, in this case, advances in medical equipment gave rise to advances in medical (or neuroscience) research, rather than the other way around.

## EXAMPLE 2: MONITORING OF CLIMATIC EVENTS

Few scientific events capture human interest as much as the weather. Weather is something that affects nearly everyone, but can be controlled by no one. Thus, it has long been the most widely covered topic in the news that people receive, and has earned the reputation of being an ideal topic of conversation. Throughout history, scientists have continued to improve their ability to predict the weather, which has benefitted society in countless ways, from preparing for disasters like hurricanes, to deciding when crops should be planted, to scheduling company picnics. Weather is also a phenomenon that is completely 'global' – it neither recognizes nor obeys national boundaries. Consequently, humanity's ability to understand and predict the weather can be attested to international co-operation in the gathering and exchange of information, and in the collaboration of scientists in their development and testing of new theories.

Yet, perhaps because weather has been studied extensively for millennia, and has become an extremely sophisticated science, some believed that progress can go just so far. By the early 1980s, many held the view that there is an inherent randomness to weather that confounds any attempt to predict it beyond a certain number of days. Others were more optimistic: they proposed that, despite fundamental limitations in our ability to predict day-to-day weather changes, it may be possible to predict seasonal averages of weather. Such a discovery would be profound: it would mean that certain aspects of weather are not as random as previously believed, and that important predictions could be made further in advance, with innumerable social and economic benefits. In the past two decades, the optimists were proven correct – a cross-disciplinary breakthrough has actually occurred in the fields of meteorology and oceanography, leading to the identification and understanding of a critical factor in the determination of global weather patterns, known as the 'El Niño/Southern Oscillation'.

The term 'El Niño', Spanish for 'the Christ Child', originated from the observation by Peruvian fisherman that, in some years, waters along the western coast of South America tended to be unusually warm during Christmas time, reducing the amount of fish but allowing the fishermen to spend more time with their families. Over time, the term became associated with a climate pattern in the eastern, tropical Pacific characterized by warm water and temperatures, few fish and fish-dependent wildlife, and heavy rainfall.[15]

Another phenomenon, first discovered independently of El Niño, was a large-scale oscillation of atmospheric pressure between the eastern and western tropical Pacific Ocean. The normal, long-term pressure, at sea level, is higher over the eastern Pacific than over the western. However, at times the pressure in the east drops below its normal level, reducing the contrast between eastern and western pressures. In the 1960s, the discovery was made that El Niño occurs when this contrast in pressures is lowest, and consequently the two phenomena were recognized as aspects of a single process: the 'El Niño/Southern Oscillation' or 'ENSO'. Still, as recently as the winter of 1982–83, one of the strongest ENSOs of the century took geoscientists completely by surprise. Only now are geoscientists able to predict and accurately measure oncoming ENSO events, using new forecasting tools and monitoring systems that were developed under a program completed in December 1994.

An ENSO event occurs roughly once every 2 to 7 years, and lasts usually between 12 and 18 months. As analyzed by the National Oceanic and Atmospheric Administration,[16] when an ENSO event does occur, its effects are substantial and global:

> leading to drought conditions in northern Australia, Indonesia, and the Philippines; and excessive rains in the island states of the central tropical Pacific and along the west coast of South America . . . drought conditions in northeast Brazil, southern Africa, and a weakened Indian monsoon . . . most of Canada and the northwestern U.S. tend to experience mild winters, and the states bordering the Gulf of Mexico tend to be cooler and wetter than normal. California has experienced a disproportionate share of its episodes of heavy rainfall during ENSO winters . . . ENSO also disrupts the marine ecology of both the tropical Pacific and the Pacific coast regions of the Americas, affecting the mortality and distribution of commercially valuable fish stocks and other marine organisms. Thus, though originating in the tropical Pacific, ENSO has socio-economic consequences that are felt worldwide.

A variety of other ENSO effects are just now being discovered and analyzed, such as its specific effects on the California water supply,[17] on the ecosystem of the northern Pacific,[18] and on hemispheric sea-ice cover.[19] In short, geoscientists have called ENSO events 'the largest source of interannual variability of temperature and precipitation on a global scale,'[20] making knowledge about ENSO events second only to knowledge about the time of year, in the prediction of weather patterns worldwide.

As one might expect, the dramatic meteorological and oceanographic effects of ENSO have other effects as well, with human health being of particular interest to many researchers and policy makers. For example, in 1995, R. Stone, a reporter for *Science,* noted:

Researchers have linked short-term climate variations . . . from El Niño to outbreaks of illness and infectious disease. Besides cholera in Latin America, Epstein and Colwell point to data suggesting a similar link between El Niño and recent cholera outbreaks in Bangladesh. An outbreak of hantavirus respiratory illness in the Southwestern United States that killed 27 people in 1993 has also been indirectly tied to El Niño. The outbreak is believed to have been caused by an explosion in the deer mouse population following heavy rains from an El Niño warming that led to a jump in the animal's food supply.[21]

Of course, predicting oncoming ENSO events, and knowing the effects that previous ENSOs have had, would not be enough, in itself, to prevent such effects from occurring again. However, as many would argue, it is a good start. Such knowledge would be expected to facilitate a wide range of preventative measures that would save lives and preserve property, although any estimation of such benefits from future ENSOs would necessarily be speculative.

There are three basic components to the current ability of scientists to predict and analyze ENSO events: (1) a physical infrastructure of equipment utilized to obtain information on ENSO conditions; (2) the development by geoscientists of sophisticated mathematical models that can take advantage of modern information-processing capabilities; and (3) a worldwide system of communication and cooperation among scientists of different countries, which makes substantial use of the Internet. To describe in greater detail each of these components would be too large a task for the confines of this section. Rather, the remaining discussion will focus on one aspect of the infrastructure, the 'Tropical Atmosphere Ocean (or TAO) Array', which is the single, most-important development to take place in recent years in advancing scientists' ability to observe, analyze and predict ENSO events.

The infrastructure for obtaining information includes satellites that relay, for example, infrared pictures of ocean temperatures; stations on the coastline that measure tide levels; drifting buoys that reveal the motion of the surface water and measure sea surface temperature; and merchant ships that are voluntary observers of water temperature, wind velocity, and so on. In addition, there is the TAO Array, which is a collection of 69 moored buoys that transmit readings on sea surface temperature, subsurface temperature, rainfall, relative humidity, and wind velocity. The TAO Array was completed in December 1994, representing the culmination of a highly successful, 10-year international effort, called the Tropical Ocean Global Atmosphere (TOGA) program. That program involved the United States and over 20 other nations, reflecting a milestone in international collaboration.

Thus far, the contribution of the data generated by the TAO Array has been substantial. By as early as 1995, nearly 200 publications had appeared making use of these data, in areas that have been expanding our knowledge of how climate is determined.[22] Moreover, these data have become an integral component of current efforts to predict climate variations, and have consequently improved the accuracy of prediction, as well as extended the time frame under which reliable predictions can be made.

## EXAMPLE 3: ELECTRONIC TOLL BOOTHS

By 1994, traffic congestion in the United States was seen as affecting some 75 million licensed drivers in heavily populated areas, robing them of a total of 6 billion hours per year that they could otherwise spend on additional work, leisure, or sleep.  On average, commuters in 1994 had demonstrated a willingness to pay an extra $1.33 to save 10 minutes (or $8 per hour) of their travel time, implying that the cost of driving delays is $48 billion per year in the United States, not including the costs of extra fuel, accidents, air pollution, and unexpected scheduling problems.[23]  Yet, new applications of economic modeling, urban planning, computer science, and communications technology have successfully been applied to combat problems of this kind.

In an article in *American Scientist* in 1994, Richard Arnott and Kenneth Small explained how history has demonstrated that traffic problems are often complex, and therefore cannot be solved with policies based simply on expanding roads where congestion occurs.  Increased road capacity may not reduce congestion, because there may be 'latent demand' for use of the road among people who have not used it before.  If a congested road is a short cut to an alternate route, and it is expanded to remove congestion, it may simply attract more vehicles until the road is just as slow-moving as it had been previously.  Arnott and Small explain that, in some cases, an expanded road may even increase congestion in the long run.  It may draw people away from mass transit alternatives, encouraging less frequent scheduling of mass transportation rides, and leading, in some cases, to even more road usage and more congestion than previously experienced.  This effect is known as the 'Downs-Thomson paradox' in transportation economics.

For decades economists and urban planners have observed these problems and have often proposed the imposition of tolls on heavily used roadways to reduce and re-route traffic, as well as encourage alternative means of transportation. The revenues generated from such tolls would reduce the need for governments to raise funds in other ways. Moreover, if the revenues from tolls are used to upgrade and expand road systems, those individuals who use the roads more often would be the same individuals who pay for, and benefit most from, road maintenance and expansion. However, while the theory behind toll collection is well established and tolls have been successfully levied for many freeway systems, there are several problems surrounding toll collection in actual practice. As many commuters already know all too well, conventional toll booths are often the cause of, rather than the solution to, congestion problems. Furthermore, they consume a portion of the revenues they collect, especially in wages for toll collectors and other employees who maintain toll-booth operations. They also consume the resources of delivery services, making them more expensive to organizations receiving shipments, and, by extension, to consumers, to whom such additional costs are imposed. While exact-change booths and highway tokens had reduced these problems somewhat, they had not solved them. Because of the logistical difficulties in collecting tolls, highway toll systems have remained much more attractive in theory than in practice.

This situation has been changing in recent years as a result of scientific and engineering advances. Electronic toll booths that require no human labor, and allow a vehicle to pass through them without reducing normal highway speed are being established. They have been adopted worldwide, and at this writing, are already operational in France, Hong Kong, Italy, Norway, Portugal, Singapore, Spain, and the United Kingdom. Plans have been made to include them in Australia, Canada, Taiwan, Japan, and Thailand. In the United States electronic toll booths exist in Florida, Illinois, Louisiana, New York, Oklahoma, Puerto Rico, and Texas, and have been planned in California, Delaware, Indiana, Maine, Maryland, New Jersey, and Ohio. As an example, an article in 1994 in *Forbes* describes an automated toll system in Oklahoma as 'lowering the state's annual toll collection costs from $180,000 a lane to $16,000 a lane – a $4 million annual savings. The system cost the state $12 million to install'.[24] This example reflects a 33 percent rate of return on the State's investment, which does not include the benefit of time saving to drivers.

Electronic toll booths require small devices on cars that send out vehicle-identification signals to toll-booth receivers. The receivers connect to a centralized computer that records charges for road use by each vehicle. In some systems a bill is mailed periodically to the user, while in other systems 'smart cards' act as road-use credit cards. Some smart cards allow for prepayments, thereby eliminating the need for recording drivers' travel history and delivering bills. Electronic toll booth payment is enforced through such means as photographing the license plates of vehicles that do not emit the smart-card signal.[25]

With the emergence of electronic toll collection, economists and urban planners have readdressed the old problems of traffic congestion in a new light, in which this new technology has provided the impetus for major changes in traffic management. A National Research Council report, funded by the US Federal Highway Administration, examined the possibility of congestion pricing, in which motorists would be charged different rates for use depending on whether it is during peak hours, not unlike billing practices for electric and telephone services.[26] When commuters face higher tolls during times of high congestion, they are encouraged to seek other means of transportation or to adjust their schedules. Consequently, the NRC estimates that, if congestion pricing is 'adopted in congested metropolitan areas nationwide, the reduced demand for new capacity because of lessened peak-period travel and the time savings for peak-period travelers would result in annual net economic savings of $5 to $11 billion'.[27] Besides the benefits already mentioned, such reductions in commuter travel time also lead to lower air pollution and fuel consumption.

## EXAMPLE 4: CONSUMER CONCERNS OVER FOOD SAFETY

In economics, four basic approaches can be identified with regard to understanding consumer concerns over food safety: (1) a traditional economic approach, in which consumers respond to the intended results of technological change, namely, cost reduction and/or quality improvement in consumer goods,[28] (2) a risk perception approach, in which consumers associate health risks with technological change,[29] (3) examination of consumer concerns that result from idealistic views about the product itself or how it is produced,[30] and (4) an eclectic approach that combines at least two of the above effects. With regard to eclectic approaches, the most common in the economic literature involves the combination of traditional 'utility maximization' (consumers deriving happiness from the consumption of goods and services) and risk perception. In these studies, a Lancaster-characteristics model is often employed,[31] where levels of risk enter into the utility function (or calculation of the consumer's happiness) in the form of a descriptive characteristic of the product in question.[32]

In the area of food safety, consumer concern over technological change has existed for generations, and in some contexts for centuries. To trace the history of such concerns, the journal *Consumer Reports* is a rich source of information, having covered the topic in a large proportion of its articles, starting in 1936. For example, the issue of pesticide residues in food has appeared in *Consumer Reports* continually from 1938 to the present. The pesticides drawing attention included lead arsenate in 1938, DDT in 1949, aminotriazole in 1960, dieldrin in 1971, a set of chlorinated hydrocarbons found in milk in 1974; and Alar (daminozide) in 1986. Attention to pesticide residues also occurred in 1963 in response to the climate created by Rachel Carson's *Silent Spring*, which had been published a year earlier.

Table 4.1 presents some examples of the specific concerns addressed in *Consumer Reports* articles on food safety over 1937–91. The year denoted in

*Table 4.1 Examples of major food safety concerns in the United States, according to* Consumer Reports, *over the time span 1937–91*

| Year | Food safety concern |
| --- | --- |
| 1938 | Lead in food, especially from lead arsenate as a pesticide and treatment for fruit |
| 1939 | Food poisoning, due to bacterial contamination (e.g., salmonella and botulism) |
| 1940 | Trichinosis in under-cooked pork |
| 1941 | Potential hazards of drinking unpasteurized milk (e.g., brucellosis) |
| 1947 | Exposure of false advertising by Fleishchmann's yeast, overstating nutritional benefits |
| 1948 | Hazards in the bleaching of flour for white bread – use of nitrogen trichloride |
| 1956 | Tooth decay caused by soft drinks |
| 1958 | Potential hazards of chemical sweeteners |
| 1959 | Radioactive fallout and its effect on the food supply, especially in milk |
| 1959 | Inadequate inspection of poultry |
| 1960 | Use of chemical additives in food, and the role of the FDA |
| 1961 | Bacterial contamination in fish |
| 1963 | False and exaggerated claims by industry on the benefits of unsaturated fats and oils |
| 1968 | High bacteria counts and filth in pork products |
| 1971 | Caffeine in coffee, and its adverse health effects |
| 1972 | Nitrites in pork products |
| 1973 | Red food coloring, and whether it is safe |
| 1974 | Presence of naturally-occurring cyanide in certain hazardous vitamin tablets |
| 1976 | Aflatoxin in peanut butter |
| 1977 | Saccharine – whether or not it is a safe product |
| 1978 | Too much added sugar in foods |
| 1985 | The issue of salt and high blood pressure |
| 1985 | Antibiotics in animal feed |
| 1987 | Chemicals found in bottled water |
| 1989 | Unsafe apples – presence of alar |
| 1989 | Pesticide residues in produce |
| 1991 | Dioxin in coffee filters |

Source:   Payson 1994b.

the table represents only one of the years in which the concern is addressed – in most cases the same concern is mentioned in several years. The causal factors underlying these concerns would include specific historical events (such as the Alar pesticide scare of the 1980s), changes in household production practices (such as microwave cooking), and agricultural and industrial innovations (such as new food additives). Other causal factors would include public knowledge of food safety issues (such as concern over cholesterol intake), the accumulation of scientific knowledge about food safety, and changes in living standards. Public attention to food safety would also depend on trends in labeling and advertising, education and sociological factors (such as consumer knowledge about preventing spoilage), and the growth of sedentary labor and calorie consciousness.

Studies that combine idealistic concerns often focus on psychological factors, in which risk is interpreted by consumers as a consequence of inadequate control mechanisms. For example, in 1993 Roger Balk remarked:

> There is a belief that the effects of biotechnological manipulation pose a risk for a possible but unknown catastrophe. To the extent that the changes biotechnology proposes initiate an element of risk to those who use its products, they demand a form of control unknown to the simple morality of a pastoral ideal in conflict with an apocalyptic vision of a mechanical universe which would destroy the Garden . . . This view of the failure to protect from risk can be dismissed as the continual failure of moral politics to understand and regulate the new face of agriculture. (p. 89)

To many food policy analysts, the tendency for some consumers to integrate their attitudes about risk with idealistic views limits those consumers' ability to objectivity evaluate technological change. For instance, Chung Huang wrote, in 1991:

> Most people desire zero risk or absolute safety, including food; but, in reality, it is unreasonable and unattainable . . . Risk is a relative concept and should be put into proper perspective to sort out sense from nonsense . . . The smaller a risk factor is, the greater tendency is that reality will be obscured with misconception. (p. 19)

Here, the outlook on risk equates the concept of risk with 'hazard', for example, the probability of fatality. In 1987, Professor Peter Sandman contrasted this outlook with a different interpretation of risk that includes 'outrage', which in turn depends on a variety of psychological, ethical, and political factors. Professor Sandman argued:

> There is a peculiar paradox here. Many risk experts resist the pressure to consider outrage in making risk management decisions: they insist that 'the data' alone, not the 'irrational' public, should determine policy. But we have *two decades of data* indicating that voluntariness, control, fairness, and the rest are important components of our society's definition of risk. When a risk manager continues to ignore these factors – and

continues to be surprised by the public's response of outrage – it is worth asking just whose behavior is irrational. (p. 22)

However, what appears to be a difference of opinion here may be little more than a problem of semantics, that is, disagreement over how the word 'risk' should be defined.

In the case of new biotechnological advances in food production, the risk perceived by consumers is a very abstract sense of risk, quite different from the type of risk that has undergone decades of experimental verification and measurement. That is, while the economic approach of incorporating a risk measure into the consumption decision might be useful in the case of relatively well-known and understood risks, like those associated with tobacco smoking and drunk driving, the same approach could not be used for products which are just now coming into existence and for which very little is known about potential hazards.

A third type of eclectic framework would see the consumer as basing his purchasing decisions on traditional economic factors (quality and price) and on idealistic factors. That is, the consumer purchases a product not only on the basis of the immediate, perceptual gratification which that good may provide, but also on the basis of what he knows about other aspects of the good, such as how the good is produced. This third eclectic approach could be the most appropriate for economic analysis of consumer demand for new agricultural products.

As mentioned above, for most biotechnology products and for most consumers, there is no specific risk–benefit tradeoff taking place like that of the tradeoff between the risk of heart disease against the pleasure of consuming foods high in saturated fats. Rather, risk itself, is not well defined – all that usually exist are psychological impressions and speculations about the potential dangers of a new good or new production process. As an example, in 1993 Margaret Visser suggested the following pattern of thought on the part of a hypothetical consumer:

> The idea of fish genes in my squash does not especially please me. I could be accused of being irrational. How awkward of me to prefer my squash without any fish genes in it. But the idea has echoes, you see. It sets up concatenations in my mind. It leads me to darker fears. These fears are neither primal nor mythological. They are technological, very up-to-date and very modern. Should we listen when scientists tell us that nothing could happen, that there is no cause for alarm? Or do we just think that they should go on trying this and that, and just wait and see whether a virulent pathogen emerges? . . . When it comes to genetic engineering, we are afraid that they [professionals] know considerably less than they let on. Oh, yes, we know that they know more than we do, but we're afraid that there's a lot that even they don't know. (p. 11)

While this type of thought pattern may not be the subject of most economic studies of consumer demand, some economists have acknowledged and verified its existence. As early as 1959, in discussing 'bounded rationality', Professor Herbert Simon noted:

> A real-life decision involves some goals or values, some facts about the environment, and some inferences drawn from the values and facts. The goals and values may be simple or complex, consistent or contradictory; the facts may be real or supposed, based on observation or the reports of others; the inference may be valid or spurious. (p. 93)

Along similar lines, the tendency for some consumers to be suspicious of, or reluctant to accept, new technologies could be attributable to Harvey Leibenstein's concept of 'ratchet rationality'. In 1980, he wrote:

> [I]ndividuals in situations where contexts are repeated are likely to have present position preference. Such a mode of behavior might be called 'ratchet rationality'. The individual works himself into a behavioral groove, so to speak, which he finds comfortable, and which he would prefer not to leave unless the potential gain of moving out of the groove, or the potential loss of not moving, are beyond some given threshold values. (pp. 88–89)

Hence, while fear of potential health hazards could be the simplest explanation for the reluctance of some consumers to patronize a particular technological change, and may be the explanation that they, themselves, provide in a survey setting, a better explanation might also take into account the behavioral patterns and personal beliefs of consumers regarding aspects of technological change.

Though consumer demand is largely studied in economics as a function of prices and the sensory characteristics of good and services, the idealistic characteristics of goods have also been important. Moreover, the historical precedents for idealistic considerations on the part of consumers is quite extensive.  Since biblical times, for example, jews were restricted to consuming only meat products that met kosher specifications, which involved not only aspects of the final meat product, but also a variety of rules regarding how the animal had been raised and slaughtered.  In addition, consumers sometimes favor goods and services that were produced with traditional, as opposed to modern, techniques, especially if those goods, themselves, have existed in a traditional setting. Handmade pottery, for instance, generally has a higher perceived quality than its mass-produced equivalent, even though the latter may have less flaws than the former.[33]

For agricultural products the preference among some consumers for traditional production methods over modern methods often coincides with health issues, environmental issues, animal rights issues, and worker safety issues. Health issues come into play with regard to a wide variety of consumer concerns, such as pesticide residues in food products, artificial hormones and antibiotics used in meat and milk production, microbial contamination in meat processing plants, chemical preservatives, artificial flavorings and sweeteners, and the addition of saturated fats to highly processed retail and away-from-home foods.[34] Environmental issues are associated with the distinction between organic and conventionally grown products, the former requiring more environmentally friendly and ecologically sustainable methods of production. Animal rights issues interrelate with the preferences of some individuals to be vegetarians, but also gives rise to identifiable levels of consumer demand for 'dolphin-safe' tuna and poultry products from 'free-range' animals. Finally, worker-safety involves the application of pesticides, thereby adding to the argument by some consumer groups for increases in organic farming methods.

Another idealistic factor that influences consumer preferences is the type of technology itself, rather than any individual, easily-identifiable effects of that technology. For example, in the case of irradiated food and genetically-engineered animals and plants, the greatest concern among consumers might be the *direction in which mankind is moving.* As John Reilly once remarked, 'It takes visionaries of bounty to achieve progress, but it also takes visionaries of catastrophe to protect us from ourselves.'[35] Nuclear radiation and genetic engineering, in themselves, could evoke negative reactions, and thus, could effectively reduce consumer demand for the food products associated with them.

It is well beyond the scope of this book, and the scope of economics itself, to evaluate, or even comment upon, the legitimacy or illegitimacy of any of these consumer concerns. As long as consumer tastes are independent of economic forces (like paid advertising), and reflect instead inherent, independent thought on the part of consumers, then they must be taken as given in any economic analysis. It would be up to historians, anthropologists, philosophers, and psychologists to iron-out the causal factors underlying these patterns of consumer tastes. Furthermore, in all economies with standards of living above subsistence levels, many forms of consumer tastes might appear eccentric to some observers and difficult to legitimize in terms of a simple, common-sense argument. Consumer markets involve as much attention to the imagery, as opposed to the substance, of products. Thus, even if some consumers are, in the opinion of some policy makers, 'wrong' about their preferences, those consumers still have the prerogative to make their own purchasing decisions. Those preferences, regardless of who does and does not share them, are relevant economic factors that determine the actual levels of consumer demand for new agricultural products.

If consumers have accurate information about the technological aspects of an item's production, then they can, in effect, vote with their wallets, by purchasing the product associated with the technology that they endorse. Production costs will likely influence any such vote. If a less-favored technology does produce a product more cheaply, then suppliers could pass that savings on to consumers in the form of lower prices, and consumers may purchase the product if the savings benefit pleases them more than the discomfort of indirectly supporting a technology that they would otherwise disfavor. Similarly, if the quality of the product is better, for example, the genetically engineered tomato tastes better, then this too might override their objection to the technology (or it might not). These are the types of tradeoffs that have occurred in economic systems throughout history. Using a prior example, consumers may prefer handmade pottery to pottery manufactured en masse in a plant or factory, all else being equal, but may actually purchase the latter because all else is *not* equal: the mass-produced pottery is usually much cheaper.

The feedback method of consumers voting with their wallets, however, relies upon three general conditions. (1) Consumers must know about the technological methods associated with the products they are consuming. (2) If society as a whole finds a technology unacceptable, then that technology would be removed by the political process, rather than the market process. (3) Markets are competitive, that is, not dominated by monopolies or oligopolies, thereby forcing industry to respond to consumer preferences. The first condition could be achieved through mandatory labeling of products, but that would not be necessary if enough consumer demand for labels induces the industry to provide its own labels voluntarily (for example, canned tuna fish labeled 'dolphin-safe'). Along similar lines, additional specialty products, like many that exist today (for instance, eggs from free-range chickens), could be created by industry to satisfy the interests of specific consumer groups.

The role of the political process in the assessment of agricultural technologies complicates the situation in many ways. For example, firms within the food industry may establish their own lobbying efforts in order to prevent, or cause (depending on their role in the market), the political banning or restriction of a new technology. Firms are also likely to attempt to influence consumer opinion through advertising techniques, information provided in their packaging of the product, and so on. Similarly, specific consumer groups might exercise a variety of strategies in order to generate support for their causes. It would then be the traditional responsibility of the media to separate fact from fiction, logic from rhetoric, and legitimate concern from hysteria.

In this separation of fact from fiction, economic analysis may also shed some light on the relevant issues. For example, such analyses might identify the vested interests associated with various policy options. If interrelationships exist between voiced idealism and economic gain, such information might be helpful to consumers, industry, and policy makers in their shaping of public opinion and public policy.

Economic arguments are often made suggesting that economic efficiency would be achieved if markets are strongly influenced by the *informed* choices made by individual consumers. For example, Professor Kelvin Lancaster, in his 1991 book on *Modern Consumer Theory*, concluded, 'since efficient choices are the same for all consumers, there is a clear argument in favour of public information on these matters and in favour of legal requirements, such as composition and contents labelling, designed to increase knowledge of the available consumption technology'. Along similar lines, Peter Dunn, Director of the Purdue University Biotechnology Institute in 1994, noted, 'Food safety and the consumer's desire to make an informed choice in selecting foods are critical issues for federal and state officials with oversight responsibility, for producers of biotechnology-derived foods and for consumers' (p. 1).

Unfortunately, certain aspects of conventional economic thought in this area may act as a constraint on policy recommendations for consumer awareness of food technology. This potential problem is not necessarily one of economic reasoning but of economic tradition. One of the most central, elementary themes in economic thought has been that demand is independent of supply, where the only linking force that exists between them is the price. Of course, as noted above, it is an observable fact that consumers do respond on occasion to supply aspects of a product that are distinct from the supply price or the perceptual characteristics of the good itself. Any argument that this perspective cannot be adopted in economics because it violates economic assumptions would be equivalent to the remark: what exists in practice must be denied if it does not also exist in current theory. Nevertheless, the dismissal of prevailing economic reasoning is not necessary in this instance. Rather, economists need only recognize each product/technology, like the genetically engineered tomato, as a distinct product (or 'differentiated product' as termed in the literature). Once this is done, then, in the absence of a 'dependence effect' in which suppliers influence demand,[36] supply and demand for that differentiated product would be independent except for price, and normal price-theory analysis could proceed.

Under a differentiated product framework, methods in applied economics might be used to approximate the costs and benefits of hypothetical technologies that have not yet come into existence. In this case, costs and benefits would be those faced by society as a whole, that is, by consumers and producers. Economic research of this kind on potential technologies might provide useful input to industry and government in terms of investigating whether a new technology is a worthwhile endeavor.

Finally, it should be noted that, regardless of the type of technological change taking place, there will always be both winners and losers.[37] Consumers who oppose a particular technology will object to its very existence, regardless of the fact that they would probably be able to avoid purchasing products that depend on that technology. Other issues, like the bankruptcy of small farms that cannot afford a new technology but cannot compete without it, may come into play as well, depending on the technological change in question. In such cases the political process could, and most probably would, have an independent influence on the direction of technological change in agriculture.[38] Thus, while economic analysis plays a key role in the establishment of policy regarding biotechnology and consumer interests, it must share that role with other areas of inquiry that also have bearing on social decision making.

## EXAMPLE 5: MODULAR ROBOTIC SYSTEMS

The study and development of robots is expanding at such a remarkable rate that science fact about robots has, in many cases, become difficult to distinguish from science fiction. According to science fact, robots are now being designed to improve greatly the mobility of the elderly and physically challenged, explore the oceans and space, assist doctors in surgery, attack military targets, and handle hazardous substances. At Johns Hopkins University, 'metamorphic' robots have been developed which act like giant building blocks that can climb over each other and reconfigure themselves to any shape, enabling, for example, the quick shoring of an unstable building after an earthquake. The 'Cog' robot at Massachusetts Institute of Technology is being developed to acquire – or imitate (depending on one's philosophy) – human sensory capabilities. Robot vehicles are being designed to navigate and maneuver on their own, and travel to pre-specified destinations. Other vehicles and robot mechanisms are being designed that are controlled by human operators, who perceive the environment surrounding the vehicle or mechanism (sometimes in a virtual-reality setting) but without being physically present in the vehicle or mechanism. In addition, basic research is being conducted on nanotechnology – the ability to produce materials and robots that operate on a microscopic, or even atomic level. While actual manufacturing using nanotechnology does not, for the most part, exist at this writing, many scientists and engineers are currently working in this area under the belief that such capability is not far from being realized.

This explosion of technological change may be attributable, in part, to advances in computer hardware, mechanical components (gyroscopes, sensors, arms, and so on), digital photographic equipment and associated software for processing and interpreting visual images, artificial intelligence software, and virtual reality software. However, robots are more than the sum of their parts, and consequently, much of their advancement should also be attributed to advances in the body of thought that falls under the general heading of 'robotics'. Robotics could be regarded as an interdisciplinary field of study, incorporating mathematics, physics, mechanical engineering, electrical engineering, and computer science. Specific areas of robotics often involve many other sciences as well, depending on the particular types of robots involved: industrial robots involve industrial engineering; medical robots, medicine; robots based on neural networks, neurophysiology; flying robots, aerodynamics; submarine robots, oceanography; space robots, astrophysics; and nanorobots, chemistry.

Given what robotics has become, the traditional utilization of robots in manufacturing, for example, robots in automobile production, may hardly seem fascinating. Nevertheless, this area of technological change is also undergoing dramatic changes, and these changes have been quite significant in their social and economic effects. Furthermore, as described in greater detail below, the entire manner in which industrial production is carried out is undergoing a paradigm shift toward 'agile', 'flexible', 'modular' and 'holonic' manufacturing, in which manufacturing processes embody features that easily allow for continuous technological improvements and alterations to accommodate changes in product specifications. This paradigm shift in industrial production is occurring hand-in-hand with a paradigm shift in the field of industrial robotics – a movement toward *modular robots* and *modular robotics systems*.

Modularity is a term that seems to have entered into common language primarily in reference to furniture and homes. 'Modular furniture', for instance, a modular sofa, consists of separable units that can be pieced together in different ways to satisfy the owner's particular tastes. The owner can purchase only a few pieces at first, for example, a small sofa, and decide later to expand the sofa by combining it with additional pieces. The shape of the sofa, as well, can be altered by the types of pieces used. Many other goods and services have modular qualities, which vary in degree. Automobiles, for example, are modular to a limited extent, as are houses (especially 'modular homes'), vacation packages, and personal computers.

In terms of economic activity, modularity exists in three general areas, as described in 1995 by Professor Kim Clark:

> Modularity-in-production rationalizes a product into components and allows parts to be standardized (e.g., all screws the same size). Modularity-in-design goes a step further: the product and its production system are decomposed into a set of independent subunits that can be mixed and matched to design a complete system. Finally, a product becomes 'modular-in-use' if *consumers* can mix and match components to arrive at a functioning whole. A significant degree of control over the design is thereby transferred from the firm to the customers. (p. 4)

In economics, business, and industrial engineering, it is becoming widely recognized that the modularity of products often facilitates their innovation and improvement. For instance, with more flexibility in the system, new specifications can be met with less alteration of existing activities. Weakness in the system can often be more easily identified, and handled more directly, without interfering with other aspects of the process. Improvements in particular components of a process can be more easily incorporated. Finally, because a modular system can be understood and analyzed in terms of its modular components, innovation *strategies* are more transparent and workable.

In effect, modularity in production embodies the same basic idea as that underlying the adage, 'divide and conquer'. In more precise terms, Professor Clark remarks, 'Modularity rests on depth of knowledge, and in an important sense is a way of creating and organizing knowledge. Moreover, because modularity creates possibilities for firms to specialize on modules, it clearly has implications for the structure of industry, for patterns of vertical relationships, and for competitive strategy.'[39]

The previous era of industrial production, and its application of industrial robots, however, often contained little, if any, modularity, due in part to the inflexibility of that generation of robots. Those industrial robots had been designed to perform a very specific task, in a very specific way. They were not generally user-friendly, and any alterations in the tasks they performed often required technical expertise from the robot's developers, who were outside the organization that purchased the robot. With expensive robots unable to 'learn new tricks', production processes were inflexible.

Recently, this problem has been greatly reduced by scientific and engineering advances in industrial robotics. At present, industrial robots are undergoing dramatic changes in user-friendliness, analogous to changes experienced by computers in the transition from mainframes to PCS. Industrial robotics engineers are also now creating robots under a 'minimalist approach', that is, making robots as simple as possible for carrying out specified tasks.[40] Simpler robots, in turn, are repaired and modified more easily, and can be controlled by user-friendly software managed directly by the firm that owns the robot.

A productive operation that relies on robots can, therefore, be made more *modular* if the robots it utilizes are more flexible in terms of their physical capabilities and programming. Because modern industrial robots are taking on these improved qualities, the benefits of modularity and flexible manufacturing are now being realized by increasing numbers of producers. The highest level of this flexibility may be characterized by the combination of computer-aided design (CAD) linked to computer-aided manufacture (CAM) in CAD/CAM systems. With these systems, factories are highly automated, and they are able to produce new designs of products without having to make costly changes in their productive mechanisms.

Modular robot systems embody this concept of modularity, but go one giant step further by permitting the automated reconfiguration of the component parts (or 'modules') of the system. That is, they enable a modular robot, or a system of robots, to alter, or even rebuild, parts of itself in order to best perform a new task, where the robot's own artificial intelligence determines what the new configuration should be. As an illustration of the modular robot system concept, Professor E.Y. Chen writes:

> Consider the robotic construction of a radio antenna on the moon's surface. The robotic system must be able to excavate soil, transport material, assemble parts, inspect constructed assemblies, etc. It is difficult to design a single robot which is simultaneously strong enough, nimble enough, and accurate enough for all of these tasks. In this kind of situation it might be advantageous to deploy a modular robotic system which can be reassembled into different configurations which are individually well suited to the diverse task requirements. By a modular robotic system we mean one in which various subassemblies, at the level of links and joints, can be easily separated and reassembled into different configurations.[41]

Modular robot systems for industrial use are now being studied primarily at a level of fundamental research which is not directed toward the production of a specific item, but, according to Professor Ken Goldberg, 'addresses basic theoretical questions such as the complexity and completeness of algorithms'.[42] Advances in both the theory and physical development of modular systems has now been achieved, for example, at the University of Southern California, California Institute of Technology, and the Institute for Robotics in Zurich. This is a topic that has turned traditional industrial robotics on its head, where, according to the Institute for Robotics, 'instead of adopting an application to a given robot system, we are trying to adapt the robot system to the application'.[43]

Continued research and advancement in modular robotics systems, and the resultant application of modular robotics systems by firms, offers to change, fundamentally, the entire way in which goods are produced. In some respects, it advances the status of the industrial robot from that of complex tool, to that of a collaborator with the engineer. In another sense, it reflects the 'mechanical empowerment' of artificial intelligence. However one might look at it, modular robotics systems have the potential to enhance, substantially, the productive efficiency of industrial operations, with the final result that more goods will be produced with less human effort. Once modular robotics systems are prominent, it is likely that modular robots themselves will be produced using other modular robots. These tendencies lead, in turn, to rather interesting questions regarding the potential for robotic systems to 'self-reproduce'.

For example, one might ask whether, in generations to come, such self-reproduction of modular robotic systems may render logarithmic increases in productive capabilities that would be independent of population increases. At that point, one might hypothesize that natural resources would pose the greatest constraint on growth, as they had done centuries ago. It follows that space colonization could be the next logical step after this 'robotics era'.

## NOTES

1. In large part, these ideas follow from Schumpeter 1934, a classic work in the history of economic thought.
2. For background on social discounting of future benefits, see, for example, Hal Linstone's discussion of 'the discounting dilemma' in Linstone 1999, pp. 215–25.
3. See, for example, Romer 1993.
4. Payson 1994a.
5. Economists often disagree as to whether certain goods or services really do meet the criteria of public goods, where welfare-state proponents usually arguing that such criteria are, in fact, met, and libertarians arguing that they are not met. For an alternative view of the lighthouse case, for example, see Coase (1992).
6. Payson 1999, p. 45.
7. Raichle 1994.
8. Raichle 1994.
9. Raichle 1994.
10. Roush 1995.
11. Roush 1995.
12. Roush 1995, p. 1897.
13. Roush 1995.
14. Raichle 1994.
15. National Oceanic and Atmospheric Administration 1994.
16. McPhaden 1995, pp. 1-2.
17. Peterson et al 1995.
18. Karl et. al. 1995.
19. Gloersen 1995.
20. Gloersen 1995, p. 503.
21. Stone 1995, p. 958.
22. McPhaden 1995.
23. Arnott and Small 1994.
24. Sullivan 1994b.
25. Arnott and Small 1994.
26. National Research Council 1994.
27. National Research Council 1994, p. 2 of the report summary.
28. Payson 1994a.
29. van Ravenswaay 1992.
30. Cude 1992.
31. Lancaster 1991.
32. Smallwood and Blaylock 1991.
33. For a detailed discussion on the precise meaning of 'perceived quality', see Steenkamp (1989). For a less detailed, broader discussion on the meaning and measurement of quality in economics, see Payson (1994a).
34. Payson 1994b.
35. Reilly 1989.
36. See Galbraith 1958 and Hayek 1961.

37. See Kuchler et. al. 1990.
38. Plein 1990.
39. Clark 1995, p. 14.
40. See, for example, National Science Foundation 1995.
41. Chen 1995.
42. Goldberg 1995.
43. Institute for Robotics 1995.

# 5. Subfields on the Economic Effects of Scientific Research

## ENVIRONMENTAL AND NATURAL RESOURCE ECONOMICS

Environmental and resource economics are two disciplines within economics that are highly interlinked and consequently often discussed broadly as a single subfield. That larger subfield frequently goes by the name of 'environmental economics' as well, making the term ambiguous as to whether it excludes or includes resource economics. Of course, this kind of ambiguity in the naming of subfields is not uncommon in many areas of inquiry. For the sake of economizing on words, the term 'environmental economics' will be used below in reference to its broader definition. That broad definition will also include 'Energy Economics' which is often associated with issues concerning environmental protection and resource depletion.[1]

An argument could be made that, among all the subfields of economics, environmental economics tends to be the most scientific on average. Aspects of the field that make it scientific include: (1) the knowledge and understanding that its practitioners have of science itself; (2) their apparent commitment toward developing useful knowledge about true causal relationships, as evidenced, for example, by their emphasis on the proper measurement of physical phenomena; and (3) their interest in observing and critically evaluating their own field in the hope of moving it in the right direction. Ironically, in contrast to experimental economists, environmental economists are too busy doing science to bother advertising themselves as scientists. In this sense, associations of environmental economists are the true associations of 'scientific economics'.

Hypotheses can be offered as to why environmental economics tends to be scientific. Perhaps the most obvious explanation is that the subject matter of environmental economics is closely associated with the natural sciences, especially the earth and atmospheric sciences. For instance, articles written in environmental economics often cite research reported in natural science journals – a practice rarely observed in most other subfields of economics. Because environmental economists need to understand the scientific aspects of environmental effects, they tend to have some background in natural science, and tend to use scientific methods in their study of environmental effects. In addition, environmental economists frequently deal with practical issues in order to meet the demands of regulatory analysis. That is, their jobs often require them to provide reports to government agencies and political organizations, rather than write theoretical articles in technical journals (although they do that as well). In catering to a more practical audience, they must be more practical. Finally, studies in environmental economics often involve issues that relate to ethical commitments, such as the maintenance of air and water quality and the preservation of endangered species. Perhaps, then, there is a bias in the selection of economists who become environmental economists, where such economists are more interested, on average, in promoting positive social change than in building theoretical models.

Professor van den Bergh and his coauthors, in their 1997 book, *Meta-Analysis in Environmental Economics,* identify the following major problems and processes studied in environmental economics: (1) pollution in production and consumption; (2) specific pollutants, which can be classified as organic, metals, reactive, toxic, and interactive; (3) congestion, noise, and disturbance; (4) extraction of resources; (5) accumulation, abatement, and treatment of waste; (6) product and materials recycling; and (7) decay, erosion, and weathering processes (p. 15). The wide variety of methods used to study these factors, according to these authors include: (1) statistical methods, that is, hypothesis testing, estimation of indicators, valuation, controlled experimentation, and econometric models; (2) partial-equilibrium analysis, in which components of the economy, rather than the entire economy, are examined; (3) systems analysis, such as input–output models and general equilibrium analysis (in which the entire economy is modeled); (4) planning and optimization analysis, which includes linear programming and the application of control theory; (5) spatial models, such as multiregional and urban models; (6) evaluation studies, for example, cost-benefit and cost-effectiveness analysis; (7) decision theory, including conflict analysis, risk analysis, and scheduling decisions; and (8) data analysis, such as statistical analysis and the application of artificial intelligence to analyze data sets.

Environmental economics is clearly a well-established subfield, that has developed a wide variety of useful analytical methods to serve public and private interests. Of course, it is not without its methodological problems, however. For instance, because the field is so integrally related to political stances on environmental issues, many researchers face difficult choices in the language they use to report their findings. The term 'sustainability', in particular, first originated as a basic, analytical concept, but has since evolved into a central buzzword for the 'green movement'. Thus, researchers who associate themselves with the term tend to be supported, indirectly, by a political constituency, but at the cost of appearing to be less objective to those who would not associate themselves with the term.

Another limitation is that environmental economists are now reversing some past mistakes, especially with regard to overemphasizing the negative consequences of continued economic and population growth. That is, certain groups of environmental economists, especially the 'Club of Rome', had made dire predictions about the depletion of resources that would supposedly force future generations into poverty.[2] They had underestimated technological change, population control, and governmental efforts to react to the very environmental problems that they had identified. The last of these underestimations is debatable, in the sense that governmental recognition of many environmental economists' concerns might not have occurred to the same extent had environmental economists not predicted doom in the first place and thereby raised public interest. Nonetheless, environmental economists involved in forecasting may still have a tendency to underpredict the positive environmental effects of future technological advances. Harold Linstone has referred to this type of problem as 'assumption drag', which he describes as follows:

> "Assumption drag," that is carrying along assumptions that were valid at the time the forecast was made but are not valid for the period being forecast, appears in many incarnations. Population forecasts for 1970 made during the 1930s depression assumed continuation of a low birth rate to 1970 and hence low estimates. Forecasts for 1970 made during the time of the post-World War II boom assumed continuation of the then-current high birth rate and resulted in high estimates for 1970.[3]

Given the inherent difficulty of predicting technological change, assumption drag in forecasting, which has tended, in effect, to be overly pessimistic about the depletion and contamination of resources, might be difficult for environmental economists to overcome. On the other hand, it is not clear that such pessimism would be socially undesirable. As economists might see it, such pessimism might conflict, to some extent, with a theoretical, optimal growth path in the economic progress of nations. Yet, the growth path under pessimism might be optimal in a broader context that includes risk aversion with regard to the well-being of future generations. Furthermore, as suggested, such pessimism might enhance the development of needed technological changes, even if environmental economists never receive the recognition they might deserve for helping to promote those changes.

Given the strong interrelationships that exist between long-run patterns of technological change and long-run environmental effects, there appears to be a severe lack of commonality and collaboration between technological-change economists and environmental economists. The absence of such interaction could be explained, in part, by the tendency for subfields of economics to be isolated, self-governing, and self-serving, as discussed in previous chapters. Another factor is that 'technological change economics' deals primarily with issues associated with industrial organization, and technological change economists, this author included, tend to have poor backgrounds in earth and atmospheric sciences. Another barrier to such interaction is political. While the majority of environmental economists probably have neutral, balanced perspectives on technological change, the strongest political advocates of environmental protection controls are inclined to be 'neo-Luddites', who are highly suspicious of, or hostile toward, technological change in general. Likewise, the strongest advocates of technological change may have an equally biased view in the opposite direction, believing that technological change in future generations can be blindly trusted to solve all cumulative environmental problems.

Nevertheless, economists seriously interested in studying future directions of technological change would benefit in two ways from greater integration of technological change economics with environmental economics. The most obvious link, which could be exploited much further than it is today, is in the recognition of new technological directions brought on by environmental concerns, such as current research leading to the development of electric automobiles.

The greatest benefit that environmental economics offers to the study of technological change, however, involves a topic that has been discussed extensively in previous chapters, and will be discussed extensively, as well, in subsequent chapters. It is the desperate need for the identification and measurement of proper elemental components of whatever phenomena are being studied. What is meant by 'proper' in this case is components that have well-defined physical meaning, thereby tying whatever is being studied to the real, physical universe. In addition, such components must, of course, be important causal determinants of the phenomena being studied. As argued previously, when it comes to measurement, economists in general are naive about, or at least do not bother to question, the elemental units in which their data are measured, often resulting in 'garbage-in, garbage-out' findings. One of the examples mentioned earlier was the tendency for some agricultural economists to measure pesticides in pounds, and then treat as a relevant analytical finding the observation that price per pound is highly correlated with toxicity per pound. Had the unit of pesticide measurement been the specified quantity that is supposed to be applied per acre per year (according to the instructions on the container), then of course the prices per relevant unit would be much more uniform and would make much more sense, though they would not lead to publishable econometric findings. The economics of technological change also suffers from an inability to identify relevant units, which will be discussed in greater detail in the next chapter.

Environmental economics, on the other hand, due largely to its scientific orientation, has devoted considerable thought to the issue of identifying proper, physical units of measure. Many of those same units, such as quantities of resources consumed in production processes, could be used equally well by technological change economists, as in their study of how production processes have evolved over time. Along these lines, in their 1998 book, *Environmental Accounting in Theory and Practice*, Kimio Uno and Peter Bartelmus wrote:

> Indeed, environmental indicators, developed by international organizations and individual countries, are mostly expressed in physical terms. Life cycle assessment also entails use of physical units. Material flow accounts enables [sic] us to trace the extraction, transformation, and disposal of industrial raw materials and the impact on . . . nature. We may say that physical measures are an indispensable part of environmental information. If efficiency of resource use is to be sought, it has to be measured in physical terms representing technological characteristics. . . .
>
> It is highly desirable to develop a scheme where long-term comparisons can be made in order to grasp dynamism running through economic development, technological change, resource requirements, environmental quality, and aspirations of the people. (pp. 415–16)

# INNOVATION, R&D, AND TECHNOLOGY TRANSFER

## Basic Research, Advancement of Knowledge, and Spillovers

Basic scientific research that is supported through public funding is carried out primarily in academic settings. Professor Mansfield examined the importance of academic research in the development of new industrial products and processes. He surveyed a total of 76 firms in seven industries and asked them about the new products and processes they developed. The firms reported that approximately 10 percent of their new products and processes could not have been developed without academic research.[4]

Professors Nathan Rosenberg and Richard Nelson have also examined the interrelationship between industrial and academic research. They observe, as many others have done, that academic research is more oriented toward acquiring fundamental knowledge in the sciences, while industrial research focuses on more immediate market applications of research and development. They remark:

> Basic research became increasingly viewed as the task of universities. . . . However, by this we do not mean that such research is not guided by practical concerns. . . . Nor does it mean that university scientists and engineers are not building and working with prototypes of applicable industrial technology. . . . What university research most often

does today is to stimulate and enhance the power of R&D done in industry, as contrasted with providing a substitute for it.[5]

Professors Rosenberg and Nelson also recognize a relatively strong association between academic and industrial research in several areas of medicine and electronics, which they attribute, in part, to research support from the Department of Defense and the National Institutes of Health. For example, they observe that in 1990, universities accounted for 18 percent of US patents in genetic engineering and recombinant DNA, 16 percent in natural resins/peptides or proteins, 12 percent in chemicals involving microbiology and molecular biology, 11 percent in organic compounds under patent class 536, and 11 percent for superconductor technology.[6]

In 1989, Professor Adam Jaffe also investigated academic research and industry patents, exploring the possibility of regional effects, in which companies conducting research may benefit from universities in their general location. He argued that such a relationship between industry and academia is consistent, for example, with 'conventional wisdom that "Silicon Valley" near San Jose, California, and Route 128 around Boston owe their status as centers of commercial innovation and entrepreneurship to their proximity to Stanford and MIT'.[7] Using data from the National Science Foundation's Industrial R&D survey, he compared research conducted in academic departments with incidences of industry patents within the same state. He carried out the analysis for 29 states for the years 1972–77, 1979, and 1981, covering five broad areas of research: pharmaceuticals and medical technology; chemical technology; electronics, nuclear technology, and optics; mechanical arts; and all other research. He found a significant positive relationship between industrial patents and university research conducted on the same topic in the same state. The strongest effect was in pharmaceuticals and medical technology; followed by chemical technology; and electronics, nuclear technology, and optics. On the other hand, he mentions that his study does not rigorously establish the causal relationship between university research and industrial patents. That relationship may be reversed, to some extent, by feedback mechanisms, in which industrial patents encourage further research by local universities. Nevertheless, Professor Jaffe's study does shed light on the relationship between academic and industrial research.

In analyzing broad categories of goods or services, useful results are often difficult to acquire because of the variation that exists within a category. If a specific product, rather than a category, is considered, then the interrelationship between scientific discoveries and economic effects can be identified more easily. In 1990, Manuel Trajtenberg investigated computed tomography (CT) scanners, which are often used in medical diagnosis and had been proven to be superior to X-ray machines. Through detailed collection of expenditure data on R&D by US firms, and econometric analysis of the economic and social benefits that result from the characteristics of different CT scanners, Trajtenberg, as mentioned earlier, approximated the annual social rate of return to R&D to be 270 percent.

A variety of issues could be raised regarding Professor Trajtenberg's study. Professor Trajtenberg himself expresses that CT scanners are only one particular product, and as such, they probably do not reflect the effects of R&D in general, nor even the proportion of R&D spent on the broader category of medical equipment. The fact that CT scanners are not necessarily representative of a broader group, but rather are the epitomic 'success story', is recognized by Professor Trajtenberg, but his work in this area has still received a fair amount of attention, as an example of how specific technological advances can be studied in terms of their economic implications.

In 1990, James Adams published a study combining the two approaches of aggregate productivity measurement and knowledge acquisition by firms. His study used a production function, as in other productivity studies, but with two added inputs: knowledge acquired by firms, and spillovers of knowledge between firms of different industries. As a proxy for knowledge, Adams used the numbers of articles appearing in technical journals in nine fields: agriculture, biology, chemistry, computer science, engineering, geology, mathematics, medicine, and physics. He attributed these quantities of knowledge to scientific and engineering personnel in those fields, and used data on personnel counts by industry to approximate levels of knowledge by industry. He measured spillover effects among industries based on the commonality of their scientific personnel. He observed that these knowledge inputs explained part of the 'residual' defining productivity, and found them to be 'sizable determinants of productivity growth' (p. 698).

The principle findings to emerge from Adams' study are the lags in time observed between the appearance of research in the academic community and the resulting effect on productivity. More precisely, Adams found that knowledge strongly contributes to growth, but lags 20 years behind the first appearance of research in the science community. The lag for interindustry spillovers is approximately 30 years. However, computer science and engineering have shorter lags of approximately 10 years, as befits their applied nature.[8]

Overall, these studies confirm the importance of the transfer, or spillover, of basic scientific knowledge to applied research and development, and likewise the movement of knowledge between academic and industrial settings. Beyond the basic qualitative picture, however, the quantitative rigor of these studies is often challenged by arbitrary aspects of how the data are defined, categorized, and interpreted. For instance, in regional studies where data are separated by state of the United States, all R&D within California is within the same 'region', while R&D in Massachusetts is distinct from R&D

in Connecticut, even though Connecticut and Massachusetts border each other and in combination are still much smaller than California. Moreover, the observed clustering of innovation by region need not be reflective of spillover effects, *per se*, but may simply be a consequence of the clustering of particular industries and/or researchers in particular fields. As Professors Jaffe, Trajtenberg and Henderson admit:

> The most difficult problem confronted by the effort to test for spillover localization is the difficulty of separating spillovers from correlations that may be due to a pre-existing pattern of geographic concentration of technology related activities. That is, if a large fraction of citations to Stanford patents comes from Silicon Valley, we would like to attribute this to localization of spillovers. A slightly different interpretation is that a lot of Stanford patents relate to semiconductors, and a disproportionate fraction of the people interested in semiconductors happen to be in the Silicon Valley, suggesting that we would observe localization of citations even if proximity offers no advantage in receiving spillovers.[9]

Similarly, 'knowledge' as measured in terms of publication counts is also limited, especially in comparisons between different fields of study, where publication differences can be as much a function of the culture and sociology of a field as they are a function of the amount of 'knowledge' produced. One might even argue that, under certain circumstances, the amount of useful knowledge generated is *inversely* related to the amount of literature published. For example, the interdisciplinary field of robotics (involving computer science, mechanical engineering, electrical engineering, and so on) tends to generate few publications relative to the amount of R&D conducted. The main reason for this is that the field is advancing too rapidly for researchers to benefit from the time-consuming process of publishing in technical journals – knowledge is transferred, instead, much more rapidly through conferences and informal working papers. Fields with slower growth not only make it easier for researchers to publish without fear of being outdated, but enable them as well to continually create new articles by mixing, matching, and repackaging the ideas they presented in previous articles. Moreover, in rapidly progressing fields genuine scientific discovery receives the most attention, and consequently the career paths of researchers depend primarily on their contribution to actual discovery, and only secondarily on their publication counts. In fields less dependent on genuine scientific discovery there is a greater tendency to treat all publications, in equally-reputable journals, as equal. In this case, career paths become much more dependent on publication counts, encouraging researchers to produce as many articles as they can, without being slowed down by the more difficult task of contributing useful knowledge.

In summary, while 'knowledge', 'spillovers', 'geographic proximity', 'technology transfer' and other terms have concrete meaning in the study of technological change, empirical observations and model testing with regard to these concepts typically use proxies for these concepts that may be highly questionable or ambiguous. Because of these and other limitations in the data, approaches to understanding technology transfer should combine observations about the data with historical and institutional details (like those mentioned above by Nelson and Rosenberg). In such studies, qualitative descriptions, and even anecdotes, may more accurately depict reality than sophisticated econometric studies using data that have not been adequately scrutinized (as in the studies by Adam and Jaffe). This 'data problem' in the study of technological change is discussed at greater length in the next chapter.

## LABOR EFFECTS OF TECHNOLOGICAL CHANGE

### The Changing Workplace

By the mid 1990s, it was widely observed that the very nature of work had changed markedly because of scientific advances, especially advances in the area of information technology. In 1994, L. Richman, a reporter for *Fortune Magazine,* wrote:

> a new worker elite . . . [is] transforming the American labor force and potentially every organization that employs them. As the farm hand was to the agrarian economy of a century ago and the machine operator was to the electro-mechanical industrial era of recent decades, the technician is becoming the core employee of the digital Information Age.

In that same year, Baker and Treece, reporters for *Business Week* observed that numbers of technical workers, primarily in the use of information technology, had grown rapidly, spanning out from the 'back office' to managing factory processes, performing customer service functions and quality control, keeping computerized records, and controlling automated laboratories. As a result, work had become more integrated, and more technologically complicated for a majority of the workforce. It had also become less routine, as the routine jobs had begun to be performed by software, robots, and 'smarter' machine tools.

Technological change has not only affected how people work, but where they work. Virtual companies and virtual offices have become much more commonplace in modern industrial society. As one example, *Forbes* magazine reported that Compaq Computer Corporation, as early as 1993, had moved its entire sales force from headquarters to their private homes. They have since interacted with headquarters via telephone, fax, and computer modem.[10] The economic and social effects of increased work-at-home employment could be substantial.   Among them are: (1) time- and income-saving benefits to employees who no longer have to commute; (2) employees with children working at home, making it easier for both spouses to work full-time; (3) reduced numbers of people commuting making commuting easier and faster for those remaining; (4) increased demand for modems, Internet access, and so on; and (5) increased digital storage of data rather than on paper, which may have positive economic and environmental consequences.

The same technological advances that enable employees to work at home, enable managers to travel and attend meetings away from the office without losing contact with the office.  Telephone and Internet services, especially e-mail, have allowed executives and professionals to maintain awareness and oversight while on extended business trips.  These trips also allow them to carry out face-to-face contact with associates (a function whose psychological benefits have yet to be adequately substituted by technological advancement). In another *Forbes* article, in 1994 by M.S. Malone, these managers are referred to as 'perpetual motion executives' or 'PMXs'.  According to that article:

> The era of the PMX will demand new business organizations, more sophisticated communications systems and regulations, and different forms of reward and compensation.  And just as the perpetual motion lifestyle affects a growing percentage of professionals, it will have a visible impact upon our culture.

Worker health and safety relates to scientific advances in several ways. The most obvious of these may be that, as new production technologies develop, they impose new potential hazards to workers, while reducing the potential hazards of the technologies they replace.  Consequently, the emergence of automated factories has reduced injuries and adverse health effects by the mere fact that human beings have been removed from the scene.  Scientific discovery may also improve worker health and safety by providing better knowledge on such health care issues as identifying hazardous materials and reducing, or eliminating, exposure to them.  Of course, when accidents do occur, scientific advances in rescue equipment, evacuation procedures, and the like, may be of great benefit.

While industry continues to use advanced production technologies, statistics on workplace injuries and illnesses indicate ample room for improving worker safety.  In 1995, the US Occupational Safety and Health Administration (OSHA) reported a drop in the overall workplace death rate to half of the 1970 level.  Particularly notable achievements by that time had been the near-elimination of brown lung disease in textile manufacturing, and a 35 percent reduction in the death of construction workers from trench cave-ins. Nevertheless, according to OSHA, 'every year over 6,000 Americans die from workplace injuries, an estimated 50,000 people die from illnesses caused by workplace chemical exposures, and 6 million people suffer non-fatal workplace injuries'.[11] Consequently, efforts at improving the safety and health of workers continues to be an important area of applied scientific and engineering research.

Incidents of musculoskeletal disorders, such as low back pain, tendinitis, and carpal tunnel syndrome are increasing, due in part to the increased use of computers in the workplace. As a result, the subject of 'ergonomics', defined by OSHA as 'the science of designing jobs to fit people', is receiving greater attention by employers, health service providers, and designers of workplace equipment. Advances in worker safety and health continue to be one step behind the technological changes that give rise to new workplace situations. On the other hand, because of legal precedents and a greater awareness of worker safety and health issues, gaps between new problems and their corresponding solutions are likely to be less severe today than in the past.

Technological change is also playing a role in enabling persons with disabilities to work. In 1995, Gopal Pati and Eline Bailey, in the journal *Organizational Dynamics*, noted 'of the 43 million Americans known to have disabilities, approximately two-thirds are willing and able to work, but only 34 percent of that group actually do work'. They find, however, that technological advances, in conjunction with proper perspectives on the part of employers, have increased the employment opportunities available to persons with disabilities. In particular, they write:

> Most workers with disabilities will not require extensive nor expensive modifications to their work stations. Our own studies, as well as studies conducted by The President's Committee on Employment of People with Disabilities and the International Association of Machinists, show that 31 percent of accommodations cost nothing, 50 percent cost less than $50, 69 percent cost less than $500, and 88 percent cost less than $1,000. (p. 56)

Recent advances, especially in information technology and communications, have greatly improved the extent to which disabled individuals can contribute to a work effort. As mentioned earlier, the most obvious advancement in this regard is the ability for many types of work to be carried out from remote locations, that is, 'telework'.[12] Research in robotics and 'telepresence' is being directed towards even greater capabilities that have yet to be realized, such as the ability for an individual to experience a workplace environment and perform physical tasks in that environment, from a remote location.

For the visually impaired, computer programs have been developed that can rapidly speak text, and verbally offer menu options to users of computer packages. Computer printers have been designed to print in both ink and braille on the same page.[13] For the hearing impaired, Gallaudet College in Washington, DC has conducted research on computer-assisted notetaking, in which notes, in the form of text, are created from the recognition of speech.

The notes can be projected on a wall or computer screen as a meeting is being conducted, thereby creating a textual account of the meeting while at the same time eliminating the need for a translator for the hearing-impaired. For individuals who rely on wheelchairs, new robotic models that enable the chair and its passenger to climb over curbs have been developed.

Recruiting and personnel operations, especially in large organizations, are also taking on new forms as they adapt to the latest technological advances in information processing and communications. In recruiting, some organizations have been using video conferencing to conduct interviews, thereby eliminating first-interview travel costs and expanding the number of potential candidates. For example, in *HRMagazine,* Karl Magnusen and Galen Kroeck described the process carried out in the Career Planning and Placement Office of Florida International University in Miami:

> The technology allows recruiters to interview students 'live' by having employer and students speak to each other with visual contact using large-screen monitors. Both parties can talk interactively while seeing each other's movements, expressions and reactions in real time.... A window on the candidate's TV screen uses picture-in-picture technology to allow the candidate to view the actual image being seen by the recruiter.... This high-tech job interviewing system has already been used by a first wave, which includes companies such as Kraft General Foods, Pfizer, AT&T, NASA-Kennedy Space Center, Underwriters Laboratories, Department of Defense, and Caterpillar. Other organizations that plan to begin using the technology include Cargill, Mobil Oil, EDS and Saturn, as well as several large school systems.[14]

In addition to convenience and cost savings for both prospective employers and candidates, this new method of recruiting may have a variety of other effects. It will expand the radius of recruiting, leading to better matches between potential employers and candidates, and may contribute to the cultural diversity within organizations as they acquire new staff from more distant regions.

Advances in communications and multimedia have made it possible for companies to train employees in certain areas with less, or even zero, professional training staff. As an example, in 1994 Liz Thach and Richard Woodman wrote that Sun Microsystems had developed a tutorial program to go with its computer 'that uses text, voice, and photos to help new Sun users learn how to operate their computers at their own pace'.[15] With such technologies, as well as videotaped lectures and lectures via video conferencing, employee training is becoming much cheaper for companies to provide, though it is also becoming less personal. This change may create a disadvantage for some trainees who learn more easily through social interaction.

New technologies have also enhanced the ability of employers to monitor employees, both in terms of actual work performance (such as keystrokes per hour in jobs requiring rapid data entry) and in communications (such as messages sent through e-mail and voice-mail systems). According to the US-based Center for Public Interest Law (CPIL), keystroke monitoring has been associated with carpal tunnel syndrome and other health problems. CPIL has also observed that, through computer networks, employers have the ability to monitor an employee's computer screen without his or her knowledge (although under certain circumstances such actions would be illegal).[16]

As more advanced information technology (IT) has entered into production and service operations, employees have found themselves more closely connected to the rest of the production or service process. Their actions have become more integrated with those of other employees, and they have been expected to understand more about the entire process. Liz Thach and Richard Woodman have noted:

> Through implementing IT, organizations not only increase process efficiency, they also change the locus of knowledge. In the eyes of many managers, this equates to changing the locus of power. If implemented in its most productive fashion, IT provides line employees with the data to perform their jobs more effectively and make decisions on job changes. . . . Coping and intellectual skills to handle these changes in information flow are critical. On the other hand, many of the lesser details, like deciding when to order additional materials, will be handled by the technology itself. In effect, work is becoming more challenging, for those gaining greater exposure to IT in the workplace. As discussed in greater detail in the Educational Indicators section of this chapter, many workers may benefit from these changes, while many others may not.[17]

## Effects of Scientific Advances on Employment Levels

Technological change has always had a profound effect on employment, and recent developments in communications and IT have had particular influence. In the prior industrial, electro-mechanical age, jobs that were lost as a result of automation tended to require relatively well-defined physical tasks, while new jobs required technical expertise. This trend continues today, as new robots, machine tools, and CAD/CAM operations replace many of the routine duties performed by workers. However, the image of robots in factories, with the only humans as robot programmers, is a very incomplete picture. White-collar employment – like law, accounting, and record keeping – is also being affected. New software developments have enabled computers to provide many of the same services previously carried out by office workers. Furthermore, communications technology has reduced the need for experts to be present physically in order to interact with clients. This means physicians can interview patients, professors can deliver lectures, and managers can supervise subordinates, from remote locations. The implication of these capabilities is that physicians, professors, and managers can perform their functions more efficiently, which may ultimately translate into less of a need for such positions.

Technological change is often associated with new goods and equipment, rather than with the services that use or sell these products. As a result, some observers may underestimate changes in the levels of expertise required for various occupations, based on outdated perceptions of those occupations. For example, a salesperson in a retail establishment today has a different set of skills than his or her counterpart 25 years ago. That expertise may include an ability to use a computer data base for looking up the features, prices, and availability of retail items. He or she may also have a more detailed understanding of the products, commensurate with the expanded technological complexity of those products.

An additional effect of communication and IT is that it allows for many jobs, like writing software, to be performed abroad, and then delivered to one's home country, and vice versa. Furthermore, cost reductions and improvements in technological change will have overall effects on income, which will influence the composition of goods and services in the economy, as well as the composition of the occupations associated with those goods and services.

In some cases, the direct effects of technological change on employment have been quite obvious. Examples include, for instance, the replacement of directory-assistance operators with automated voice-recognition equipment, or the replacement of gas-station attendants with self-service gasoline pumps and automated credit-card billing. In most cases, however, the effects on employment are more subtle and indirect. In general, one cannot assume that occupations that have less complex duties will tend to employ fewer people. For example, closed circuit cameras enhance the efficiency of security guards, but that does not necessarily mean that security guards will be in lower demand as this equipment improves or falls in price. On the contrary, guards could be in greater demand, if organizations that previously could not afford labor-intensive surveillance are now able to the afford the same surveillance with fewer employees.

As these changes continue, their implications are two-fold: on the one hand, some work is becoming less mundane, more challenging, and perhaps more intellectually rewarding for those fortunate enough to be on the high-technology wave. On the other hand, some workers were, in fact, displaced by the technological advances. Such displacements, however, tend to be short-term, on average, and most displaced workers can find new jobs (though they may not be a preferable). In 1998, for example, the Progressive Policy Institute – a pro-labor organization in the United States – presented a overall favorable view of technological change, stating:

New technologies (e.g., tractors, disease resistant crops, etc.) spurred the decline in agricultural jobs. However, as food became cheaper (American consumers spend less of their income on food than any other nation) consumers spent their increased income on other things (e.g., cars, appliances, entertainment), creaing employment in other sectors. The 30-year low for unemployment after the wave of corporate downsizing and technology introduction makes it clear that technology doesn't reduce the total number of jobs in the economy. As new information technologies begin to raise productivity growth rates, this same positive dynamic will continue, leading to higher incomes, not fewer jobs.[18]

## Education, Wages, and Technology

Several economic studies have implied that, on average, people with relatively low levels of education have faced declining wages, while people with relatively high levels have enjoyed wage increases. For example, Gregory Acs and Sheldon Danzier compared the earnings of men in 1979 and 1989, and found a direct relationship between the average change in their wages and their level of education. One must be careful in interpreting data of this kind, however, because an association between education and wages does not necessarily mean that the former causes the latter. In some cases, the reverse causality applies: individuals from high-income families can more easily afford to attend college, and also have additional advantages in seeking employment, such as benefits deriving from possible family-based connections.[19][20]

In 1995, a team of researchers led by Mark Doms[21] performed an analysis of the interrelationships among education, employment, and scientific advancement. They first identified 17 possible advanced technologies that manufacturers could employ, such as computer-aided design (CAD), and then categorized manufacturers by how many of these technologies they possessed. They then interrelated their classification of plants by level of technological advancement with three levels of education for their employees: (1) high school diploma or less, (2) some post-secondary education but not a college degree, and (3) a college degree (including graduate degrees). Although there is a slight break in the observed trend between plants with 9–10 of the identified technologies and those with 11–13, the overall trend for all types of plants was clear. Low-tech plants with less than four of the technologies have as many as 66 percent of its workers with high school completion or less, and only 9 percent with a college degree, compared with 37 percent and 33 percent, respectively, in high-tech plants with over 13 technologies. This observation easily leads to the conclusion that technologically advanced plants rely more on educated workers and generally employ a higher fraction of workers in skilled occupations. Several other studies have confirmed that technological change leads to a shift in labor composition and compensation in favor of workers with higher levels of education. These results are consistent with the notion that 'skill-upgrading' occurs after new technologies are implemented on the factory floor.[22]

Because well-educated employees cost more for a firm to hire, the best explanation for their doing so is simply that they benefit more from those employees. Since higher technologies tend to require advanced skills, like computer programming, this willingness of high-tech firms to employ well-educated workers is consistent with the utilization of advanced technologies. Given the findings observed, it is reasonable to assume that the future will bring greater relative demand for employees with more education, and lower demand for those with less. In the aggregate, if the efficiency of production processes depends on the level of education of its employees, then how much a society produces in total depends on its overall level of education. This idea has already been established in economic thought, long before the information age. According to Professor Fellner, for example, in his presidental address to the American Economic Association in 1970, long-run increases in output per person-hour can be 'interpreted as developing from additional per capita knowledge'.[23] The incredible growth of information technology in the 1990s, of course, is now reinforcing that idea.

# EVOLUTIONARY ECONOMICS

'Evolutionary economics' could be considered a relatively new area, even though it has roots that trace back to certain classical theoreticians, such as Schumpeter and Marshall. In a nutshell, the theory of evolutionary economics is analogous to Darwin's Theory of Evolution, where economic institutions and economic activities, especially at the level of the firm, undergo a process of mutation (or innovation) and natural selection. The process of selection occurs as the entities that evolve, for example, firms, compete for limited markets, where the best managed, and/or most successfully innovative firms have a greater chance for survival and expansion.

Useful comparisons could be made between evolutionary economics and other subfields already mentioned. For example, as already remarked, environmental economics tends to be one of the most scientific subfields of economics in terms of its subject matter, methods, and culture. However, although most economic activity can be related to environmental effects, most of economic thought, for better or worse, is focused elsewhere. Similarly, the study of innovation is largely constrained by its focus on intellectual property and R&D expenditures, without much linkage to the rest of economic thought, except when it is occasionally correlated in time series analyses with overall economic growth or productivity change. In short, economic subfields that attempt, with various degrees of success, to achieve scientific advances in knowledge can only go so far, as they are limited by either the scope of their subject matter (for instance, the environment or intellectual property) or by the scope of their analytical methods (for instance, experimental economics or applied econometrics). The subfield of evolutionary economics, in contrast, is quite different – it is not constrained in terms of a specific set of topics or methods, but rather, embodies a distinct perspective on how phenomena change over time. That overall perspective is relevant to all, or nearly all, areas of economic inquiry. Consequently, evolutionary economics continues to pose the greatest challenge to mainstream economic thought. Its wide applicability, plus the fact that it is scientifically oriented, suggests that it is the one subfield that offers the most promise and hope for the improvement of economic discourse. For this reason, the third and largest part of this book, 'New Attitudes, Philosophies, Frameworks and Models', presents new areas of economic inquiry that are based on an evolutionary perspective.

As one might expect, evolutionary economics is rooted in the belief that there is a process of selection occurring for the economic variables in question, analogous to Darwin's 'natural selection'. Esben Andersen defines an 'evolutionary-economic explanation' of such a process as:

> an explanation of a fact of economic life by reference to previous facts as well as to a causal link which (immediately or in reconstructed form) may be shown to include (1) a mechanism of preservation and transmission, (2) a mechanism of variety-creation, (3) a mechanism of selection, and which includes or may be enhanced by introducing (4) a mechanism of segregation between different "populations".[24]

In broader terms, Professor Richard R. Nelson writes:

> The general concept of evolutionary theory . . . involves the following elements. The focus of attention is on a variable or set of them that is changing over time and the theoretical quest is for an understanding of the dynamic process behind the observed change; a special case would be a quest for understanding of the current state of a variable or a system in terms of how it got there. The theory proposes that the variable or system in question is subject to somewhat random variation or perturbation, and also that there are mechanisms that systematically winnow on that variation. Much of the predictive or explanatory power of that theory rests with its specification of the systematic selection forces. It is presumed that there are strong inertial tendencies preserving what has survived the selection process. However, in many cases there are also forces that continue to introduce new variety, which is further grist for the selection mill.[25]

Given this broad mandate, economists have applied evolutionary theory to a wide range of alternative analytical approaches. The breadth of the subfield is consequently quite wide, as reflected for example in the 'Aims and Scope' of the *Journal of Evolutionary Economics*:

> Following the tradition of Joseph A. Schumpeter, it [the journal] is designed to focus on

original research with an evolutionary conception of the economy. The journal will publish articles with a strong emphasis on dynamics, changing structures (including technologies, institutions, beliefs and behaviours) and disequilibrium processes with an evolutionary perspective (innovation, selection, imitation, etc.). It favours interdisciplinary analysis ... Research areas include: industrial dynamics; multi-sectoral and cross-country studies of productivity; innovations and new technologies; dynamic competition and structural change in a national and international context; causes and effects of technological, political and social changes; cyclic processes in economic evolution; the role of governments in a dynamic world; modelling complex dynamic economic systems; application of concepts, such as self-organization, bifurcation, and chaos theory to economics; evolutionary games.[26]

Unfortunately, the breadth of the subfield can have adverse consequences, especially in the sense that the subfield is partly immobilized by its own internal diversity.

For example, one of the major thrusts of evolutionary economics has been its contribution to theories on technological change and organizational behavior (for example, work by Nelson and Winter which is discussed in detail shortly).   A completely different area of evolutionary economics involves political and social change, in which neoMarxist theory is often expressed, which has its own tradition of studying evolutionary processes of social change.[27] Ironically, political hype about evolutionary economics by business journalists occasionally focuses on the 'survival of the fittest' regarding organizational behavior, portraying the subfield as an anthem for corporate competitiveness and savvy entrepreneurship. At the other extreme, radical viewpoints are also expressed in treatises on evolutionary economics, many of which condemn the 'military-industrial establishment'.  Still other research in evolutionary economics simply involves theoretical modeling, in which the process of evolution is interpreted in terms of sophisticated mathematical constructs that exist largely as intellectual works for their own sake, with little if any policy implications.   In essence, by the above definitions, any economic research that involves an evolutionary process of any kind could be classified as 'evolutionary economics', allowing for 'strange bed fellows' within the subfield.[28]

In accordance with the theme of this book – the interrelationships among economics, science and technology – the remainder of this section will focus on a specific branch of evolutionary economics. That branch, referred to hereafter as 'evolutionary studies of technological change', will be restricted to empirical, applied approaches to evolutionary economics that are directed toward the study of technological change. This branch will also be restricted to the realm of economic discourse, as opposed to interdisciplinary frameworks that significantly involve themes from sociology, law, political science, history, and so on. The reason for this latter restriction is simply that of the space limitation – any decent coverage of such interdisciplinary frameworks would warrant at least another chapter of its own, if not another book.

There are three features of evolutionary studies of technological change that distinguish it from conventional economic theory. First, they rely heavily on the idea that technical changes made by firms occur as a result of variation, much the same way that Darwin's theory relies on variation of phenotypes among organisms. In and of itself, this perspective on economic change represents a substantial departure from the 'deterministic' qualities of conventional theory. Secondly, these studies allow for, and in fact focus on, unsystematic or 'random' changes over time in the economic system's very structure. As a result, they are not preoccupied with mathematical minutiae, such as creating a model that leads to a steady state equilibrium. Thus, evolutionary studies of technological change have more leeway than most other economic approaches to explore the behavioral and institutional causes of economic change. These studies of technological change open up a new area of economic thought, that creates a need for the economist to look underneath the old economic variables in order to understand economic change. In essence, they are scientific, not because of any 'imitation' of a theory in biology (as some might naively suspect), but because they call upon a search for a new set of elementary components – components which could explain the causality of how economic institutions and processes change over long periods of time. (The search for such components, in fact, is the primary objective of the third part of this book.)

Evolutionary studies of technological change have, thus far, focused primarily on the behavior of firms.[29] According to Professors Richard Nelson and Sidney Winter, for example, firms perform three types of activities: standard operating activities, investment planning decisions, and decision making whereby 'people within the firm may engage in scrutiny of what the firm is doing and why it is doing it, with the thought of revision or even radical change'.[30] Not surprisingly, it is this third type of activity that is the major focus of evolutionary studies of technological change. Viewing technical change in this context, evolutionary economists regard it as endogenous, in contrast to its common treatment in traditional economics.

As already suggested, there is a tendency for evolutionary economists to draw an analogy between evolutionary studies of technological change and Darwin's Theory of Evolution. For instance, Professors Nelson and Winter state:

> [P]rofitable firms will grow and unprofitable ones will contract, and the operating characteristics of the more profitable firms therefore will account for a growing share of the industry's activity. . . . The selection mechanism here clearly is analogous to the natural selection of genotypes with differential net reproduction rates in biological

evolutionary theory. And, as in biological theory the sensitivity of a firm's growth rate to prosperity or adversity is itself a reflection of its 'genes'.[31]

An important implication of this perspective is that it allows for a distinction between the day-to-day forces that keep a system in balance (or in 'equilibrium') and the subtle, evolutionary forces that work more slowly but lead to substantial long-run effects.[32] This distinction among influential forces may be obvious to anyone familiar with technological change, but it is nonexistent in most areas of economic thought (other than evolutionary studies of technological change), and its absence is an important barrier to useful economic analysis of technological change.

A very simple example, from biology, of this distinction among forces, might be expressed as follows: the number of rabbits and the number of foxes in a forest may vary over time according to systematic forces, such as the tendency for rabbits to multiply rapidly when there are few foxes, and the tendency for foxes to starve when there are few rabbits. Yet, these balancing forces in themselves tell little about the characteristics of future generations of rabbits and foxes. They do not explain why rabbits have a tendency to hop greater distances, and foxes to run faster, with each passing generation. That is, evolutionary theory, in short, calls for a new set of considerations, or variables, for understanding long-term change.

Once a commitment is made toward an evolutionary framework, however, an evolutionary economist must continue to make methodological distinctions. In particular, within any evolutionary framework, there are two major areas of inquiry. One area addresses the question of 'how' and the other the question of 'why'. With regard to organisms, the question of 'how' organisms evolve is explained in two parts: how genetic material (DNA) encodes and evokes the characteristics observed in phenotypes, and how that genetic material is continually revised between generations as a consequence of both random mutation and natural selection.

The question of 'why' organisms evolve, in contrast, requires a more detailed explanation of the selection process associated with the 'survival of the fittest', for example, a discussion about population pressure and limited food supplies, and about rates of reproduction among alternative varieties.

The answers to the questions of 'how' and 'why' are essential components of any evolutionary framework. For clarity, let us redefine them, respectively, as the 'transmission mechanism' and the 'selection process'. These phenomena are obviously interrelated, and in this sense they support, and to some extent validate, one other. For example, it is unclear in which of these categories one would place variation in the rates of reproduction, since it could involve phenotypes that bear directly on the molecular biology of the reproductive process. Nevertheless, for the most part, the transmission mechanism and the selection process are independent.

In both biological and economic evolution, the selection process is subject to change over time, as conditions in the world change, and as entities evolve thereby creating new selection criteria for themselves and other entities that interact with them. In biological evolution, however, the transmission mechanism does not, itself, change to any notable extent. As a result, evolutionary biologists are able to study the effects of the selection process without paying much attention to the transmission mechanism (unless they have a specific interest in the genetic coding itself, for instance, for cloning experiments). In fact, Charles Darwin's theory of evolution was able to maintain its widespread acceptance among biologists, for its analysis of the selection process, long after its discussion of the transmission mechanism had been discarded.

In economic evolution, in contrast, the transmission mechanism is, itself, subject to change over time. In fact, one might even say it, too, evolves, suggesting the mind-boggling notion of 'dimensions' of evolutionary processes. That is, economic entities evolve, but the transmission mechanisms and selection processes through which they evolve, themselves evolve. This implies that the survival of such entities depends not only on their own survival within each given mechanism and selection process, but depends, as well, on the survival of the transmission mechanisms and selection processes that best favor the survival of those entities.

A concrete example of this abstract framework would be the current state of affairs with regard to communication services. Television networks used to compete against each other to draw the largest audiences to their programming. That general selection criterion of drawing the most audiences has not changed, but the television network as an individual entity in a well-defined market is no longer the case. In the United States, one major television network, NBC, is now linked to Microsoft, the software and Internet giant, and another network, CBS, is linked to America Online (AOL), another Internet giant. The mechanism whereby NBC and CBS will be passed on to future generations will be through the Internet, not the air waves, and they will be selected, in part, on their Internet presentation in addition to their television programming.[33]

The above example illustrates that, in economics, there is another phenomenon, besides the transmission mechanism and the selection process, that needs to be clearly identified, which is not a problem at all for biology – that phenomenon is the *actual entity that is evolving*. It is on this issue that this book will diverge from the rest of the economic literature on evolutionary studies of technological change. As displayed in Table 5.1, in biological evolution there are clear distinctions among: the entity that evolves; factors associated with its ability to be selected; the selection criteria for fitness; and the transmission mechanism between generations. In economic studies of

*Table 5.1  Comparisons among evolutionary frameworks*

| Type of phenomenon | Evolutionary framework | | | |
| | | Economic studies of technological change | | |
| | Biological | Emphasis on the firm | Emphasis on technologies | This book's emphasis on goods and services |
| --- | --- | --- | --- | --- |
| Entity that evolves | Species | Firm | Technologies | Goods and services |
| Factors associated with its ability to be selected | Phenotypes | Organizational characteristics and routines | Description of the technology | Physical characteristics of the good or service |
| Selection criteria for fitness | Organism's ability to live and reproduce | Firm's profitability | 'Path dependencies' of the technology | Profitability of the good or service |
| Transmission mechanism between generations | Process of reproduction – information storage in DNA | Economic expansion of the firm | Process of technological diffusion | Economic expansion of the firm; process of technological diffusion |

technological change, however, each of these distinctions is unclear. As illustrated in the table, the framework adopted in this book will be different from the two other major frameworks adopted in economic studies of technological change.

In brief, the following arguments could be made for the preferability of the framework adopted here – these arguments will be expressed in greater detail in subsequent chapters:

1. Firms, technologies, and goods and services are all undergoing long-run changes over time. However, it is goods and services that are truly and ultimately being selected more than any other type of entity in the economy. For example, a single firm may sell thousands of products, and those products can be highly diversified. In terms of changes in the physical nature of production and consumption, there is, therefore, an enormous

amount of pertinent evolution taking place, though this evolution would not be well understood if observed at the aggregate level of the firm.

2. With the goods and services identified as the type of entity that evolves, it is easier for this evolutionary framework to be integrated with other areas of economic thought. In particular, technological change could be linked to national accounts of goods and services.

3. As discussed in subsequent chapters, the physical characteristics of goods and services, if properly chosen, can be identified, measured, and analyzed in ways that would enable us to better understand patterns of technological change. The same cannot generally be said of the factors associated with selection in the other two economic frameworks in Table 5.1, which are difficult or impossible to measure at any aggregate level.

4. Unlike the other two economic frameworks, but like the biological framework, the framework chosen here allows for a clear distinction between the entity that evolves and the transmission mechanism between generations. In doing so, it allows for a clearer understanding of each.

Nevertheless, there is no ultimate, 'correct', evolutionary economic framework – each has its own set of advantages and disadvantages with respect to the others. What is most important, perhaps, is that evolutionary economics, in general, offers the best, overall perspective on how technological change should be studied in economics.

## NOTES

1. See, for example, the journal, *Energy Economics*.
2. See, for example, Meadows et al 1992.
3. Linstone 1999, p. 228.
4. Mansfield 1994.
5. Rosenberg and Nelson 1994, p. 340.
6. Rosenberg and Nelson 1994.
7. Jaffe 1989, p. 957.
8. Adams 1990, p. 676.
9. Jaffe et al 1993, p. 579.
10. Sullivan 1994a.
11. Occupational Safety and Health Administration 1995.
12. Pati and Bailey 1995.
13. Pati and Bailey 1995.
14. Magnusen and Kroeck 1995, pp. 71-72.
15. Thach and Woodman 1994, p. 36.
16. Center for Public Interest Law 1994.
17. Thach and Woodman 1994, p. 30.
18. Atkinson and Court 1998, p. 45.
19. Acs and Danziger 1993.

20. Still another issue is whether the learning, itself, is what employers are looking for, or if it is just the credential of a degree, which might serve merely as a signal to employers of the ability of a prospective employee to accomplish an intellectual and long-run goal (see Spence 1973).
21. Doms et al 1995.
22. Siegel 1995, p. 15.
23. Fellner 1970, p. 1-2.
24. Andersen 1999.
25. Nelson 1995, p. 54.
26. *Journal of Evolutionary Economics* 1999.
27. It is commonly known that the early 1990s witnessed a sharp fall, worldwide, in political support for Marxist theory. However, the fall in academic and intellectual interest in Marxism was less sharp. In particular, many Marxist scholars did not attribute the fall of the Soviet Union to an inherent failure of Marxist principles but to a failure in the Soviet Union's attempts to implement those principles. Nonetheless, the political fall of Marxism carried with it a fall in the overall acceptance, in academic settings, of scholarly contributions that are explicitly Marxist or 'radical'. Institutional and evolutionary economics have since become more popular venues for analyses that are generally Marxist in orientation, but not explicitly stated as such. I mention this only in order to describe the literature that now exists in the subfield – any value judgements about the subfield in this regard would, of course, be anachronistic, as the cold war has been over for some time now.
28. As examples of how different groups interpret and expand on evolutionary economics, an article in 1994 in *The Economist* states, 'So both evolutionists and economists found themselves arguing that individuals do things for the good of the larger group only if it is also for the good of the individual' (1994a, p. 94). In contrast, Gowdy (1991) writes, 'The idea that the economic process is an evolutionary one in the narrow Darwinian sense is so ingrained in our way of thinking that it is almost impossible to conceive that reality might be different. . . . The theme of co-operation is a strong one in social economics' (p. 9).
29. See, for example, the review article in by Dosi in 1988.
30. Nelson and Winter 1982, pp. 16-19.
31. Nelson and Winter 1982, p. 17.
32. This argument also appeared in Payson 1991 and 1994a.
33. The transmission mechanism in biological evolution may also be seen as evolving in future generations as a result of cloning, depending on whether one thinks of biological evolution as pertaining to natural environments only or all environments, natural or synthetic. At this writing, cloning has already become significant in the breeding of agricultural organisms (both plants and animals) and laboratory organisms. If, at some point, cloning is practiced in humans, then the fact that it would be cost prohibitive would suggest that, at that point, economic evolution and biological evolution would be fused together, with biological evolution (in humans) being subservient to economic evolution. Of course, if human cloning begins to occur, how the process relates to discourse on evolutionary theory would be the least of our concerns.

# 6. Economic Literature on Technological Change

## A PRODUCT-CYCLE MODEL OF ECONOMIC STUDIES

Economic literature on technological change could offer a great deal more than it does now. Nearly all of it falls into three general categories: (1) *highly theoretical*, primarily involving the presentation of a sophisticated mathematical model that serves much more as an intellectual curiosity than as a guide to any kind of policy analysis or business decision making; (2) *highly empirical*, presenting the results of surveys, but with little analytical content; and (3) *historical/anecdotal*, providing heuristics for decision making but often not well connected to modern circumstances. The first of these is most commonly viewed as strictly within the purview of economic thought – the others tend to attract a variety of audiences interested in economics, public policy or industrial management.

Economic theory on technological change (and on other topics in economics as well) often undergoes the following 'product cycle':

1. Prominent economists within a prestigious economic organization first coin a new concept, or buzzword, such as, in chronological order, 'technological trajectory',[1] 'technological discontinuity',[2] 'knowledge as a form of capital',[3] 'national innovation system'[4], 'general purpose technologies'[5], and the 'internationalization of R&D'[6]. (The second-to-last of these is examined below as an example.)

2. The new concept has broad, common-sense appeal, though among economists it is couched in technical and/or mathematical jargon. As a result the concept is publicly perceived as something that many people might want to know about, but only experts in the field can truly understand. The impression conveyed, at least to naive observers, is that the new concept reflects a true, scientific breakthrough in the field of economics.

3. The concept is published in top technical journals, or in working papers of leading institutions, and may also be summarized in laymen's terms in the popular press if the founding economist(s) is a famous figure.

4. At first, the concept is recognized informally by the economics profession as the intellectual property of the economist(s) who developed it. Once this recognition is clearly in place, the peer-review process often allows other economists to build on the original model, provided the founding economists are properly and favorably cited. Criticism of the new concept is much less welcome for the variety of sociological reasons discussed in earlier chapters, as well as the fact that the founding economists, being the leading experts on the topic at hand, are often chosen to peer review those new papers.

5. A paradigm is vaguely defined by the initial new concept, the initial model that defines it technically, its interpretation in the popular media, and the flow of secondary articles that build on the initial model. Within academic circles the paradigm becomes 'hot' – that is, it provides new, fertile ground for getting papers published, for dissertation topics, and for grant proposals.

6. The novelty of the new concept and paradigm eventually plays out. It becomes old news, journal editors become less interested in publishing additional articles on it, and thus new concepts and paradigms are sought to eventually replace it.

7. As economists and others look retrospectively at, what is now, an old paradigm, the actual benefits it offered become obscure in the light of more recent paradigms. The only unambiguous, cumulative effect it might have had was to help enhance the quantity of literature attributable to its author(s), and to the subfields and institutions to which its author(s) belonged.

For ease of discussion, let us call this process 'buzzword specification and expansion', or BSE for short.

As an example of a recent BSE, consider the concept of a 'general purpose technology'. In 1998 a book came out entitled *General Purpose Technologies and Economic Growth*, which is a collection of theoretical papers by various prominent economists. The book was edited by Elhanan Helpman of Harvard University and published by the MIT Press. In the third chapter of the book, Helpman and Trajtenberg define a general purpose technology as follows:

> In any given "era" there typically exists a handful of technologies that plays a far-reaching role . . . The steam engine . . . electricity . . . and microelectronics . . . Bresnahan and Trajtenberg (1995) refer to the them as general purpose technologies (GPTs hereafter).
>
> GPTs are characterized by the following features: (1) They are extremely pervasive; that is, they are used as inputs by a wide range of sectors in the economy. (2) Their potential for continual technical advances manifests itself ex post as sustained improvements in performance. (3) Complementarities with their user sectors arise in manufacturing or in the R&D technology.[7]

Here one observes a broad concept with common-sense appeal. The quoted paragraph above uses a fair amount of words to describe, in sophisticated language, what anyone would normally expect from an important technological breakthrough like the discovery and use of electricity. On the other hand, thus far no harm is done. In fact, depending on one's perspective, it might be useful, for the sake of clarity, to have these aspects of technological breakthroughs spelled out in this manner.

The above quotation was at the very beginning of Helpman and Trajtenberg's chapter, and it is followed by another two pages of similar discussion. By the third page of their chapter, however, an abrupt change is made as a new section on 'building blocks' is introduced. That section begins as shown below (readers who might have difficulty following the equations should not be concerned – they are provided here only as an illustration of the technical complexity of the literature):

> Suppose that a final good is produced with the aid of a general purpose technology (GPT) $I$ and an assembly of a continuum of components $x_i(j)$, $j \in [0, n_i]$ . . . where $n_i$ denotes the number . . . of available components. The production function is given by

$$Q_i = \lambda^i D_i, \qquad \lambda > 1,$$

> where $\lambda^i$ stands for the productivity level of GTP $I$, and

$$D_i = \left[ \int_0^{n_i} x_i(j)^\alpha \, dj \right]^{1/\alpha}, \qquad 0 < \alpha < 1.$$

> The elasticity of substitution between any two components is thus $1/(1-\alpha) > 1$.[8]

This type of discussion – the presentation of strong (and often unrealistic) assumptions, complex equations, and associated graphs – continues throughout the remaining 26 pages of their chapter, with only an occasional break from the mathematics in which text is used to describe what the mathematics has implied. As an example of this intermittent text, Helpman and Trajtenberg remark:

> Thus the main inference from our analysis is that even if substantially more efficient, new technologies may barely make a dent at first in actual growth, since they have to await for the development of a sufficiently large pool of complementary assets to make a significant and lasting impact.[9]

There are two fundamental problems with this analysis, which may already be obvious:

1. The 'main inference' mentioned above was based entirely on the assumptions made, and the mathematics that followed from those assumptions, without taking into account a single observation or datum about the real world. Therefore, it is as scientifically valid as the proof in Chapter 2 that a castle is better than a queen in chess.
2. That main inference offers no new information beyond what is commonly known about technological change by the general public. Indeed, instead of using 16 pages of mathematics to reach that conclusion, the authors could have reached the same conclusion, and more convincingly, with the sentence, 'The first electronic television was introduced in the 1939 World's Fair in New York City, but was not widely used by households in the United States until the late 1950s.'

Of course, the main objective of the Helpman–Trajtenberg study was to develop economic theory as an end in itself. As will be demonstrated further on in this chapter, through a census of the economic literature, this type of economic treatise of technological change is much more the rule than the exception. Moreover, in the minority of cases in which data about the real world are actually used, the data themselves are often superficial and of questionable scientific value. In only a very small number of cases do these data provide useful information about how technological change actually occurs.

## THE DISTANCE BETWEEN DATA AND THEORY

As suggested earlier, even when data are used, technical change economists have considerable difficulty in identifying important causal relationships in their economic constructs. One explanation for this is that they do not have much in common with the economists, statisticians and other practitioners who define, classify, and provide the information about how technological change is actually occurring. As shown in Figure 6.1, these differences exist within three layers of behavioral determinants: areas of inquiry, expertise, and motivation/orientation. At the upper left corner of the figure is the cell 'Specification of the Economic Model' which is the process through which technical change economists purport to understand and explain the underlying causality of technological change. However, analysis can only be a good as the data that go into it.

In contrast to the study of theory, the data can be seen as coming from the upper right corner of Figure 6.1, entitled, 'definition, measurement, and classification of data'. Not only is this area of inquiry distinctly different from economic modeling, but the two are separated by two other distinct areas of inquiry, 'econometric estimation' and 'compilation of data'. Each of the four areas of inquiry has its own unique perspective or orientation. For example, the definition, measurement and classification of data is an area of inquiry that must address concerns like the comparability of data acquired by different statistical agencies worldwide, so that meaningful aggregate statistics could be developed by organizations such as the United Nations and the Organisation for Economic Cooperation and Development (OECD). Issues in this area are often resolved at international conventions attended by government officials who have little or no background in economic theory, but who know 'all there is to know' about how their governments measure various statistics. As one might expect, issues in this area are sometimes interrelated with issues pertaining to a nation's image in the world community.

Similarly, the 'compilation of data' acquired through surveys (the cell to the left of one just described) is an area of inquiry that must address issues that are far removed from those addressed by economic theory. For instance, surveys to acquire data are based, in large part, on the anticipated willingness of survey participants to answer the questions posed, and on the likelihood that they would understand those questions. Here, the effort to acquire as much useful information as possible is greatly compromised by the need to make the

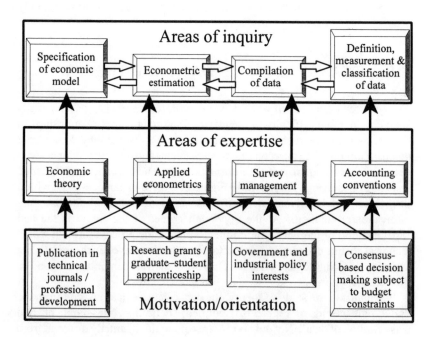

*Figure 6.1  The long distance between data and theory*

survey as least burdensome as possible to participants. The less burdensome the survey, the more it will encourage participation and promote beneficial relations between the agency conducting the survey and the public.

As an example of the difference among these perspectives in terms of the type of thinking that goes on, I once heard a panel discussion in which experts were called in to advise an institution on how a survey of industrial firms could be improved. One of the experts was a prominent economist known for his work in theoretical modeling. His advice to the organization conducting the survey, which he stated formally as a panel participant, was that it should conduct a new study on the perverse incentives that firms might have to provide misleading information. In particular, he believed that firms participating in the survey, rather than reporting accurate information might realize that they could look better to potential investors if they exaggerated certain aspects of their operations. Thus, according to the panelist, a new economic model should be developed that could investigate, as a measurable parameter, this tendency for surveyed firms to exaggerate. The justification he gave for proposing this research effort was that it would be 'interesting from a game-theoretic perspective'. Such 'expert' advice, however, neglected the idea that it would be suicidal (from a public-relations standpoint) for any organization that administers a survey to support research that explains *why people lie on it.*

The cell entitled, 'econometric estimation' has its own set of issues. Interaction does exist between econometric testing and economic theory, with many articles in economics containing some of each as they examine a particular subject. On the other hand, several econometric studies appear to be designed primarily to explore thoughts in the theory and practice of econometrics itself, where data on technological change act primarily as fodder for those exercises. Other studies that involve some of each are primarily explorations in economic theory, but which throw in some data and testing as an afterthought that, indirectly, may help to support the theory being postulated.

Like the child's game of 'telephone', where a message is sequentially whispered from one child to another until the last message whispered is completely different from the one originally intended, the true nature of original data on technological change is lost by the time it gets to economic theory. As Figure 6.1 demonstrates, this distance between data and theory exists in other layers besides 'areas of inquiry', namely, in the layers of practitioners' areas of expertise, and in their motivation and orientation. As a case in point, economic theoreticians who claim to know something about the causal relations between technological change and other economic phenomena usually have little expertise in applied econometrics, survey management, and R&D accounting procedures, which underlie the three other areas of inquiry.

This diversity of expertise explains some of the methodological problems that continue to plague the study of technological change in economics (as well as other subfields). For example, it is not uncommon for technical-change economists to complain about the limited applicability of technical-change data to useful theory, but it is very rare for those same economists to make suggestions as to how, precisely, the problem of applicability could be fixed with better data. Ironically, many technical-change economists simply recognize that they are not qualified to discuss issues about where data come from, in spite of their reliance on data to write their papers and peddle their theories. As Professor Robert Solow has remarked:

> From the point of view of the econometrician, I think there is really much less data available than is suggested. The only possible solution that I see is to enlarge the class of eligible facts, or class of observations, that one is willing to take account of. I think you have to include anecdotal facts, impressions, and direct observation. Most of the economists I know, including myself, do not have any talent for direct observation, nor, by the way, do we have any methods for dealing with it, which is not a reason not to deal with it.[10]

As Figure 6.1 suggests, differences in motivation and orientation are substantial. Theoreticians are motivated by the desire to publish and to be recognized in their profession. Empirical, econometric work is often integrally related to the process of grant acquisition for graduate-student support in exchange for their participation in data analysis. Survey management is an area that lies mostly outside the academic world, but well within the world of public policy, in which particular governmental and industrial interests come into play. Finally, those who define, measure, and classify technical-change data are oriented toward consensus-based decision making, subject to budget constraints, and heavily subservient to precedents.

Indeed, when all of the layers of the distance between data and theory are accounted for, one might wonder why the situation is not even worse than it actually is. Nevertheless, what should stand out most is the immensity of the problem. The distance in any one of the three layers mentioned (inquiry, expertise, or motivation) would be enough alone to perpetuate the problem. The solution to acquiring data that are more useful for developing theory would require nothing less than a three-pronged attack on all layers – requiring a new, interdisciplinary approach to studying the topic (in the dimension of inquiry), an alteration in the background and training of practitioners (in the dimension of expertise), and a global commitment toward making useful discoveries about the causes and effects of technological change (in the dimension of motivation/orientation).

A natural criticism that many economists might have about the perspective outlined in Figure 6.1 is that it is not unique to the study of technological change. Other areas of economics, if not every one of them to some extent, could be described as having similar problems. For example, in the area of economic inequality, measurement of actual economic hardship is often far removed from economic theory about the causes and effects of skewed income distributions. Nevertheless, if our primary concern is to improve economic inquiry in the area of technological change, then we must first identify the most relevant problems, regardless of whether those same problems also exist in other areas. In short, our focus must be on progress, not guilt. If the universality of the problem makes the problem less interesting to technical-change economists, then that is not a good thing, that is, it might reflect too great an interest in theory as an intellectual pastime in itself, as opposed to a means of understanding the world as it actually exists.

It will be argued here that, in fact, the study of technological change in economics presents a very special case with regard to the problem of distance between theory and data. To understand this argument, we must return to the discussion of elemental units. Precisely because technological change, by definition, involves changes in the nature of economic phenomena, a scientific approach to the topic requires elemental units that look underneath traditional economic categories. By analogy, again, general chemistry works well for understanding how atoms of various types behave, but when one atom changes into another, the makeup of atoms, as studied in quantum mechanics, must be employed.

An alternative, perhaps overly simplistic, interpretation of the same problem, is that it is a matter of accountability. As mentioned above, in most cases in which technical-change economists analyze data, they simply acquire the data from someone else. Any problem in the accuracy and relevance of the data is something they can attribute to the data provider, and so a technical-change economist is able to publish his results in a guilt-free and scrutiny-free environment. Moreover, since everybody does it, no one throws the first stone. This situation is extremely different from the way in which most natural science is practiced. In natural science, scientists are generally responsible for the data they analyze, which they acquire themselves, or from the graduate students and laboratory assistants under their direction.

A unique feature of technological change is that it very often involves changes in the very nature of the data used to assess it. Therefore, for progress to be made, continual revisions must be made in our understanding of how to measure the appropriate data. Such revisions, for the purpose of more useful economic discourse, will never become a reality unless they are heavily endorsed by theoretical economists, who, in effect, dictate any new initiatives in the profession. Unfortunately, as already argued, most theoretical economists have little or no expertise in how the data are defined and compiled, have little understanding themselves of the scientific and engineering advances underlying technological change, and simply do not have the incentive, the interest, or the confidence to make the necessary recommendations.

In the absence of a deliberate and conscious effort by technical-change economists to advocate better data, movements could still be made in the right direction as long as there is some commitment to understanding the actual physical events that underlie technical change. The hope is that, wherever useful discoveries *are* made with regard to trends in technological change, there will be greater impetus for improvements in data definition, measurement, and classification.

Figure 6.2 illustrates this point by outlining the differences between causes, effects, and results in the study of technological change. In particular, the figure illustrates why data cannot rely on traditional methods, because such methods would typically leave out some of the most important aspects of how technological change is manifested. Technological change involves the development of new and improved products, processes, and human skills. Consequently, economic studies of technical change can vary substantially in the way such changes are measured and understood.

Economic studies of technological change can, and should, be assessed in terms of their tendency to accurately describe the relationship between physical change and economic change. In short, one might call it a tendency to be scientific.

Figure 6.2 acknowledges that actual effects can be properly measured 'by cautiously using *traditional* definitions, measurement techniques, and classification of data'. However, there is a greater tendency to be scientific if researchers allow for '*revised* definitions, measurement techniques, and classification of data'. Such tendencies are merely that – tendencies; it is certainly possible for a study that uses revised methods to be less scientific than one that uses traditional methods.

## ARTICLES CATEGORIZED BY THE DATA THEY USE

The tendency for economic studies of technological change to be more scientific, in terms of the data they examine, is expressed in greater detail in Table 6.1. The table provides eight categories of analytical frameworks for how data on technological change are examined. The first category, 'physical characteristics of technological change related to economic variables', is the most scientific in nature in the sense that it involves direct observation of

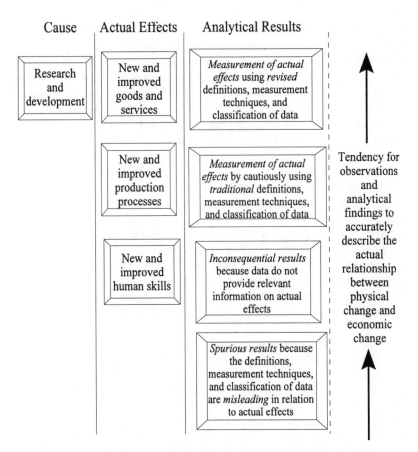

*Figure 6.2 Causes and actual effects of technological change versus analytical results*

physical change, even when economic concepts are included in the model. (The articles appearing in this category will be discussed shortly.)

The second category, 'descriptive proxies for technological change related to economic variables', does not involve physical measurement but the computation of proxies, symbols, or other abstract ideas reflecting technological change, such as patents, innovations, or scientific publications. Such counts are rarely weighted by their economic, physical, or scientific importance, primarily because that kind of information is rarely available. When it is available, it is usually the result of arbitrary or circumstantial assumptions.

As discussed in the previous chapter, publication counts and geographic proximity are each poor proxies for levels of knowledge and measures of spillover, respectively. Efforts to correct for such imprecision in measurement are often made, but such corrections are sometimes as questionable as the initial measure itself. For example, publication counts, in the rare event that they are weighted by their relative importance, are weighted by their citations, where citations to articles regarding work that is sharply criticized (that is, cited as 'the wrong way to do it') are counted in the exact same way as citations to articles regarding work that is applauded.

Another proxy for technological change is the number of 'innovations' based on industry surveys which basically ask firms how many innovations they have achieved within a specified period of time. These numbers reflect the level of innovative activity of a firm, as well as the firm's inclination to exaggerate about its innovative character for public relations or other purposes. Also completely unclear is the relative importance of an 'innovation', which might range in importance from a new design for a paper clip to the cure for AIDS. As David Audretsch, for instance, has noted, 'the innovation data are not weighted by sales or some other indicator of the value of the innovation. Thus, it is conceivable that the quality or significance of innovations is not constant across either firm size or with respect to the R&D effort'.[11]

Each of the next six categories reflects, sequentially, frameworks with still lower likelihoods of accurately depicting any true relationships that might exist between physical change and economic change. The last, as one might expect, is 'theory without measurement' where observation itself plays no role in the analysis.

In order to examine how scientific or unscientific economic studies tend to be in this regard, I conducted a census of every journal article that is listed under the topic of "technological change" in the *Journal of Economic Literature* (JEL) in its four 1996 issues. This amounted to a total of 135 journal articles, excluding the small number that were not in English and would have thus required the expense of translation. This number of articles – 135 over an entire year – appears to be quite small relative to the importance of the topic and the enormous number of economics articles on other topics cited in the JEL. However, given the weakness of economic approaches to technological change that this and other chapters discuss, such a lack of attention to the subject by economists may, unfortunately, be justified.

While no single year is 'representative' of subsequent years of economic research, because of evolutionary patterns of change in field, the general findings acquired for 1996 are indicative of problems that are likely to persist well into the twenty-first century. Figure 6.3 illustrates the distribution of the eight categories of Table 6.1 among the 135 economic articles on technological change. In the determination of this distribution, articles were

*Table 6.1   Incidence of articles on technological change by data category*

| Type of Data Used to Analyze Technological Change | Conceptual Example (not necessarily among the studies listed) | N | Studies Listed Under Technological Change in the *Journal of Economic Literature* in 1996 |
|---|---|---|---|
| I. Physical Characteristics of Technological Change Related to Economic Variables | A hedonic price study that attributes quality-measurement values to improved characteristics of computers. | 11 | Baltagi et al. 1995, Bashin 1995, Brown 1995, Clark et al. 1995, Daugherty et al. 1995, Dufournaud et al. 1994, Huang & Rozelle 1996, Ionov & Popov 1995, Koomey et al. 1996, Ofori-Amoah 1995, Saloner & Shepard 1995 |
| II. Descriptive Proxies for Technological Change Related to Economic Variables | Counting 'innovations' in the computer industry – without details on physical properties – and determining how many follow from government support. | 14 | Alexander & Flynn 1995, Bertschek 1995,Casavola et al. 1996,Cohen & Klepper 1996, den Butter & Wollmer 1996, Gu 1996, Henderson & Cockburn 1996, Koboldt 1995, Koeller 1995, Konan et al. 1995, MacPherson 1994, Meghir et al. 1996, Niosi 1995, van Reenen 1996 |
| III. Economic Resources for Technological Change related to Other Economic Variables | With industrial groups as the units of observation, e.g., 2-digit SICs, performing a cross-sectional regression analysis of output growth onto R&D expenditures. | 25 | Angel & Savage 1996, Ashcroft et al. 1995, Audretsch 1995b, Audretsch 1995c, Audretsch & Feldman 1996a, Audretsch & Feldman 1996b, Basant & Fikkert 1996, Bernstein 1996, Harris & Trainor 1995, Karier 1995, Khoroshilov 1996, Kokko et al. 1996, Kumar 1996, La Croix & Kawaura 1996, Leung & Wu 1995, Loginov & Kulagin 1995, Noland 1996, Park 1995, Perelman 1995, Pfirrmann 1995, Raut 1995, Schnabl 1995, Sivitanidou & Sivitanides 1995, Suarez-Villa & Karlsson 1996, Taylor M. 1995 |
| IV. Summary Statistics on Proxies related to Economic Variables | With industrial groups as the units of observation, e.g., 2-digit SICs, performing a cross-sectional regression analysis of output growth onto number of innovations. | 8 | Doi 1996, Geroski and Walters 1995, Gould & Gruben 1996, Lee & Mansfield 1996, Lerner 1995, Martin & Taylor 1995, Maskus & Penubarti 1995, Sjöholm 1996 |

*Table 6.1  Incidence of articles on technological change by data category*
*(concluded)*

| Type of Data Used to Analyze Technological Change | Conceptual Example (not necessarily among the studies listed) | N | Studies Listed Under Technological Change in the *Journal of Economic Literature* in 1996 |
|---|---|---|---|
| V. Broad Industry Groups linked to Technological Change | Measuring the share of output in 'high-tech' industries. | 5 | Acs 1996, Audretsch 1995, Freeman et al.. 1995, Goldin & Katz 1996, Kholdy 1995 |
| VI. Qualitative Discussion of Aspects Involving the Process of Technological Change | Discussions on the political and historical factors that have accounted for changes in patent regulations. | 29 | Amirahmadi & Wallace 1995, Cowan & Gunby 1996, Curry 1996, Dam 1995, Deardorff 1995, Frank 1996, Garrison & Souleyrette 1996, Heertje 1995, Hutter 1995, Kenny 1995, Kuri Gaytán 1995, Leontief 1995, Levy & Murnane 1996, MacQueen & Peacock 1995, Maillat et. al. 1995, McCulloch et al. 1996, Metcalfe 1995, Menasse Noble & Adler 1996, Merges 1995, Nelson & Romer 1996, Niman 1995, Pfouts 1995, Pianta 1995, Salomon 1996, Scott 1995, Stein 1996, Taylor 1995, Teubal 1996, Tisdell 1995 |
| VII. Measurement Without Theory | Discussion of R&D accounting or compilation rules only. | 2 | Carson et al. 1994, Chen 1995 |
| VIII. Theory Without Measurement | Economic models that are purely theoretical, without any hypothesis testing or the reporting of empirical files. | 41 | Agliardi 1995, Anton & Yao 1995, Athey & Schmutzler 1995, Bag & Dasgupta 1995,Balmann et. al. 1996,Bhattacharjya 1996, Birchenhall 1995, Bloch & Markowitz 1996, Caballero & Hammour 1994, Chen 1996, David & Rothwell 1996, De Bijl & Goyal 19 95, De Bondt & Henriques 1995, Duménil & Lévy 1995, Eicher 1996, Frenkel & Shefer 1996, Gandal & Rockett 1995, Goel 1995, Harris & Vickers 1995, Huizinga 1995, Jensen & Thursby 1996, Jin 1995, Jones 1995, Joshi & Vonortas 1996, Justman & Mehrez 1996, Keller 1996, Krusell & Ríos-Rull 1996, Matsumura & Ueda 1996, Matutes et al. 1996, McCulloch et al. 1996, Morasch 1995, Parente 1995, Purohit 1994, Redding 1996, Richardson & Gaisford 1996, Scotchmer 1996, Stadler 1995, Stokey 1995, van Dijk 1995, van Dijk 1996, Vega-Redondo 1996 |
| TOTAL | | 135 | |

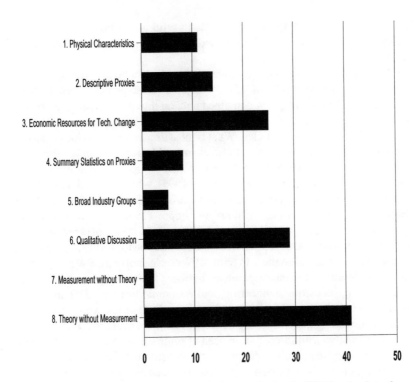

*Figure 6.3  Distribution of technological change articles in 1996 by the data they examine*

classified in terms of the lowest-numbered category for which they could qualify.  For instance, any article that contained any data on physical characteristics was placed in Category 1, even if most of the data it contained were on descriptive proxies.  Articles that focused almost entirely on economic theory, however, were placed in Category 8, even if they contained a smidgen of data at the end to 'illustrate the theory'.  As the figure indicates, there is clearly a predominance of 'theory without measurement' among these articles.

This distribution of articles does lend support to the notion that technological-change economics, like most other areas of economics that are published in technical journals, is dominated by empty formalism. Nevertheless, care should be taken in not drawing strong conclusions about these particular 135 articles.  It is quite possible that any article in any of the eight categories has, in fact, made an important and useful contribution to economic thought.  Since this may be the case for any one of the articles, it is certainly possible, though less probable, that a majority of the articles in any of the higher-numbered categories is also useful as a whole. In short, the value of these articles cannot be assessed on the basis of their data categories alone.

What may be most important about this distribution, however, is the observation that only 11 out of 135 articles (or 8 percent) belonged to Category 1. That is, very few contained data on the 'physical characteristics of technological change'. Table 6.2 presents the physical characteristics contained in these eleven articles. What is most immediately obvious from the table is that all of these eleven articles examined 'microeconomic' effects.

The closest any one of them came to a macro analysis of some general aspect of the overall economy was Bashin (1995), which focused on machine components, but for a variety of manufacturing industries in Russia. Both Bashin's article and the one by Ionov and Popov (1995) were from Russian economists, who dealt with Russian economic issues from a perspective quite different from the kind of capitalist discourse common to North American and Western European economics. In terms of Western subfields, that perspective could be described as interdisciplinary between the economics of industrial organization, industrial engineering, and economic history. This may be a useful combination of approaches, but their discussions were at least as journalistic (citing government statistics, government mandates, and so on) as they were analytic, and were thus in need of some sort of model. That is, they reflected the opposite of empty formalism – unstructured empiricism.

The article by Dufournaud et al. (1994) was a borderline case between Category 1 and Category 8, in that it was primarily about theory, not observation. This leaves only eight articles cited in 1996 by the *Journal of Economic Literature* that appear to have looked solidly into the physical characteristics of technological change, though at a microeconomic level. Furthermore, all of these eight studies were primarily retrospective, rather that prospective – that is, they tended to examine current and historical effects, but contained very little about the future characteristics of goods or services. They are obviously the products of economists who have some interest in science or engineering. Nonetheless, because of their limited scopes and historical orientation, they are unlikely to effect any significant change in economists' overall approach to technological change. That overall approach, as shown in Figure 6.3, appears to be dominated by 'theory without measurement'.

## NOTICING THE PROBLEM

The lack of attention among economists to the physical nature of technological change has not gone entirely unnoticed. In 1999, for example, Gregory Tassey of the United States government's National Institute of Standards and

Table 6.2  *Physical characteristics mentioned in eleven articles on technological*
*change cited in 1996 in the* Journal of Economic Literature

| Study | Physical characteristics of technological change |
|---|---|
| Baltagi et al. 1995 | In airline transportation: 'Average seat miles flown per gallon of fuel' |
| Bashin 1995 | Percentage of 'standardized parts' in machine building |
| Brown 1995 | With regard to commercial jet aircraft, the average age of the aircraft and the percentage of 'high bypass engine equipped jets in an airline's fleet' |
| Clark et al. 1995 | Percentages of firms in a geographic area that use different types of communication and computer equipment (e.g., fax machines, personal computers, mainframe computers, and cable networks) |
| Daugherty et al. 1995 | Incidence of the adoption by firms of electronic data interchange (EDI) |
| Dufournaud et al. 1994 | Quantities of firewood burned and incidence of alternative types of stoves in the Sahelian region of North Africa (though most of the paper is theoretical) |
| Huang & Rozelle 1996 | Characteristics of rice production in China, e.g., incidence of hybrid rice adoption, chemical fertilizer use per hectare, and cultivated land area per capita. |
| Ionov & Popov 1995 | Costs of generating electric power (per kWh) and thermal power (per thousand gigacalories), before and after specific innovations at particular power plants |
| Koomey et al. 1996 | 'Engineering . . . characteristics of standard and energy-efficient magnetic ballasts for fluorescent lighting' |
| Ofori-Amoah 1995 | The physical features of twin-wire, paper-making machines as they have evolved over time |
| Saloner & Shepard 1995 | Adoption of automated teller machines (ATMs) by banks over 1972–79 |

Technology wrote a report, entitled *R&D Trends in the U.S. Economy:*
*Strategies and Policy Implications.* In that report, he remarks:

> Few economists have focused their research on technological change and, of those that
> have done so, most have failed to target their research toward the needs of policy
> makers. . . . A consensus economic model that accurately represents the complex role
> of technology in economic growth has not been achieved. As a result, data
> identification and collection are not driven by a coherent set of analytical
> requirements. . . . Even if such a model were available and accepted, current economic
> data in general and R&D investment data in particular are highly inadequate for
> effective R&D policy analysis. . . . As a result, policy recommendations are poorly
> constructed and have a weak track record of successful implementation. (p. 2)

Nevertheless, efforts at acquiring useful data are frequently compromised by
the translation problems illustrated in Figure 6.1. In particular, ideas for new
economic data on technological change are expressed largely in a public-
policy/public-relations environment. As such, those ideas build on anecdote,
common sense, and historical precedent and involve concepts that nearly
anyone can understand. The problem is that important considerations as

fundamental as whether a measure can be unambiguously defined, or whether a concept has physical meaning that can facilitate a physical understanding of the world, are rarely addressed in this type of discourse. In short, the *science* of technological change is *absent*.

As an example, in 1999, a report entitled *Securing America's Industrial Strength* was put out by the Board on Science, Technology, and Economic Policy (STEP) of the National Research Council of the US National Academy of Sciences. The STEP board was chaired by Dale Jorgenson of Harvard University, one of the most famous and widely-known economists of the past three decades. Other famous economists on the STEP board included Ralph Landau of the Stanford Institute for Economic Policy Research, and Joseph Stiglitz, former Chairman of the US President's Council of Economic Advisors and currently the Senior Vice President and Chief Economist at the World Bank.

In its appendix on 'R&D and Innovation Data', written by Stephen Merrill and Ronald Cooper, the STEP report provides the standard 'boilerplate language' on the topic:

> Ideally, the collection of national and international data on innovation should be guided by a solid theoretical understanding of the process and its impacts. Such understanding of causes and effects, while being developed, is not very far advanced. It is possible to elaborate a conceptual framework that encompasses direct indicators of innovation, influences on innovation, and its effects. (pp. 99–100)

The last sentence of this quotation is a reflection of the type of euphemistic, yet nebulous, statements that are often made about R&D 'indicators' in science policy discussions. They are public statements made largely to support existing, or already planned, data-collection efforts, as opposed to shedding light on new analytical approaches.

In this vein, shortly after this quotation, a huge list of existing indicators is provided in the report. The list includes, for example, 'invention/innovation disclosures', 'new product announcements', 'innovation counts', 'patent counts', 'shares of sales attributable to new products and services', 'strategic technology alliance counts', and 'licensing agreements'. All of these indicators are already provided by well-established governmental and non-governmental organizations, many of whom were the sponsors of the report to begin with. The language and nature of the report, and its association with Dale Jorgensen and Joseph Stiglitz, provide excellent advertising for currently-available data on R&D indicators.

Yet, Stephen Merrill's and Ronald Cooper's appendix of the report ends with the conclusion, 'What is certain is that without a concerted effort to improve R&D and other innovation indicators, we will continue to be in a relatively poor position to assess industrial innovation trends' (p. 116).

Among the problems they listed included the idea that data on industries are too aggregated, so that one cannot identify precisely where R&D is taking place. Another is 'accounts of discrete transactions fail to indicate their value in monetary or other terms'. Basically, all of the problems they identify are description of limitations and failings in existing indicators, suggesting that those indicators be improved with more 'robust' data. In effect, the implicit message is that the existing data-collecting institutions are doing the right thing – but they just need to use more resources to do it better. As in nearly all such reports, no methods are seriously criticized or challenged, and no new methods of analysis are offered. This limitation in such reports occurs in spite of the fact (if not partially *because* of the fact) that highly-prominent economists were affiliated with the study.

In short, our most highly-respected members of the economics profession have offered little in the way of new directions for the acquisition of data on technological change. Yet, as argued in this chapter, without better data, economic research on technological change will continue to be severely constrained. Moreover, as also suggested in this chapter, there may be very little economic literature on technological change, beyond formalized common sense and anecdote, that offers any real hope for understanding true causal relationships. The next three chapters of this book will provide examples of how new kinds of data on technological change might be conceived, obtained, and analyzed.

## NOTES

1. Dosi 1982.
2. Tushman and Anderson 1986.
3. Romer 1986.
4. Freeman 1987.
5. Bresnahan and Trajtenberg 1995.
6. Mowery 1998.
7. Helpman and Trajtenberg, 1998, p. 55.
8. Helpman and Trajtenberg, 1998, p. 57.
9. Helpman and Trajtenberg, 1998, p. 73.
10. Solow 1993, p. 40.
11. Audretsch 1995a, p. 582.

PART III


New Attitudes, Philosophies, Frameworks and Models

# 7. Product Evolution and the Case for Function-Based Classification

## INTRODUCTION

One of the essential functions of any science is to examine a set of phenomena, and develop hypotheses and theories on the underlying causal factors that best explain them. What happens, however, when there is a process in which the phenomena being studied are not constant, but are subject to change? When this occurs, scientists divide and conquer: they establish two fields – one for the original set of phenomena, and the other for the processes through which those phenomena change. This is essentially why genetics is distinct from the rest of biology, kinetics is distinct from general chemistry, and history is distinct from political science, to name a few.

To many scientists this discussion may be quite elementary, but it may warrant greater attention in the field of economics. In economics many different sets of phenomena are studied, but, for the moment, let us just focus on two of these sets: firms (and firm behavior), and products (both goods and services). What firms are, and the differences among them in terms of their features and behavior, is studied in separate subfields: industrial organization and the supply side of microeconomics. In contrast, products are examined in all aspects of microeconomics: how they are made is explored on the supply side, and why they are purchased by consumers on the demand side.

Both firms and products change, especially over long periods of time. In a competitive market system, these changes are associated with the need for firms, and for products, to compete among themselves for their own survival. In short, both firms and products evolve. With regard to *firms*, two interrelated subfields have been established for understanding evolution: 'evolutionary economics' and 'the economics of technological change'. Some would argue that these subfields also address how *products* evolve. However, in the case of product evolution, an alternative framework is warranted.

When product evolution is examined in the existing economic literature, it is almost always done in the context of particular products coming from their respective firms. The firm is seen as the active agent in the process, causing the creation of new products. However, as argued below, over long periods of time, the survival, expansion, or demise of a product could be peripheral to the innovative processes of firms. The essential determinant of a product's evolution is based on the broad function that it serves, and more precisely on how well it serves that broad function in comparison to other, competing products that serve the same broad function. In this chapter, the firm is not seen as the source of change, but largely as a messenger between scientific and engineering advances, at one end, and product evolution at the other.

## THE CASE FOR FUNCTION-BASED CLASSIFICATION

Examples in support of a function-based classification of products are not difficult to find, and they can clarify what is meant by the term 'broad function' mentioned above. For instance, the Pony Express is often hailed as one of the most innovative companies of its time. It was very successful at delivering mail across the continental United States in 1860–61, using an elaborate, and truly innovative, network of 420 horses, 80 riders and 190 relay stations – a system that, under other circumstances, might have been considered ahead of its time. Yet, it had a short life of only 18 months, as it was unable to compete with the newly-established telegraph. Consequently, the quick downfall of the Pony Express may best be seen not as a failure in *innovation*, but perhaps as a failure in *precognition* – the future is hard to predict, especially with regard to technological breakthroughs.

The idea that the Pony Express was replaced by the telegraph is widely known. Yet, one might ask how this product evolution would have been analyzed in traditional economic analysis of innovation. At present, courier services are categorized under the broader heading of 'transportation' in standard industrial classifications, with SIC 4513 for courier services by air (SIC 45 for all air transportation) and SIC 4215 for non-air courier service (SIC 42 for all 'motor freight transportation and warehousing').[1] This categorization of courier services with transportation is certainly justified on the basis of similar technologies, plus the obvious fact that packages *are* transported. In contrast, the telegraph, telephone services, and so on, fall under SIC 48, communications.

A firm/innovation study would typically separate out, based on available data, 'transportation firms' like the Pony Express, or a more modern courier that uses trucks, from communications firms. Product evolution, like the telegraph replacing the Pony Express would simply not be observed, because the development of telegraph services, and the demise of the Pony Express, would be treated as separate events occurring in separate groups of firms, or separate 'sectors of the economy'. As a result, the causality underlying the observed decline in the 'transportation sector' would not be known.

Ironically, what might be concluded is that transportation firms, on the basis of their low growth rate, do not appear to be innovative.

The story of the Pony Express and telegraph is being repeated today on a much grander scale. The Internet is now replacing an enormous amount of courier services worldwide, through the transmission of documents in electronic, rather than hardcopy form, while it is simultaneously increasing courier services as the Internet is beginning to replace retail shopping. With the Internet and many other new technologies, if economic analysis of technological change could occasionally free itself from the 'world-according-to-industrial-codes', and focus instead on the broad functions served by products, then it might be able to offer better explanations of the causality underlying the evolution of products. Once product evolution is better understood, then the evolution of the economy as a whole would be better understood as well.

Underlying the above discussion is the very-basic idea that the actual competition that exists among products (including services) is based on the broader functions that those products serve. While this notion does not surface very often in the economic literature on technological change, it does do so in the business and marketing literature, though in a slightly different form. Joseph Juran, for example, a famous historical figure in the business literature on quality control, had distinguished between the 'stated needs' of consumers and their 'real needs', with the former being a superficial labeling of a product and the latter a broader-based categorization that allows for a wider range of substitutions.[2] As examples of pairs of stated needs vs. real needs, Mr Juran listed: 'food / nourishment, pleasant taste; automobile / transportation; color TV / entertainment; house / living space; house paint / colorful appearance and freedom from maintenance'. As his own example of the above distinctions, Juran discussed the history of women's hair nets. Many women used to wear hair nets in order to hold their hair in place after visits to the hair dresser. Companies competing in this market developed high-quality nets of different colors, fabrics, and so on, in an effort to out-do one another. However, both companies perished when a chemical hair spray was developed that could perform the same basic function invisibly, with the mere push of a button. Along similar lines, in 1975 Theodore Levitt discussed the business problem of 'marketing myopia' in which companies are seen as often making the mistake of focusing too much on the narrow functions of products, thereby missing out on opportunities in new products that serve the same broader functions.

In the economics literature, function-based categorizations of products appears primarily in the literature on quality measurement. The economic approach may be seen, in part, as rooted in Lancaster's (1991) classic assumption that consumers do not purchase products for their own sake, but for the 'characteristics' they possess and the functions those characteristics serve. Professor J. Steenkamp, in 1989, noted that a limitation in the Lancaster framework is that it relies on measurable characteristics, while important factors like the taste of complex food products cannot be easily or objectively measured on the same scale for all consumers. Taken together, these ideas suggest that the function served by a product may be a useful piece of information, even when the exact magnitude with which it meets that function is difficult to measure. Amartya Sen has also emphasized the functions of products, by relating them to the overall well-being of consumers: 'In judging the well-being of the person, it would be premature to limit the analysis to the characteristics of the goods possessed. We have to consider the 'functionings' of persons . . . what the person succeeds in *doing* with the commodities and characteristics at his or her command'.[3]

In the above discussion on courier services and electronic communication, it was argued that more would be understand about the causes of change if observers recognized the broader function served by both products – the transfer of information. Thus, attention to the broader function served could spell out many of the important interrelationships that currently exist among 'horizontally-competing' consumer products. In addition, attention to functionality could shed light on 'vertical' relationships among products, allowing for better understanding of how intermediate products are best utilized to make other products.

Furthermore, any examination of vertical relationships associated with technological change that does not consider functionality could have a bias toward overemphasizing 'scientifically interesting' changes, while giving too little attention to changes that may be less scientifically interesting but otherwise important. As an example, in an earlier study[4] I examined the technological changes in five household products over the period 1928–93, based on characteristics observed in items sold in the *Sears Catalog*. In discussing these characteristics, I contrasted an innovation that occurred in one of these products – polyurethane foam replacing springs in sofas – with one that occurred in another – an electrical self-ignition device replacing the pilot light in some gas ranges. As I have argued, in the firm/innovation framework, it is likely that the innovation in sofas would either be ignored entirely, or at best, receive little attention. The reason is that polyurethane foam would be seen as a product innovation in the chemical industry, but then not be given the credit it is due in the furniture industry. As a new chemical, polyurethane foam is 'scientifically more interesting' than it is as a physical substitute for coils in sofas. Moreover, the idea of adding to a piece of furniture a material that someone else had invented in another industry does not convey quite the same intellectual worthiness that is normally associated with product innovation. Yet, the same firm/innovation approach would likely find the electrical self-ignition device in a gas range to be an important advancement. Rather than reflecting a simple replacement of one spring-like object for another, it involves electrical components, and the conversion of one form of energy to another, both of which appear more 'scientific' in nature, especially to observers with limited backgrounds in science. In addition, in this latter case, there is a seamless connection between the invention of the device and its incorporation into the final product. In the case of polyurethane foam in sofas, the raw material and the final product are developed in distinctly different industries, making it harder for observers to interpret as a single, identifiable innovation.

These and similar differences between the technological advances in sofas and gas ranges would cause the firm/product innovation approach to be much more likely to conclude that gas ranges underwent *more* technological change than sofas, reflecting a bias against technological advances that are not scientifically interesting and against advances that cross over product sectors during the production chain. In actual fact, the vast majority of sofas today do have foam rubber cushions of one sort or another, while the vast majority of gas ranges do not have electrical self-ignition switches. Consequently, the polyurethane foam advancement is more important, at least economically, but in order for that importance to be recognized, a link was needed between the chemical/materials industry and the furniture industry. That link could have been established if the polyurethane-foam invention had been associated with improvements in the quality of furniture.

Another benefit of the functional categorization of products is that more meaningful and/or accurate evolutionary trends can often be observed. Because of technological similarities rather than functional similarities, video cameras had been placed in the same industrial classification as television sets, SIC 3651, while older 'movie cameras' purchased by many households in the 1970s, for example, appear in the same category as photocopy machines and X-ray film, SIC 3861. Similarly, household window fans are found under 'electric housewares and fans', SIC 3634, which includes crock pots and waffle irons, while window air conditioners are under SIC 3585, along with refrigerators, furnaces, and snow-making machinery. In my earlier study of household products in 1993, I combined household cameras, movie cameras, and camcorders to focus on household photographic equipment, and combined household fans and air conditioners to form room-cooling devices. Quality improvement based on these broader, functional definitions revealed remarkable quality improvement rates of 9.3 percent per year for photographic equipment, and 7.5 percent per year for room-cooling devices, over the entire period 1928–93.[5]

A fascinating study by William Nordhaus in 1994 examined every major device that human beings have ever used to produce light, such as open fires (beginning in prehistoric times), the neolithic lamp (40–15,000 BC), the candle (1800), the kerosene lamp (1855), the electric filament lamp (1900), and the compact fluorescent bulb (1992). He estimated the cost, in terms of hours of work required, to produce one 'kilolumenhour', which is a well-defined, physical quantity of light emitted. The number of labor hours required to produce this quantity of light dropped from approximately 100 in the good-old days of 500,000 BC, to about 3 hours in 1850, 0.010 hours in 1930, 0.0010 hours in 1960, and 0.00012 hours in 1992. Because official price estimates of the cost of lighting had been based on factors much more removed from the functional concept of physical lumens of light, they varied greatly from Professor Nordhaus's findings. Consequently, Professor Nordhaus concluded that official price estimates of the fall in lighting costs for the period 1800–1992 were off by a factor of at least 900.

While discussing the topic of price indices, Professor Nordhaus, too, makes an appeal for a broader-based classification system for products:

> During periods of major technological change, the need to construct accurate price indexes that capture the impact of new technologies on living standards is beyond the practical capability of official statistical agencies. . . . If we are to obtain accurate estimates of the growth of real incomes over the last century, we must somehow construct price indexes that recognize the vast change in the quality and range of goods and services that we consume, that somehow compare the services of horse and automobile, of facsimile machine and Pony Express, of Xerox machine and carbon paper, of television with dark and lonely nights, of magnetic resonance imaging with brain surgery.[6]

## CONNECTIONS BETWEEN SCIENTIFIC ADVANCES AND THE FUNCTIONS OF PRODUCTS

Many of the economic effects of scientific discoveries may be understood more clearly in the context of the functions that products serve. In the case of product evolution, consider, for example, the evolution over the past 50 years of four household products: footwear, vehicles, photographic equipment, and computing devices (from manually powered adding machines to modern-day computers). While all of these products have experienced considerable evolution, vehicles have evolved at a greater rate than footwear, photographic equipment at a greater rate than vehicles, and computing devices at a greater rate than photographic equipment, begging the question of why these rates differ.[7]

To a physicist there should be little mystery as to why computing devices have evolved at a much greater rate than vehicles. Vehicles are heavily constrained by physical laws of energy and inertia. The energy required to transport any cargo (or passenger) will always be at least as great as $\frac{1}{2}mv^2$ where m is mass and v velocity, even ignoring other factors like air resistance, friction, and directional acceleration. Thus, even if the mass of the vehicle itself were somehow made negligible in comparison to the mass of the cargo, the absolute minimum energy requirements associated with the mass of the cargo would remain unchanged. Transportation of a fixed mass can never be less costly than the cost of the minimum amount of energy required. In contrast, computing devices require the processing of information, where information itself has *no physical requirements* in terms of mass, except at an atomic level, and no speed restrictions except at the speed of light. The same may also be said of electronic and photo-electronic communication devices that do nothing more than move information from one location to another. In the final analysis, the laws of science best explain why information processing and communications have evolved faster than transportation.

To a neuro-psychologist, or a psychologist specializing in human perception, the fact that cameras evolve at a greater rate than footwear should come as no surprise. Although comfort in walking and running plays a definite role in sensory perception and cognitive processing, that role is minuscule in comparison to the role of visual input (and auditory input provided by a camcorder).

More generally, by focusing on the broad functions served by products, reasonable hypotheses could be set forth on their evolutionary patterns of technical change. For example, products designed primarily to appeal to the senses, especially in the form of entertainment, would be expected to undergo continual quality improvements as firms compete among themselves for providing customers with the most-stimulating and/or thought-provoking products. This might explain, for instance, the dramatic changes that have taken place in the progression of entertainment media from the silent movies of the 1920s to the virtual reality experiences of the late 1990s. In contrast, products that are standardized, or designed to meet a specific physical requirement that remains unchanged, would not be expected to undergo rapid growth in quality, because competing firms would be expected to focus, instead, on lowering costs, though such costs could include not only pecuniary costs, but costs in terms of the consumer's use of time, space, and other resources. Basic transportation is an example of this latter case, in which customers are only interested in cost, once a certain standard of comfort and safety are met.

# BARRIERS TO THE STUDY OF PRODUCT CLASSIFICATION BY FUNCTION

An unavoidable question is likely to arise: If a function-based classification of products has the aforementioned potential benefits, then why does one not already exist instead of the type of classification used today? However, the need for function-based classification should not be misinterpreted as any lack of need for the industrial classification that already exists. The benefits of the existing classification are so widespread, and so obvious in many instances, that any discussion along these lines would not be productive. All that is advocated here is that a function-based classification system be established that could *add to*, or *supplement* the existing system of classification. Moreover, as already suggested, a function-based classification of products would be used for different purposes in any event, and would not, therefore, take any role away from the existing system.

Nonetheless, the first and most obvious barrier to function-based classification is the view, held by some, that only one classification should exist, regardless of the variety of purposes that could be served by different classifications. Part of the underlying problem lies in the context in which classification is done, which can range from 'customer-service' in the case of economic classifications, to 'scientific-inquiry', as mentioned in Part I.

Another barrier to the classification of products by function is that it is inherently an interdisciplinary task, requiring an understanding of the ways in which products are used. For example, if a new rifle is developed, an industry-based approach would simply place the new product in SIC 3484, 'Small Arms'. A function-based approach might ask whether it will be used primarily for hunting, criminal activity, local law enforcement, or military purposes. An answer to this question would require some knowledge of the topic by people who would perform the classification. Ultimately, this would make a function-based system more expensive to develop and maintain.

More generally, the direction of technological change is explainable, in part, by the *strategies* and *objectives* of firms and other organizations, as opposed to their particular actions or organizational structures. (Empirical evidence of this perspective will be provided in the next chapter.) This perspective is uniquely different from the firm/innovation approach that dominates the field of technical-change economics, in which the particular actions of firms are seen as the central factor explaining causality.

The popularity and dominance of the firm/innovation approach to technological change may involve, in part, a fallacy of composition. Without a doubt, the short-term innovative activities carried out by the firm are responsible for, and in this sense, cause, the short-term creation of new products by that firm – a product evolution approach would not deny this basic fact. *However, in the aggregate, and over long periods of time, the differences in rates of technological change among products could not be explained by differences in the average, initial, innovative capabilities of firms.* For instance, innovation in food products has resulted in some improvement in products, like the genetically-engineered 'Flavor-Saver' tomato, but such improvements, in terms of product quality, are indisputably minuscule in comparison to those experienced, for instance, in computers. One could not, with the least bit of rationality, claim that this difference between food and computers is due to computer producers starting out with greater innovative capability than food producers. Surely, the difference is best explained by the inherent aspects of food and computers themselves, namely, the improvements consumers want and how much they would be willing to pay for them, and the scientific and engineering advances that have been recognized and adopted by both industries. Nevertheless this fallacy of composition may pose a barrier to the product evolution framework. As an analogy, when people are accustomed to relating the height of a tree to its age, they are inclined to think of the average height of a forest as a function of the average age of its trees. However, in a long-run perspective, what would really matter for the height of a forest, in comparison to other forests, is the *species* of trees that forest contains.

As if these barriers were not enough, there is one other barrier that might make the others pale by comparison. The variety of products that exist in the economy, and the number of purposes they serve, are simply enormous. One might envision that a classification system based on function would require nothing less than the establishment of a new government agency to collect, interpret, and process aggregate data. In the absence of aggregate data, one could only rely on anecdotal findings associated with one or a few specific product groups, such as Professor Nordhaus's 1994 findings on lighting mentioned earlier.

This 'data-collection problem' is actually not a problem at all if one confines the product-based classification to the specific context under which it is being used. As mentioned earlier, product-based classification should be used in order to ask the question of how scientific and engineering advances become manifested in new products. Consequently, one need only look at the products that have recently been influenced by scientific discoveries. This context also implies that products, classified by function, need not be weighted by sales, nor associated with particular firms. In other words, no efforts at reproducing 'national accounts' should be attempted – an entirely different area of inquiry is being explored. With regard to 'confusion among users' resulting from multiple classifications, the opposite view is taken here: multiple classifications would add clarity; perhaps it is the very absence of multiple classifications that creates the most confusion.

# AN EMPIRICAL DEFINITION

Once categories are established, the stage of evolution for any category and time period could be approximated by the observed quality of a specific good within the category and period, designated as the 'representative good'. This representative-good approach (RGA) to product evolution is not meant to be more rigorous than currently established methods of quality estimation. Rather, *it is a less rigorous method by design*. However, unlike many price-linking and hedonic methods of quality measurement, the RGA has less tendency to drift from an accurate measure of change as more periods are added. The reason is that the process of identifying a representative good for a given period is independent of any results obtained from previous periods. By starting from scratch in each period, there is no systematic accumulation of bias from one period to the next.

The RGA makes the measurement of product evolution possible using data found in historical documents such as the *Sears Catalog* (in existence from 1893 to 1993), *Consumer Reports* (1936 to present) and the *New York Times* (1851 to present). What is necessary for the RGA is a consistent and logical means of designating a representative good (and its price) in each period, and an ability to find that same representative good (and its price) in an earlier period. The period itself could be long or short depending on the rate of product evolution for the good in question. Personal computers, for instance, should have periods of less than one year, while goods that have not changed much over time, like items of jewelry, could have periods as long as a decade.

The representativeness of the 'representative good' would always be one of the most important concerns. For instance, in the transition from one period to the next, if only a single, but markedly different new item is introduced to the category, it is hoped that the presence of this new item would lead to the identification of a new representative good, thereby reflecting the product evolution that has occurred from the introduction of the new item. In the present study the representative good is defined as the item with the median price among the items in the category (and the median quality to the extent that price reflects quality).

Once representative goods are identified, standard price-linking techniques can be used to measure rates of product evolution. For instance, consider one of the products examined in this study – sofas. Let $A_{1988}$ denote the set of all sofas in 1988, and let the representative item be the sofa with the median price, $p_{1988}$. Using five-year intervals, and examining every fifth Spring/Summer issue of the *Sears Catalog*, in 1993 another representative item is observed, with price $p_{1993}$. Given this situation, any comparison of $p_{1988}$ and $p_{1993}$ would have little meaning in itself, because several factors besides quality change could have influenced them, since the two representative items exist at different points in time. On the other hand, one could ask the following question: was the representative sofa of 1993 on the list of items available in 1988, and if so, what was its price in 1988? Assuming the 1993 median item was available in 1988, let us call that item the '1988 future median item', because the item itself will become the median item in the future, but its price is observed in 1988. To draw a clear distinction between designated items, let us call the median item of 1988, based on 1988 prices, the '1988 present median item' (see Figure 7.1).

There are two main differences between the 1988 present median item and the 1988 future median item: characteristics and price. Because both items exist at the same time, a cost reduction effect, a pure price effect, and an income effect on demand cannot account for any of the difference in their prices.[8] Their prices vary only because of their characteristics. Thus, the difference in their price reflects quality improvement, and defines product evolution, from 1988 to 1993. As for the 1988 future median and 1993 present median items, both are identical in characteristics, so quality is not a factor. Their price differences could have only resulted from a cost reduction effect, an income effect on demand, a pure price effect, or some combination thereof. This approach is no different from any other price-linking method, except for its identification and utilization of the 'representative good' for each period.

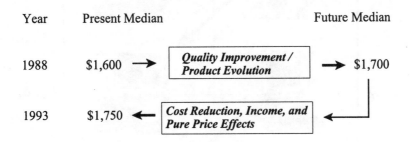

*Figure 7.1 Use of price linking to measure product evolution*

## REPRESENTATIVE GOOD APPROACH VERSUS CONVENTIONAL PRICE LINKING

Figure 7.2 illustrates another example of quality change among items in consecutive periods. Period 0, the base period, contains five models, A–E, with corresponding prices $a_0=1$, $b_0=2$, and so on. In Period 1, Model A drops out; Model F is added; and the prices of Models B–E are reduced by one unit.

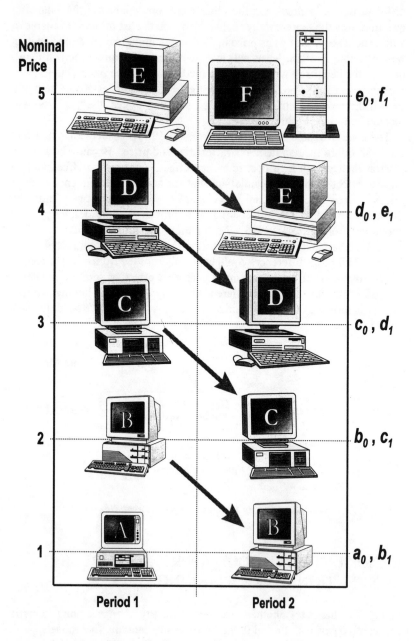

*Figure 7.2 Quality change and product evolution in two consecutive periods*

(If these are computers, the prices shown could be thought of as being in thousands of dollars.) Prices in Period 1 are $b_1=1$, $c_1=2$, and so on.

For simplicity, assume that the quantity sold is divided equally among the five models in each period. Let $Q_0$ and $Q_1$ be scalars that serve as index numbers of the quality of all items in Periods 0 and 1. Under these conditions, qualities in Period 1, measured by conventional price-linking (CPL), would be proportional to values in Period 1 at base-period prices. The only item that does not exist in the base period is Model F. However, under a price-linking approach, the hypothetical value of F in Period 0 could be estimated as:

$$\tilde{f_0} = f_1 \frac{e_0}{e_1} . \tag{7.1}$$

Thus, one has:

$$Q_0 = a_0 + b_0 + c_0 + d_0 + e_0$$

$$Q_1 = b_0 + c_0 + d_0 + e_0 + f_1 \frac{e_0}{e_1} . \tag{7.2}$$

The proportional change in quality, based on conventional price linking is then given by:

$$\left( \frac{Q_1 - Q_0}{Q_0} \right)_{CPL} = \frac{f_1 \dfrac{e_0}{e_1} - a_0}{a_0 + b_0 + c_0 + d_0 + e_0} . \tag{7.3}$$

Under the RGA, the proportional change in product evolution would be based exclusively on the representative good in each period. Because Model C is the present median good and Model D is the future median good, one has:

$$\left( \frac{Q_1 - Q_0}{Q_0} \right)_{CPL} = \frac{21}{60}$$

$$\left( \frac{Q_1 - Q_0}{Q_0} \right)_{RGA} = \frac{20}{60} . \tag{7.4}$$

With the numbers provided in Figure 7.2, we find:

$$\left(\frac{Q_1-Q_0}{Q_0}\right)_{RGA} \equiv \frac{d_0-c_0}{c_0} .$$ (7.5)

In this example, the RGA serves as a close approximation to the conventional price-linking approach.

In actual practice, however, it is quite possible that the uniqueness of Model F may not be discovered and/or accounted for in Period 1. Suppose, for example, that Model F is treated as equivalent to Model E, even though its price is higher in Period 1. This could occur quite easily if the higher price of F is simply attributed to a pure price effect, because the unique features of F that distinguish it from E are not recognized by individuals collecting or analyzing the data.

If F is not recognized as distinct from E, then its estimated base-period price, $\tilde{f}_0$, could be taken as $e_0$, implying:

$$\left(\frac{Q_1-Q_0}{Q_0}\right)_{CPL} = \frac{e_0 - a_0}{a_0+b_0+c_0+d_0+e_0} .$$ (7.6)

Using the hypothetical values in Figure 7.2, the estimated proportional change in quality would be 26.67 percent, in comparison to 35 percent if F were recognized as a unique model. Yet, such an error would not alter the estimated proportional change under the RGA, 33.33 percent, because Model D would still be regarded as the representative good in Period 1.

The more subtle the changes in quality between periods, the greater the tendency for conventional price-linking to underestimate quality change. Of course, over long periods, any small but systematic underestimation of quality change between consecutive periods could lead to a dramatic underestimation of quality change for an entire time span. For instance, suppose the true quality change were, in fact, 35.00 percent in every five-year interval. Suppose the RGA consistently measured 33.33 percent instead, while the CPL approach went back and forth between the underestimate of 26.67 percent and the correct estimate of 35.00 percent. Let the initial quality index at time 0 be 100. After 100 years (or 20 five-year periods), the true quality index would be 29,946; the RGA product evolution index would be 23,650 (79 percent of the true index); and the CPL quality index would be 15,835 (53 percent of the true index).

One could argue that the mix-up between Model F and Model E in this example would not create a problem for the RGA in Period 1, but would lead to its underestimation of quality change in Periods 2 or 3, when E and F are being considered as potential representative goods. However, such a mix-up between E and F is much less likely to occur, because under the RGA all of the focus and attention is placed on the analysis of representative goods. Consequently, the characteristics of potential representative items would be studied much more thoroughly than in the conventional approach. This additional attention would be feasible, because rather than having to rate all items in relation to each other, we would only need to determine how other items fare in relation to the representative item.

Depending on the type of good being investigated, the time span considered, and the rigor with which comparisons are made, the RGA and product evolution framework could have certain advantages over conventional methods of quality adjustment. The RGA allows for easier recognition of new items, even uniquely different items, that appear first at the top of the quality spectrum. In conventional methods of quality measurement, when a good that is unique first appears on the market, it is often not accounted for until much later. For example, Professor Robert Gordon found that the room air conditioner had appeared in the *Sears Catalog* and in *Consumer Reports* for 11 years before it became incorporated into the consumer price index.[9] Furthermore, conventional and hedonic methods often have a bias toward the under-reporting of minor and subtle quality improvements.[10] The RGA is less likely to display this bias in the comparison of representative goods, although it could create a less precise estimator for certain pairs of consecutive periods, due to imprecision in the initial identification of representative goods.

Over long time spans, for example, 100 years, the higher period-to-period fluctuations in the RGA due to inefficiencies in the identification of the representative good would be of minor importance. In contrast, a continual and cumulative drift away from accurate quality assessment (due to a systematic bias in measurement) in a conventional or hedonic approach to quality adjustment could be an important source of error.

It should also be noted that the concept of a representative good has a great deal of precedence in economic thought. The consumer price index is based on a bundle of representative goods, which are occasionally changed to reflect quality improvements over generations. The representative good approach, if applied to several different categories of goods, could provide a more accurate representative bundle for each period.

One of the most advantageous features of the representative good approach is that it allows for the empirical investigation of product evolution through the examination of historical documents. The designation of the median of the sample of items as the representative item could be justified if the mean and median prices, based on equal weight per item, are very similar throughout the time span, as are the ratios of minimum/median and median/maximum.

Nevertheless, in terms of rates of change, the minimum, mean, median, and maximum prices grow at roughly the same rate (Payson, 1994a).

An index was established for each of the five goods examined with the value of 100 in the year 1928, which would increase or decrease in proportion to changes in the quality of the representative item. The rates of product evolution for (1) window fans and air conditioners, and for (2) cameras, movie cameras and camcorders, dramatically exceed the rates for the other three goods: men's shoes, sofas, and gas ranges. These findings constitute strong evidence that certain types of goods undergo, in a consistent fashion, much greater rates of product evolution than others. In fact, the magnitude of the estimated rate for cameras, *14,000 percent over 65 years*, is hardly representative of most goods and services.

## OBJECTIONS TO THE APPROACH

Four areas of concern have surfaced regarding the product evolution/RGA framework: (1) ambiguity in defining the product group and the representative good within it; (2) inaccuracy of price data; (3) disinterest among researchers due to the simplicity of the approach; and (4) territorial issues between different economic schools of thought. *The question that must be asked with regard to each of these concerns is whether a problem exists with the framework itself, or with the environment surrounding the framework.* The first concern regarding ambiguity will always exist, because the researchers will always have the option of defining a product group to fit their own research interests. The definition of a product group and representative good within it merely forces researchers to do the analytical homework that they would need to do in order to ensure meaningful and definitive conclusions. Any methodological alternative, for example, the use of SIC code categories taken at face value simply because data are available in that form, may relieve researchers of that responsibility, but at the cost of rendering little useful information about the underlying reality of product evolution.

Price data will always be suspect. For example, an anonymous referee of an earlier paper of mine (Payson 1995) noted:

> The fact that the representative good is being replaced by an improved good in period 2, suggests that the representative good is overpriced in period 2 and thus the quality change taking place is understated. The assumption that relative prices at a given moment of time reflect true valuations does not allow for the fact that different consumers have different information and ability to judge different products. At any one time, some products are over priced and other products are underpriced. The over priced products may be in excess supply, and there may be a shortage of underpriced products. This will

result in gradual correction of the situation, but in the short run such price disparities will exist and will affect price measurement.

The mechanics of price adjustment, however, are highly dependent on the product and time interval. For example, in some markets a new, superior product may have an exclusively high price that exceeds marginal cost. Initial overpricing could serve a dual purpose to the supplying firm, of exaggerating a good's relative quality for the sake of winning more customers after a planned price reduction, and/or providing a means of price discrimination where certain households, early on, would gladly pay a premium to be the 'first on the block' to own the new item. Overpricing of future median goods (as defined above) would lead to overestimates, not underestimates of product evolution; hence, the overestimation or underestimation of quality is highly dependent on the particular market situation. Ultimately, the scrutiny of a price datum should depend as much on market share as on a discrepancy between supply and demand. For instance, if only three units of an item exist, and four people would each be willing to buy one unit at the current price, then the novelty aspect of the item, or Veblen effect, could cause it to be 'overpriced' in a broader sense of the term, in spite of demand exceeding supply. Of course, these limitations in the use of price data apply equally well for the representative good approach as for conventional price linking and hedonic methods. They are limitations inherent in the consumer price index, producer price index, GNP implicit price deflator, and so on. As demonstrated here, observed differences in the rates of evolution across different products can be quite substantial, thereby overshadowing the inaccuracies inherent in the use of price data.

Disinterest in the approach because of its simplicity may be the greatest constraint that it faces. The application of the approach is not meant to be an intellectual end in itself. The intellectual reward lies in the findings that the approach can generate. Why, we may ask, do cameras evolve faster than furniture? Though this is an interdisciplinary question, it is one that could be useful for economists to answer. However, without some feasible and affordable means of measuring product evolution to begin with, economists would not be able to ask such questions.

Finally, the greatest objection to this approach has been its misinterpretation as some type of primitive price index, for example, a deflator like the GDP implicit price deflator, or the consumer price index (CPI), but where the researcher is too lazy to manipulate as much data as would normally be required in the development of an official price index. The key purposes of price indices are not to measure product evolution, but to guide monetary policy regarding inflation and business cycles, and to enable cost-of-living adjustments in wages, benefits, rents, and so on. In this regard, the economic impact of a price index like the CPI is enormous. For instance, Joseph Juran had once noted that for every 1.0 percent increase in the CPI in 1986, Federal outlays, in nominal terms, were increased by $2.8 billion, and personal income tax receipts were reduced by $1.8 billion (from what they would have otherwise been) due to a redefinition of tax brackets.[11] Surely, it would be absurd for the *Sears Catalog*, or any other historical document, to be used in this role. Hence, those who use the RGA to measure product evolution should acknowledge that the RGA can never be a *replacement* for the consumer price index or any other deflator. Conversely, those who construct and/or advocate the methodology for constructing price deflators should not be opposed to other measurement techniques that are designed to answer entirely different questions.

The product evolution approach is not, in itself, a plea for simplicity. It only reflects a relative lack of interest in sophisticated issues of price indexation, which is peripheral to its main area of interest – the causality underlying different rates of quality change among broad categories of goods. As already suggested, perhaps the most subtle advantage of the product evolution/RGA framework is that it will always force the researcher to have a concrete, and fairly specific, understanding of the particular product being studied and the manner it which it evolved. Once that well-defined problem is specified, and initial observations are made, sophistication of an interdisciplinary nature would be warranted in interpreting why different rates of quality change exist.

## THE BASIC PROBLEM REGARDING NEW ECONOMIC APPROACHES TO TECHNOLOGICAL CHANGE

The above problem with regard to a product-evolution approach may be seen as a reflection of a more general problem that faces most economists who choose to investigate the causality of technological change. That problem may be summarized as follows:

1. Historically, economic theory had been devoted primarily to comparative-static problems of how the economic system, as an entity in itself, responded to various circumstances. Thus, traditional economic variables, such as prices, the money supply, capital, interest rates, and the like have been studied *ad infinitem* in thousands of economic models, which have defined the territories of subfields within the profession.
2. In the last decade those models have become less important. One reason for their decline in importance is that they are victim to their own success. For example, when I was in graduate school in economics in the latter half of the 1980s, debates existed regarding the perilous effects of inflation,

which fueled the 'rational expectations revolution' in economic thought.[12] Like the monetarist models before them, the rational expectation models proved that one could be infinitely complex in arguing the simple idea, 'inflation is bad'. Since that time, it has become much more widely accepted that inflation is bad – consequently, the need for those models has been diminished. Another reason for their decline in importance is simply the principle of diminishing returns – the remaining ground for new models is less fertile than the ground already cultivated.

3. Technological change, on the other hand, becomes more important as traditional economic problems get solved. In other words, traditional economic analysis tends to address 'how can we produce and distribute optimally'? The closer we get to such optimality, the more interested we become in improving our technological capability, so that growth can continue in spite of society already knowing what it is doing in terms of solving basic, traditional macroeconomic problems.

4. As economists recognize the greater importance of technological change, however, their territory in terms of concepts, variables, and models remains constrained by the history and sociology of the economics profession. Technological change economics, if it is to contribute significantly to intellectual achievement and positive social change, must encroach upon the traditional methods of mainstream economic thought. The *status quo*, however, resists any such encroachment for the variety of reasons already mentioned.

The product evolution approach is one of five new methodological approaches offered in this book. The remaining four, in the order in which they will be covered in the book, are: (1) new methods classifying and studying business interest in scientific discoveries; (2) the separation of technological change into cost-reduction versus quality-improvement categories; (3) a new, interdisciplinary approach toward the measurement of physical capital; and (4) developing artificial intelligence programs capable of generating economic analyses. Each of these approaches, however, may face the same kind of problem that the product evolution approach has continued to face. That problem is a dismissal of such approaches by traditional economists who are basically uninterested in technological change issues, but who would interpret the encroachment of new ideas regarding traditional economic variables as amateurish (because they are not built upon previously established models), disrespectful (for the same reason), and not entitled to recognition (for lack of proper institutional affiliation if the case may be). Hopefully, others will focus on more substantive issues, and either accept or reject these approaches on the basis of scientific usefulness.

# NOTES

1. See Office of Management and Budget 1987.
2. Juran 1992, pp. 73-74.
3. Sen 1985, pp. 9-10.
4. Payson 1994a.
5. Payson 1994a.
6. Nordhaus 1994, pp 1-2.
7. See Payson 1995.
8. See Payson 1994a.
9. Gordon 1990, p. 426.
10. See, for example, Cagan 1965 and Siegel 1994.
11. Juran 1992, p. 468.
12. See the discussion of the Rational Expectations school of thought in Chapter 3.

# 8. Business Interest in Scientific Discoveries

## INTEREST OF PRIVATE INVESTORS IN SCIENTIFIC RESEARCH

Many of the most important benefits to society, and the largest profits to investors, often derive from scientific and engineering breakthroughs, and these breakthroughs are associated with only a very small proportion of the activities commonly described and measured as 'research and development'. In 1962, Willard Mueller emphasized the association between scientific breakthroughs and new, as opposed to slightly improved, products or processes:

> I recognize that the cumulative effects of many small changes in existing products and processes may have an important aggregate effect on product quality and production costs. The reason for placing special emphasis on the social and economic processes generating *new* products and processes is that they involve a basic breakthrough in scientific knowledge – often based on fundamental research – upon which subsequent product and process improvements are based.[1]

Therefore, while much of R&D efforts reflect business as usual, investors, especially the most aggressive ones, are most concerned with the fraction of R&D devoted to finding the next breakthroughs. This focused interest is consistent and compatible with the reporting of scientific advances in business journals, which highlights only the most noteworthy, and often most profitable, scientific advancements.

In discussing the importance of entrepreneurial interest in novel discoveries, Chrisopher Freeman notes:

> [T]he crucial contribution of the entrepreneur is to *link* the novel ideas and the market. At one extreme there may be cases where the only novelty lies in the idea for a new market for an existing product; at the other extreme, there may be cases where a new scientific discovery automatically commands a market without any further adaptation or development. The vast majority of innovations lie somewhere in between these two

extremes, and involve some imaginative combination of new technical possibilities and market possibilities.[2]

Thus, investors are constantly searching for business opportunities that arise from scientific advances, as they have done throughout history. As argued in the previous chapter, in studying how investors analyze information on scientific advances, one would benefit most from a classification system based on the broad functions served by products. Such functions coincide directly with what customers want, which forms the basis of business success in a competitive market place, as investors well know.

## NEW INFORMATION ON BUSINESS OPPORTUNITIES FROM SCIENTIFIC RESEARCH

The interest and curiosity that private investors have toward scientific research is reflected strongly in the information they receive. In order to develop an understanding of this information, four business journals were examined that have extensive coverage of scientific advances and their business implications: *Business Week*, *Forbes*, *Fortune*, and *The Economist*. These magazines were chosen on the basis of the highest number of subscriptions among business journals with extensive coverage of scientific advancement. In 1994 alone, these journals contained a total of 783 articles whose main themes were the discovery and/or commercial application of new scientific or engineering advances. The information contained in these articles is examined below as an indicator of the importance of science and engineering developments to entrepreneurs and other business leaders.

The information was measured according to the length and importance of an article, with a weight of 1 for an article occupying less than one full page, 2 for an article between 1 and 3 pages, 4 for an article with over three pages, and 8 for a cover story. With these weights, an information index was developed that was aggregated over main areas, major categories, and subcategories of topics. The breakdown of the information index by main area is presented in Table 8.1, illustrating that the four sources were similar in the type of information they contained. In fact, the same news stories on scientific advances were frequently covered by more than one magazine, reflecting the responsiveness of these magazines to new information of interest to investors. Figure 8.1 illustrates the overall importance of main areas and their major categories for all of the four sources taken together. The definition of a main area is best explained by the major categories that it contains. The main areas used are: communications, health, information processing, public concerns and interests, and traditional production.

Table 8.1  Business information index by source and main topic area,
January 1 – December 31, 1994

| Main area | Source | | | | Total |
| --- | --- | --- | --- | --- | --- |
| | *Business Week* | *Forbes* | *Fortune* | *The Economist* | |
| Communications | 77 | 65 | 63 | 53 | 258 |
| Health | 99 | 42 | 37 | 67 | 245 |
| Information | 160 | 164 | 111 | 60 | 495 |
| Public concerns and interests | 86 | 32 | 12 | 68 | 198 |
| Traditional production | 42 | 5 | 12 | 17 | 76 |
| Total | 464 | 308 | 235 | 265 | 1,272 |

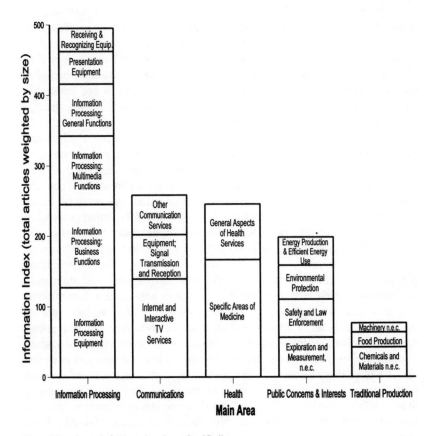

Note: 'N.e.c.' stands for 'not elsewhere classified'.

Figure 8.1  Business information in 1994 by main area and category

In the identification and classification of the information analyzed, particular attention was placed on the purpose the information served, which in most cases was to convey new business opportunities associated with scientific discovery. In the case of new consumer goods that derive from scientific or engineering advancement, only products that might be sold to a reasonable number of people were considered. Finally, the information describes international scientific advances, though, especially in the case of the three US-based magazines, these were scientific advances that tended to originate in the United States and were likely to be of particular interest to US investors.

As Figure 8.1 demonstrates, the main area that received the most attention in 1994 was information processing, followed by communications, health, public concerns and interests, and traditional production. Public concerns and interests, other than health, was defined as including scientific exploration and measurement that was not included in any of the other categories, (for example, particle physics research); safety and law enforcement; environmental protection; and energy production and efficient energy use. The category, 'traditional production' included food production, and also included aspects of machinery and vehicles, and chemicals and materials, which were not already counted under information processing, communications, health, or public concerns or interests.[3]

Advances that may have involved information processing, but which served the purposes of communications, health, public concerns and interests, or traditional production were counted under one of these three areas. For instance, computer hardware developed for a medical purpose was counted under health, and software used in food production was counted under traditional production. Consequently, as large as the information processing component appears in Figure 8.1, it is actually an understatement of the relative importance of information technology as reflected in the business information examined. To provide a clearer view of the relative importance of information technology to business, Figure 8.2 displays the same main areas and categories presented in Figure 8.1, but shows how much information in any area and category was associated with new computer hardware or software. Nearly all of the business information on information processing and communications involved new hardware or software, as did substantial portions of the other three main areas of health, public concerns and interests, and traditional production. While the predominance of information technology in communications may not be surprising, its degree of importance in such areas as health services, and in safety and law enforcement, may not have been as obvious. For example, in health services a great deal of business attention is being paid to issues like the digitalization of medical records, and software to assist doctors in making diagnoses. In areas of safety research,

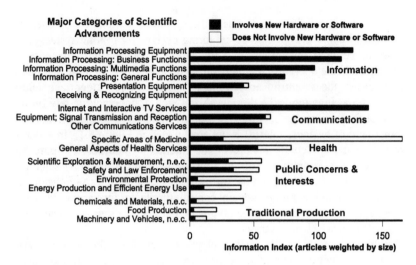

*Figure 8.2  Scientific advancement involving new computer hardware or software*

such as advances in the design of buildings with better evacuation capabilities, there has been increased use of computer simulations that test alternative building designs against possible emergencies. In farming, computers are now used in a variety of functions, such as analyzing soil samples and identifying species of insects. Figure 8.2 indicates the use of these and other applications of relatively new software and hardware that are linked to the scientific advances in question. However, the figure does not account for the use of information processing techniques in broader contexts. For example, it does not include the use of modern software packages for databases, spreadsheets, and statistics, as well as modern computers, that are not tied to a specific area of research, even if they are likely to be used extensively in many types of scientific research. Such general advances in hardware or software, however, were included under advances in information processing if that was the topic of an article.

Another topic that pervades the main areas identified in this analysis is the Internet. The first major category in the area of communications involves business interest in the development of new capabilities for the Internet and interactive TV. However, several other areas of scientific advancement, that do not involve improvement in the Internet itself, are closely associated with the Internet. For example, a new type of advanced, telephone answering machine would be counted under 'Communications' and under 'Equipment; Signal Transmission and Reception'. That answering machine might record a message and then play it back on a remote multimedia computer, where the digitalized audio information is sent through the Internet. Researchers in biomedical engineering could be exploring designs for robotic systems that assist in surgical operations, and that allow a physician to observe or participate in the operation remotely through the Internet. In these and many other cases, the scientific advancement would not be categorized under 'Internet and Interactive TV Services', but would, nonetheless, rely on the Internet for its usefulness. In this sense, the importance of the Internet as a component of business interest is underestimated in Figure 8.1. In order to provide a more accurate picture of the Internet's importance, Figure 8.3 identifies the proportion of all business information on scientific advancements that depend on the utilization of the Internet. As indicated in the figure, the Internet is an essential contributing factor for various advances in information processing, other types of communications advances, and general aspects of health services.

Robotics, virtual reality (VR) technology, and biotechnology are also alternative categorizations of scientific advances that transverse the main areas of interest which were identified in Figure 8.1. The greatest interest in robotics resides in the category of 'information processing: business functions', which includes the role of robotics in manufacturing operations. However, robots are receiving significant attention in other areas, especially health. For example, robot 'snakes' or 'worms' are being designed to enter the human body in order to acquire information and/or perform physician-controlled microsurgery without the need for surgical incisions.

Similarly, virtual reality technology is being used in, and being considered

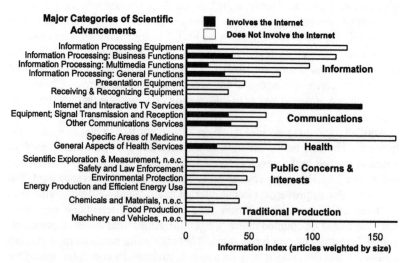

*Figure 8.3 Scientific advancement involving the Internet*

for, business interests that extend well beyond its use as a form of entertainment. For example, virtual reality is finding applications in training programs for a variety of different professions, from construction-equipment operators to surgeons, where the social and private costs of mistakes during on-the-job training might otherwise be much higher. Virtual reality has been used by engineers at Ford, for example, in their computer-aided design (CAD) systems, in which vehicle parts are represented and 'fitted together' in a virtual world.[4]

Virtual 'telepresence' is a technology that allows people to interact with one other as if they were in the same place, for example, the same room, while they are actually in physically different locations, perhaps thousands of miles away. In this sense, telepresence is analogous to video conferencing but with virtual-reality perception and interaction, as opposed to people seeing one another on opposite ends of a television screen. Telepresence technology combined with advanced robotics, for example, would enable a physician to participate in a medical operation from a remote location, in which a robot in the true physical location of the operation translates the physician's movements.[5] While this area of interest is relatively new, and has yet to be applied extensively, it has been actively researched at several universities in the United States and throughout the world, and it has also been receiving attention in the business literature. Other applications of virtual reality technology, besides those already mentioned, include architectural design, scientific research instruments, military training and operations, and tools for the handicapped.

As shown in Figure 8.4, biotechnology advances are primarily related to health applications, although they also play important roles in food production and several other business and legal interests. The occurrence of biotechnology in the category 'information processing: business function' reflects the fact that computer-aided manufacturing design has entered into a new era in which 'designer molecules', especially for medical purposes, are being conceived of and produced.

# INTERRELATIONSHIPS AMONG ECONOMIC AND SOCIAL INSTITUTIONS

Another important aspect of these business-information data is that they are not constructed in relation to a specific economic or sociological framework, but rather, they reflect interdisciplinary ideas. For this reason, the data may be able to reveal effectively the interconnections that exist among economic and social institutions with regard to the discovery and application of scientific

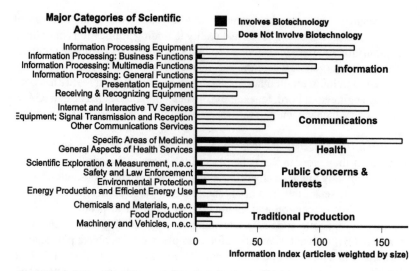

*Figure 8.4  Scientific advancement involving biotechnology*

knowledge. In particular, four interconnections are easily observable, and they appear to be quite strong, although they may not be consistent with the underlying assumptions sometimes made in economic research on technological change. These four interconnections are described below.

(1) *Scientific advancement and household consumption.* As noted earlier, most studies on technological change, especially in economics, examine improvements in the productive capabilities of firms. Consequently, there has always been a great deal of attention paid to capital goods. In contrast, with few exceptions[6] technical change has not been given much attention in economics in relation to 'consumer goods and services', that is, the final products and services that households purchase. The business-information data, as illustrated in Figure 8.5, shows that in the four business journals examined for 1994, as much as 44 percent of the business information index is attributable to interest among investors in scientific advancements in *household* goods and services. As might be expected, this interest was particularly strong in the areas of communications and health, as well as information processing related to household computing and entertainment. There was also considerable interest in other types of household products and services, such as alarm systems, food products, and vehicles.

(2) *Business ventures and university research.* Business interest in university research, both applied and fundamental, is strong according to the 1994 business-information index. For any article describing a scientific advancement that would be of interest to investors, a notation was made

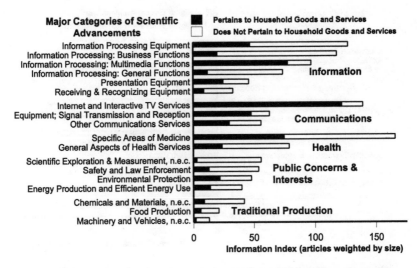

*Figure 8.5 Scientific advancement pertaining to household goods and services*

whether the article mentioned research in higher education as a direct contributing factor to the advancement in question. (*All* scientific research may be seen as having been *indirectly* dependent on university research, in the sense that colleges and universities have provided the fundamental scientific knowledge and the personnel training that allowed such research to be possible.) Higher education as a direct contributing factor accounted for 28 percent of the information index, as illustrated in Figure 8.6. This direct contribution, as a proportion of the total information index in each of the major categories, was particularly high in specific areas of medicine, scientific exploration and measurement, n.e.c., and chemicals and materials, n.e.c. This is not surprising in view of the fact that these categories tend to involve more fundamental science. In addition, Figure 8.6 indicates significant, direct university involvement in nearly all of the major categories of scientific advancements, with the exceptions of 'other communication services' and 'machinery and vehicles, n.e.c.'

(3) *Interdependency of Sectors and Fields.* Drawing a clean distinction between goods and services and between fields can be difficult enough in itself for any researcher, and the difficulty increases when one tries to categorize the effects of scientific advances. In order to add clarity to the distinction between goods and services, one needs to make a distinction between (1) the institution or industry that *carries out the scientific research and can be credited for the scientific advancement* and (2) the institution or industry that *puts the scientific advancement into use.* Often these two industries are not the same, and it is

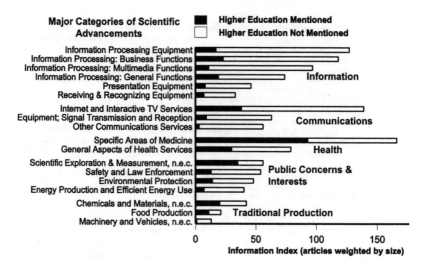

*Figure 8.6    Scientific advancements in which higher education is mentioned as a*
*direct contributing factor*

quite possible for one of the two to be in the service sector and the other to be
in the manufacturing sector. Furthermore, when (1) and (2) involve different
companies for the same scientific advancement, there is no hard and fast rule
that determines which of the two would benefit most from the advancement.
In many cases, a third group, the households that consume the final product,
benefit as well. Who benefits most would generally depend on a variety of
circumstances including legal issues, market clout, and bargaining capabilities,
among other factors. Thus, in cases in which close to half of the financial
benefits of an advancement go to a service company and the other half to a
manufacturer, it may be arbitrary for one to categorize such an advancement
as either a service-sector or manufacturing advancement based only on which
company happens to have received the greatest benefit.

As an typical example, consider a new type of medical device, such as the
latest model of a magnetic resonance imaging (MRI) machine that enables
hospitals to perform more accurate diagnoses and, as a result, better health
care (see Chapter 4, Example 1). The scientific and engineering R&D to
create the MRI machine took place primarily in the manufacturing sector,
although any new software that would be needed to enable the machine to
work would be a service-sector advancement. The machine is then used by a
hospital, which is in the service sector. The three potential beneficiaries of the
device are the manufacturer, which acquired a profit from selling it; the
hospital, which would probably never have purchased the device if it could not
gain in terms of increased revenues and/or reduced operating costs; and the

patients who are examined with the device. A fourth group of beneficiaries are health-insurance companies which likely played a direct or indirect role in the hospital's decision to purchase the device. This entanglement of service-sector and manufacturing aspects of the causes and effects of the MRI advancement demonstrates that there is no simple means of determining whether the advancement should be attributed, overall, to services or manufacturing.

The above example also serves to demonstrate the strong interdependency of fields of science and engineering. The MRI device is primarily a product of applied physics, biomedical engineering, and computer science – not only 'medical research'. Physicians (the primary users or clients) will only need to know how to use the device in conjunction with their diagnoses, and have enough of an understanding of how it works to interpret its output correctly. In essence, the quality of medical services was improved from research in physics, engineering, and computer science – one cannot simply attribute the quality of medicine to advances in medical research alone.

In recent decades, service-sector activities have become increasing dependent on sophisticated equipment, that is, on products from the manufacturing sector, especially for the purposes of information processing. Banking is another typical example in this regard, with its current dependence on ATM machines. At the same time, manufacturing has also become more dependent on information processing, and is utilizing more sophisticated computer-aided design (CAD) and computer-aided manufacturing (CAM). This means that manufacturing operations are relying much more heavily on software development, which is a service-sector industry. These interrelationships among services and manufacturing are measured and discussed below on the basis of observations using the business-information index.

(4) *Unique role of office equipment.* The business-information index sheds light on the interrelationships among three types of products: (1) manufactured goods, (2) services, and (3) office goods and services (office services might include software developed for office purposes). These groups were not mutually exclusive; for example, a new type of computer, like a Pentium-based PC in 1994, was included as a manufactured product and an office product (as well as a household/consumer product in Figure 8.5). Office products were identified for the following reasons: a substantial proportion of the scientific and engineering advancements described by the business journals involved improved office equipment and software, and it might be useful to examine the extent of this effect. Furthermore, office products reflect the necessary operations and expenses of all types of companies and institutions. Consequently, improvements in the quality of office products would be expected to have the end result of lower prices and/or improved quality in

virtually all consumer goods and services due to improvements in the operations of their businesses. For example, more efficient hardware and software devoted to maintaining customer records would be expected to reduce the operating costs of a wide variety of companies.[7]

## MEASUREMENT OF INTERRELATIONSHIPS AMONG GOODS AND SERVICES

For each of the scientific advancements described by the business information, a notation was made as to whether the advancement involved an 'input' or an 'output' in relation to office functions, production (manufacturing), or the provision of services, where such categorizations were not mutually exclusive. That is, anything that was produced through a manufacturing process was identified as a 'production output', and anything provided through a service process a 'service output'. Anything that was employed in a manufacturing process in order to produce something else was regarded as a production input, and anything employed in providing a service, a 'service input'. A communications satellite, for instance, was a manufacturing output that was a service input. Software to operate machine tools was a service output and manufacturing input. Experimental research that might eventually lead to the discovery of a new drug was identified as a service output and manufacturing input. A drug that was already developed was identified as a production output, and if it was expected to be administered by doctors, it was also identified as a service input. Computer components were identified as production outputs as well as production inputs, while communication services for delivery companies were identified as service outputs as well as service inputs.

Based on these notations, it was found that advances in production outputs that were also service inputs, like the MRI equipment described above, accounted for 42 percent of the business-information index for 1994. As shown in Figure 8.7, scientific advances in production-outputs/service-inputs accounted for more than 50 percent of the business-information index for communications and health, which may not be surprising because these major categories heavily involve services. The production outputs/service-input factor was also high for scientific exploration and measurement, n.e.c., and for safety and law enforcement, which are also dominated by services (including public services). The figure provides strong evidence in support of the notion that advances in the quality of services depend on research and development in manufacturing, as well as in the services industry.

This interdependence can work in two directions: service outputs that are

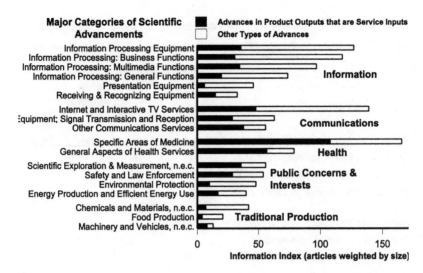

*Figure 8.7 Scientific advancement involving production outputs that are service inputs*

product inputs accounted for a total of 11 percent of the 1994 information index. While this effect was not as strong as its converse shown in Figure 8.7, it was equally widespread across the vast majority of major categories of scientific advancement (see Table 8.2). Its particular importance in 'specific areas of medicine' is attributable to the importance of research (a service) as an input into pharmaceutical manufacturing, while its importance in 'information processing: business functions' is attributable to software development for CAD/CAM. Finally, production outputs also often serve as office inputs. As one might expect, this factor largely involves information processing and communications equipment and services, as evidenced in the figure. The factor also appears to play a significant role in 'general aspects of health services' and in 'safety and law enforcement', which may not be surprising in view of the heavy dependence of these categories on office equipment.

Admittedly, these categorizations and numerical tabulations of scientific advances by type of input and output are not very robust. In the absence of a rigorous manual on how every type of case should be scored, some of the data are bound to be the result of somewhat arbitrary judgment calls. Furthermore, these data are dependent on the appearance of articles in only four journals, during only a single year, and thus the idea of generalizing these findings to conclusions about technological change in the economy as a whole would be highly questionable. The intent here is not to draw such conclusions, but to

*Table 8.2 Interrelationships among manufacturing, services and office functions*

| Major categories of scientific advances | Business-Information Index (total articles weighted by size), for | | | |
| --- | --- | --- | --- | --- |
| | All advances | Production outputs and service inputs | Service outputs and production inputs | Production outputs and office inputs |
| Information processing equipment | 127 | 36 | 12 | 71 |
| Information processing, business functions | 118 | 31 | 25 | 33 |
| Information processing, multimedia functions | 97 | 35 | 0 | 13 |
| Information processing, general functions | 74 | 20 | 9 | 23 |
| Information presentation equipment | 46 | 6 | 2 | 17 |
| Receiving and recognizing equipment | 33 | 15 | 2 | 18 |
| Internet & interactive TV services | 139 | 48 | 13 | 36 |
| Equipment / signal transmission and reception | 63 | 29 | 0 | 23 |
| Other communications services | 56 | 38 | 8 | 26 |
| Specific areas of medicine | 166 | 108 | 36 | 1 |
| General aspects of health services | 79 | 57 | 8 | 7 |
| Scientific exploration & measurement, n.e.c. | 56 | 36 | 6 | 0 |
| Safety and law enforcement | 54 | 29 | 6 | 11 |
| Environmental protection | 48 | 10 | 6 | 1 |
| Energy production and efficient energy use | 40 | 17 | 7 | 1 |
| Chemicals and materials, n.e.c. | 42 | 7 | 4 | 1 |
| Food production | 21 | 4 | 2 | 1 |
| Machinery and vehicles, n.e.c. | 13 | 8 | 0 | 0 |
| Total | 1,272 | 534 | 146 | 283 |
| Percent of total | 100 | 42 | 11 | 22 |

Note: These categories are not mutually exclusive, nor do they encompass all scientific advances.

illustrate the potential this type of analysis might have in aiding our understanding of how technological change is actually manifested in the economy.

## QUALITY IMPROVEMENT VERSUS COST REDUCTION

Table 8.3 contrasts the perspective adopted in this chapter with three others: (1) the history of science and engineering (S&E), (2) education in S&E, and (3) the economics of technological change (as it currently exists). As indicated, differences in perspectives on the causes and effects of scientific advances can be identified in terms of the effects being studied, the main causal factors attributed to them, and the manner in which causes and effects are categorized. The present perspective offered in this book is applied microeconomics of science and engineering. It includes the treatment of new goods and services, and quality improvement in existing goods and services,

*Table 8.3   Alternative perspectives on the causes and effects of science and engineering advances*

| Perspective | Examples of main effects studied | Examples of main causal factors | Categorization of causes and effects |
|---|---|---|---|
| History of science and engineering (S&E) | Scientific advances in their own right | Pivotal experiments, paradigm shifts, succession of discoveries | Fields of science and engineering |
| S&E education | Public understanding, labor skills, educational achievements | Governmental initiatives, policies of educational institutions | Subgroups of the population of scientists and engineers |
| Economics of technological change | Improved production of goods and provision of services | Industrial innovation, managerial reorganization | Industries (e.g., standard industrial classification) |
| Applied microeconomics of S&E | Quality improvement and cost reduction | Consumer behavior and firm strategy | Functions served by goods and services |

as important effects of scientific and engineering advances. The causal factors associated with these effects are aspects of consumer behavior and firm strategy. Finally, causes and effects are categorized, or grouped, in relation to the *functions served by goods and services.*

Figure 8.8 provides an schematization of the interactions that exist among the four perspectives discussed, but with the applied microeconomics perspective adopted here broken into its two main components: quality improvement and cost reduction. The figure merely attempts to illustrate important sequences of events, and does not purport to explain the causality of events, which is much more convoluted due to feedback mechanisms. As the figure suggests, the economics of technological change is central to the system being studied. However, it is a limited framework that has been oriented primarily toward *how* innovation is achieved within the firm. The notions of quality improvement and cost reduction help to explain, in a broader sense, *why* innovation is achieved. (See the discussion of 'how' and 'why' with regard to evolutionary effects in the section on Evolutionary Economics in Chapter 5.)

A dichotomy exists between scientific advances devoted to cost reduction (CR) and those devoted to quality improvement (QI) where each of these factors may be defined as follows: *cost reduction* in the present context occurs whenever a scientific or engineering advance *frees resources from an existing function,* by allowing *more to be produced or provided with less resources.* This includes not only reductions in production costs but savings to consumers in terms of additional resources they would exhaust in using a product themselves, including their use of time. *Quality improvement* occurs whenever a scientific or engineering advance *leads to the creation of new* products, or new features of existing products, *that directly enrich human existence.* This interpretation of quality improvement is consistent with other approaches to quality measurement, as, for example, that expressed by Professor Scott Maynes:

> An acceptable, empirically measurable concept of quality should have three major uses:
> (1) as an *index of possible payoffs* to searching (shopping) by consumers, (2) as an *index of the 'informational effectiveness'* of markets, (3) as a *building block in economic theory*, facilitating the development of market demand/supply relationships for differentiated products.[8]

In essence, CR advances expand production/consumption possibilities, while QI advances raise the utility of existing production/consumption possiblities.

In spite of the distinction between CR and QI advances outlined above, one could certainly find ambiguities in which certain types of advances could apply to both. In this case, we may simply identify CR and QI components of those advances. For example, the current system of household movie

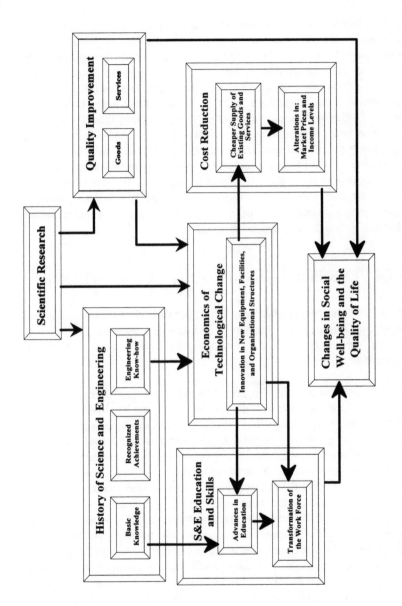

*Figure 8.8 Interaction among perspectives in terms of the effects of scientific and engineering research*

watching, requiring television sets, VCRs and video rental services could be interpreted as QI over the prior system requiring film projectors, movie screens, and rental services for film reels. There has also been substantial CR in the movement from the prior system to the current one, as evidenced by the fact that the former system could only be afforded by wealthy households, or by institutions, like student unions, that would distribute the cost among viewers. Furthermore, some advances may reflect one of the effects, CR or QI, at the expense of the other. For instance, the invention of instant coffee led to a lower-quality product, but a product associated with substantial CR in the consumers' use of time and resources. Window air conditioners reflect a QI over window fans, but they also consume more fuel. In cases in which one effect occurs at the expense of the other, one could categorize the scientific or engineering advancement in terms of its apparent goal, for example, instant coffee as CR, and the air conditioner as QI.

## CR/QI VERSUS PROCESS/PRODUCT INNOVATION

The CR/QI dichotomy is analogous to that between product innovation and process innovation in the economic literature on technological change. However, the former dichotomy encompasses a wider variety of effects, in four respects:

1. When products are defined in terms of functions served, the concept of QI should include the creation of new products that may be physically unique from pre-existing products, but which serve the same broad function. For example, as previously suggested, hair spray would represent a QI – broadly defined – over hair nets. In contrast, most studies of 'product innovation' have been oriented toward products defined, to begin with, in terms of their physical characteristics. That is, one could only have a 'product innovation in hair nets' rather than in 'hair-holding mechanisms'. As argued below, this limitation may constrain our ability to understand the true causal forces of economic change, especially over long periods of time.
2. QI is generally associated with any change in a product making it more desirable to consumers, including artistic and conceptual changes, while product innovation focuses only on physical changes that tend to be of most interest to industrial engineers. For instance, artistic and literary work could certainly change in quality, but would not be treated as 'product innovation' unless the physical medium changes, for example, the transformation of musical records to compact disks.
3. Process innovation is studied in a context in which the magnitude of a change is perceived as the extent of physical change in an industrial

process, whereas CR relates more generally to any sources of production costs. For instance, new machinery on a factory floor directly involved in the production process could reflect both process innovation and CR. More efficient control of the factory's employee records, due to the utilization of better accounting software, would only be included under CR.

4. As suggested, for the final consumer, a broad definition of CR would not only include advances leading to a reduction in the product's price, but could include advances that save consumers time, space (for example, room space or counter space), energy, or other resources. This effect would generally not be captured by most economic analyses of process or product innovation.

As argued in the previous chapter, the CR/QI dichotomy, in combination with function-based classification, could be a useful device for understanding the determinants of long-run technological change in the overall economy. Cost-reducing sectors tend to shrink over time in terms of revenues, while quality-improving sectors tend to increase. These tendencies explain why food production (especially for food products that have not changed much in terms of sensory effects) has fallen as a proportion of the economy, while entertainment has risen. At the same time, CR and QI need not be conflicting influences. Quite the contrary, high levels of QI, as experienced, for instance, in medical services, photographic equipment, and information-processing entertainment, must *coincide* with substantial CR. Otherwise, the price of high quality products would be so great that only the highest-income stratum would be able to afford them, which would not generate the sales volume needed to justify the initial development and mass production of these products.

Scientific and engineering advances that improve quality and reduce costs are, therefore, encouraged by market demands for these types of changes, which is based on the functions served by products. On the other hand, scientific advances should not be seen as being driven by market demand alone, as they often derive from fundamental aspects of nature (influencing the direction of science), from the initial intellectual motivations of researchers, and from the resources available to different sets of researchers.

Moreover, there has long been strong, anecdotal evidence for the idea that the actual applications of scientific advances may be far removed from the original intended application. A classic example in this regard is the application of laser technology in compact disk players and supermarket check-out devices, whereas the initial research was originally intended for military applications that never materialized. Nevertheless, when scientific advances do come about on their own, or even by accident, they may still render greater technological improvements in certain types of products than in others, suggesting that functionality remains an important determinant of patterns of technological change.

A particular case in point is in the area of medical research, which, in terms of industrial classifications and the firm/innovation approach, is split right down the middle between 'pharmaceutical research' which falls under chemical manufacturing (SIC 2834), and health services (SIC 80). If an AIDS vaccine is developed, for instance, then, of course, it would have enormous economic and social effects. Thus, if all products (goods and services) that were devoted to the treatment of AIDS were classified under a single heading, such a medical breakthrough would be clearly observed, and its effects easily evaluated. Yet, under the current industrial classification system, there would be some 'disturbance' in the pharmaceutical industry, and a delayed decline in the amount of medical services provided (all else being equal) but researchers would need to look at the news on television or in the newspaper to understand why the decrease in health service revenues came shortly after an increase in pharmaceutical revenues.

Again, such an alternative classification scheme would not be, and should not be, mutually exclusive. There is no scientifically-justifiable reason for disallowing multiple classification schemes, as suggested earlier by the fact that biologists use three different taxonomies of organisms in order to answer different types of questions. The only requirement for multiple classification schemes is that each scheme uses a uniquely different set of concepts (for example, type of production operation vs. type of function served by the product). Otherwise, summary findings could wind up being circumstantial if variation in the classification of the same concept leads to variation in aggregate results.

The 'innovation framework' adopted by technical-change economists has been oriented toward product and process innovation, while business strategists have focused on the 'larger picture' of market survival, which is better characterized by CR and QI advances. Thus, historically, economists have paid little attention to the CR/QI dichotomy, with the exception that it has occasionally surfaced in 'development economics', in the area of devising strategies for third-world development. In the early 1950s, the economists Raúl Prebisch,[9] Hans Singer,[10] and Arthur Lewis,[11] for instance, had argued that primary commodities undergo CR, while manufactures undergo QI, implying that third world countries specializing in primary commodities would tend, over time, to grow more slowly than industrialized countries specializing in manufactures. This primary commodity versus manufactures distinction is of little use today, as many manufactured products, like standard computer chips, act very much like traditional agricultural and mining commodities of prior generations. Nevertheless, the basic intuition that some products are continually quality improving, and others continually cost reducing, in response to technical change, is as relevant today as it ever was, and should never have been limited to development economics alone.

As suggested in Table 8.3, greater consideration of the CR/QI dichotomy, and its implications for long-run change, could bring together three interrelated areas of inquiry: the economics of technological change, applied microeconomics of science and technology, and studies of trends in scientific and engineering research. In order for this integration of ideas to happen, however, four conceptual barriers to a CR/QI framework would need to be broken in current economic treatise of technological change:

1. Economic measurement of 'quality change' in industrial statistics has often been conducted on the basis of changes in production costs, when better information has not been available. While such estimation is often justifiable for the sake of useful statistics, it might also be recognized as conceptually flawed within the theoretical context of long-run economic change. That is, QI and CR are, more often then not, different phenomena, and estimating one in terms of the other would only take us further away from understanding the true causes of change.

2. Economic theory has correctly related QI to the concept of consumer utility, and CR to production. In terms of empirical evidence for either, the two are linked by their opposite effects on the price of the final product. However, an economic model incorporating both price effects tends to be more mathematically problematic than mathematically intriguing, and thus has not generated much interest among theoretical economists. Such a model would also fly in the face of current methods by economists in some statistical organizations of using cost as a proxy for quality. Nevertheless, for the sake of thoroughness, such a model is presented in an appendix at the end of this chapter.

3. 'Quality change', as a concept in economic thought, has too often been associated with trivial exercises involving the definitions of units of measure. For example, a good would be said to 'increase in quality' if it is measured in 'numbers of boxes', and the only change that occurs is that the boxes are made larger to carry more weight – the so-called 'repackaging case'. This kind of simplistic definition of quality change is peripheral to any efforts to understand quality change as an aspect of long-run, technological change. Therefore, in efforts to understand causality, empirical observations on *meaningful* quality change would need to adhere to a general principle of *unitless quality change* – quality change that would be recognized as such regardless of trivial circumstances involving the definition of units.[12]

4. The importance of CR and QI can be assessed in terms of their economic importance, which would be based on the magnitude of their effects on

price. Innovation studies should be recognized as not having any such metric for measuring economic importance. In this sense, innovation studies may be seen as having a greater tendency to be anecdotal, with a bias toward changes that are more scientifically interesting than economically important, as argued in the previous chapter. Moreover, studies that use R&D expenditures as a proxy for scientific advancement are measuring the *desire* for economic change, more than economic change itself.

## INCIDENCE OF CR AND QI AMONG INDUSTRIAL CATEGORIES

Figure 8.9, which is comparable to Figure 8.1, provides a breakdown of the business coverage by main area and by QI versus CR advances. One sees immediately that the ratio of QI coverage to CR coverage varies greatly by main area, with QI dominating advances in communications, health, and public concerns and interests, and CR dominating in information processing and traditional production. In terms of absolute amounts of coverage, the bulk of CR is strongly captured by information processing, while QI is spread nearly uniformly among all main areas of advances except traditional production.

As shown in Figure 8.10, CR in information processing occurs generally within three categories of advances: information processing equipment (for example, computers and computer components), business functions (for example, software for computer-aided design and computer-aided manufacturing), and general information-processing functions (for example, operating systems and new theories in software development). As is commonly known, these areas of CR in information processing have dominated the business climate of the 1990s, as in accordance with the modern credo: 'smaller, faster, cheaper, . . . better'.

Fueled by the continual advent of faster and cheaper calculations through better hardware and increased computer science know-how, QI has been expanding rapidly as well in information processing. As shown in Figure 8.10, quality improving advances have occurred primarily in multimedia development (for example, 'edutainment'), presentation equipment (for example, virtual reality apparatus), and receiving/recognizing functions (for example, automated dictation). Of course, the economic relationship between CR and QI has been symbiotic – CR making QI more feasible and affordable, while consumer demand for the latest QI, in turn, increasing the demand for additional CR.

In the area of communications (Figure 8.11), CR is associated with new

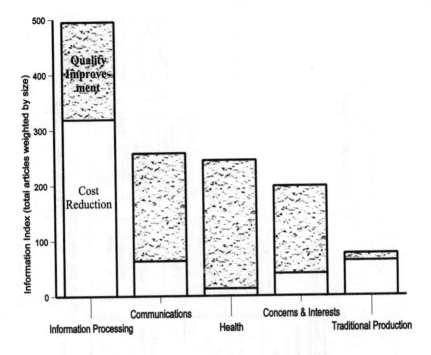

*Figure 8.9  Business information by main area and by quality improvement versus cost reduction*

equipment (for example, modems), and with advances in signal transmission and reception.   QI is associated with new and improved aspects of communications services, with most of the coverage devoted to Internet and interactive TV advances.

Advances in health are quality improving, in nearly all cases, as they directly affect consumer well-being (Figure 8.12).  One exception is advances in medical records processing, especially advances deriving from the digitalization of medical records, whose primary purpose is to reduce administrative costs.  On the other hand, it is important to note that improved medical services are inherently cost-reducing to the consumer in the sense that improvements to patients' health reduce the need for further medical services. In this sense, medical services appear to shrink in economic importance as a result of their own success.

Advances in public concerns and interests (Figure 8.13) are also mostly quality improving according to business coverage in 1994.  The QI categories of advances in this area are: scientific exploration and measurement n.e.c. (in

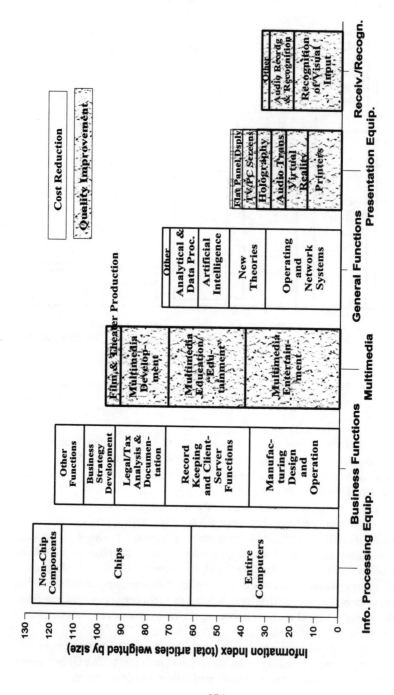

Figure 8.10 Business interest in information processing by major category and subcategory

174

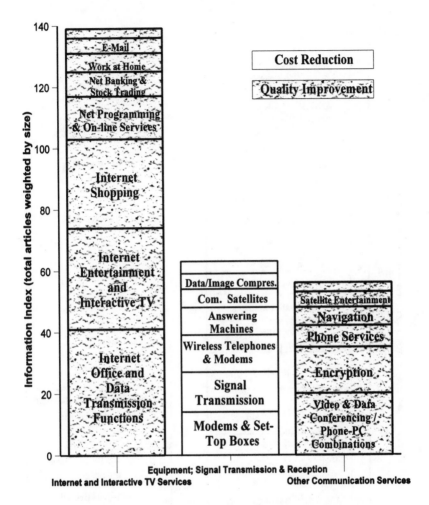

*Figure 8.11  Business interest in communications by major category and subcategory*

which scientific knowledge acquired, especially in fields like astronomy and theoretical physics, tend to be seen as a social end in itself), safety and law enforcement, and environmental protection. CR may be associated with advances in energy production and efficient energy use. However, in the main area of public concerns and interests, the CR/QI dichotomy is ambiguous in certain instances. For example, safety and law enforcement could be interpreted as reducing costs more that improving quality, if one is focusing on factors that affect firms rather than households.

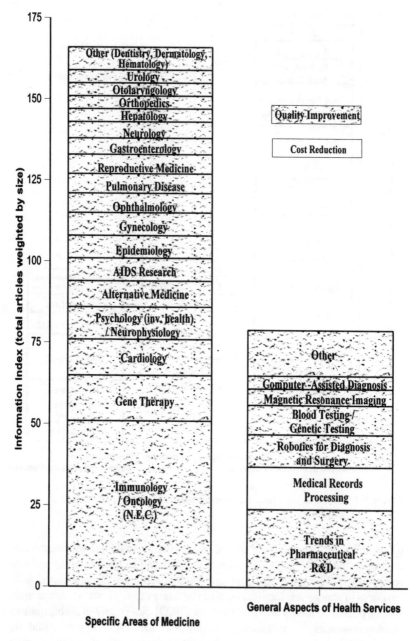

*Figure 8.12  Business interest in health by major category and subcategory*

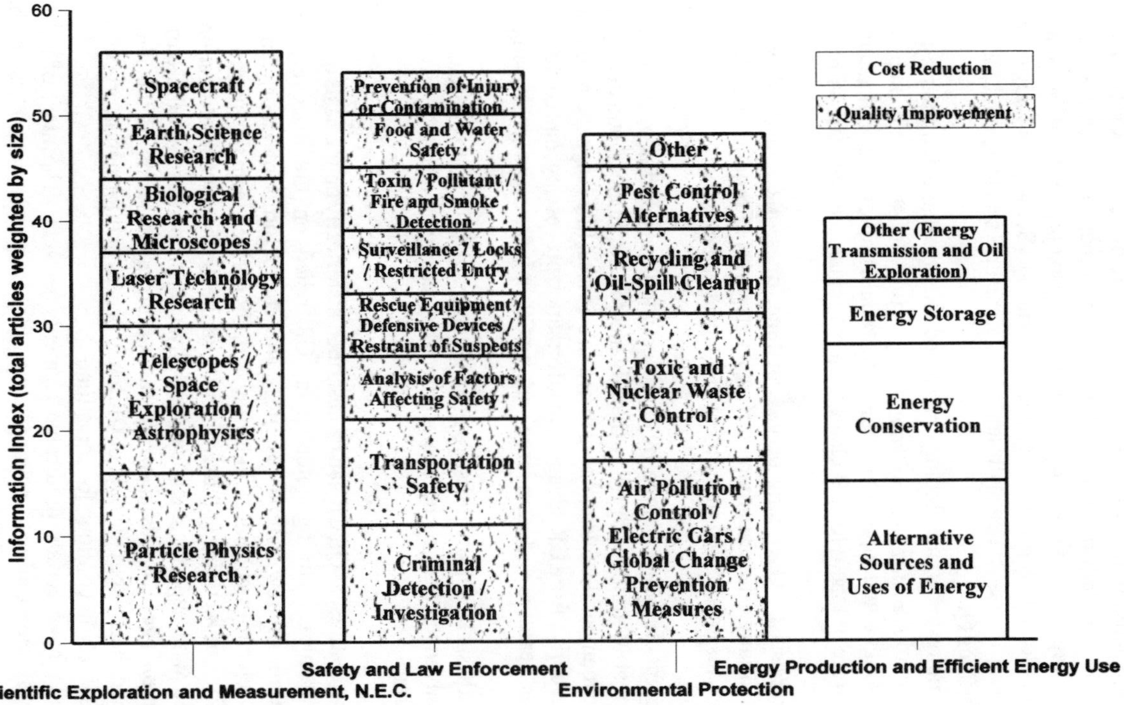

Figure 8.13  Business interest in public concerns and interests by major category and subcategory

Finally, advances in traditional production (Figure 8.14), like food production and chemicals and materials, n.e.c., are more closely related to CR than to QI. Advances in many forms of machinery and vehicles, n.e.c., however, can reflect QI if the these items are used primarily by households (for example, household vehicles and appliances). Some recent advances in aircraft can be associated with amenities in airline services, could also be interpreted as QI.

In some respects, the findings presented thus far could fall victim to the accusation of *measurement without theory*. However, as already suggested, these findings could support hypotheses that could improve our understanding of the nature of technological change. In particular, we can start with:

Hypothesis I. Over long periods of time, rates of CR and QI will be substantially different among different categories of products where these categories are defined in terms of the purposes they serve.

This is evidenced, for example, by the observation that information processing advances are dominated by CR, while advances in health are dominated by QI. Because many of the QI advances in health services, like magnetic resonance imaging, derive from CR advances in information processing, one could argue that QI in health is *fueled*, in large part, by CR in information processing.

Hypothesis II. QI advances are often diverse and difficult to predict, while CR advances tend to be characterized by easily-identifiable, historical patterns.

In fact, in contrast to QI, CR can be described historically on the basis of fairly simple themes. During colonialism, CR relied on the discovery and exploitation of new natural resources and cheap forms of labor. In the previous electro-mechanical, industrial age, CR derived from the invention of more efficient facilities and machinery, and the discovery and utilization of materials with superior chemical and physical properties. In the current information age, CR advances are still occurring in terms of the above-mentioned factors, but the bulk of CR today occurs in information processing which is likely to continue for some time.[13]

QI does have certain predicable elements as well. The most obvious, perhaps, is the continued enhancement of sensory stimulation, as in the expansion of visual fields through the continual increase in the size of computer screens, the emergence of virtual reality, and so on. Health, of course, is a form of QI in itself, which also has easily-identifiable trends in terms of final effects (for example, the continual increase of life expectancy). However, QI also takes on conceptual and idealistic elements, which often

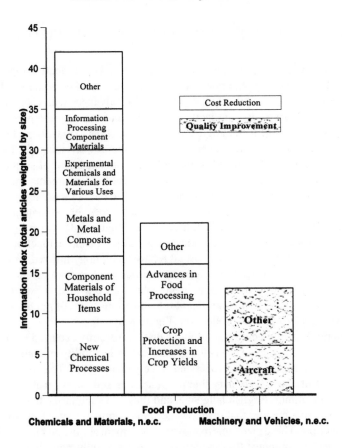

*Figure 8.14    Business interest in traditional production by major category
            and subcategory*

defy its simpler elements. For instance, for some consumers, one of the
appeals of reading a book, in contrast to seeing a film, lies in the fact that the
reader is *not* bombarded with a high frequency of sensory input. Quality may
depend as well on how consumers perceive a product's role in relation to
society overall, rather than to their own consumption of it. As discussed in
Chapter 5 in the section on food safety, they may, for instance, prefer products
whose production is consistent with environmental objectives, or other
idealistic principles. In short, quality, unlike cost, is multidimensional, and
consequently represents a much larger area of inquiry.

## CONCLUSION AND PROSPECTS FOR THE FUTURE

The business-information index and function-based classification represent, above all, an interdisciplinary approach to the study of the economic effects of scientific advancement. By linking scientific advances with categories of the purposes served by products, one can arrive at useful observations regarding patterns of technological change, as well as explanations for why those patterns occur. These explanations include, for instance: (1) a strong reliance on new hardware and software for the advancement of science and engineering, especially with regard to new scientific instruments and better computers and software for analyzing scientific data; (2) wide usage of the Internet for many existing and potential advances in communications, information processing, and health services (Figure 8.3); (3) progress in robotics leading to improved manufacturing (under 'business functions') and health services (Figure 8.3); (4) virtual reality technology utilized, or having the potential to be utilized, in information processing, communications, and health services; and (5) discoveries in biotechnology playing a substantial role in medical advances, and a significant role in various types of public-concern endeavors and traditional production (Figure 8.4).

Among the many new breakthroughs that has recently occurred in the area of artificial intelligence (AI) is the greatly-expanded ability of computers to perform 'natural language processing' (see Chapter 10). That is, they can identify central and secondary themes in articles and papers that have been written in common English language, and they can summarize these articles and papers in a manner that displays the same command over language as a human writer. These programs require that documents be in machine-readable form, that is, computer files, which is a constraint only now, but could be trivial in the future as historical documents and published papers become available on compact disk, the Internet, and the like, and as scanners and their associated software became more adept at translating hardcopy into digital form. Given this ability, some AI programs are also able to generate literature searches, not only on key words, but on actual topics and themes, as demonstrated, for example, by the work of Gerald Salton.[14]

If such AI technology could be applied to the current task of classifying and counting articles, then many of the problems now observable with this process could be eliminated or substantially reduced. That is, through the application of artificial intelligence programs, text summarization and category analysis could become relatively inexpensive, precise, and detailed. Furthermore, the categorization process may not only provide useful data for economic analysis of technological change, but could also allow for a highly-sophisticated referencing system, in which researchers could easily find articles on specific subjects and themes.[15] For these reasons, the classification of products by function, and the utilization of business articles on scientific advances to do so, is an endeavor worth exploring.

From an applied microeconomics, or business management, perspective, scientific advances are driven by two basic incentives that are associated, respectively, with the dichotomy between supply and demand: CR and QI. Beyond this simple division lies the much more important taxonomy of the functions served by products to both immediate consumers and to society overall. By overlaying the CR/QI distinction with the classification of products by function served, one can observe some useful patterns of the effects of scientific advances. Moreover, the CR/QI dichotomy, and the functions served by products, may be seen as representing the main underlying forces that *motivate* applied scientific and engineering research, and consequently, may represent, as well, an important component of the *causality* underlying technical change in society.

## APPENDIX A: ECONOMIC MODELING OF THE QI/CR DICHOTOMY

Quality changes in products over time could be seen as shifts in the $g_i$ parameters of the utility function:

$$U = U[g_1(t)x_1, g_2(t)x_2, ..., g_n(t)x_n] \tag{8.1}$$

where $g_i$ is a function of $t$, and $x_i$ is the number of units of product $i$ consumed. The representative consumer thus faces the static maximization problem:

$$\max U = U[g_1(t)x_1, g_2(t)x_2, ..., g_n(t)x_n] - \lambda[\sum_{i=1}^{n} p_i x_i - I(t)] \tag{8.2}$$

yielding:

$$p_i = \frac{u_i g_i(t)}{\lambda} \; ; \quad \lambda = \frac{\sum_{i=1}^{n} u_i g_i(t)}{I(t)} \quad \rightarrow \quad p_i(t) = \frac{g_i(t) u_i I(t)}{\sum_i x_i g_i(t) u_i} \tag{8.3}$$

On the supply side, let $C_i(x_i,t)$ be the minimum cost of producing $x_i$ at time $t$, for the representative firm. Increased productivity, or cost reduction, could be interpreted as the tendency for the marginal cost to decline over time, that is:

$$\frac{\partial}{\partial t} \frac{\partial C_i(x_i,t)}{\partial x} < 0 \ . \tag{8.4}$$

In perfect competition, marginal cost will equal the price:

$$p_i(t) = \frac{\partial C_i(x_i,t)}{\partial x} \ . \tag{8.5}$$

In this simple model, there are $n$ quality-related functions to be estimated, $g_1$, $g_2$, ..., $g_n$, and $n$ cost-related functions $\partial C_1(x_1,t)/\partial x_1$, $\partial C_2(x_2,t)/\partial x_2$ , ..., $\partial C_n(x_n,t)/\partial x_n$. Thus, with data on prices and quantities at various points in time, there are $2n$ equations for estimating the parameters of these $2n$ functions: $n$ equations of the form of Equation 8.3 and $n$ of the form of Equation 8.5. However, the system is far from linear and would be difficult to estimate, even if each function, ($g_i$ or $\partial C_i(x_i,t)/\partial x_i$) contains a single parameter, for example, $g_i(t) = q_i^t$ or $\partial C_i(x_i,t)/\partial x_i = k_i^t$.

One approach that has made the system feasible for estimation in a partial equilibrium model requires quality to be interpreted as an elasticity [$U = U(x^{g(t)})$] rather than the standard specification shown in Equation 8.1. With a Cobb–Douglas utility function, quality then becomes synonymous with expenditure share, that is, the quality of a product doubles when its share of income doubles, all else being equal. This set of conditions, combined with a simple production function allowing for constant rates of productivity growth in the competitive firm, does allow for a solution for the parameters of Equation 8.1 in terms of the parameters of Equations 8.3 and 8.5.

Nevertheless, the apparent difficulty in deriving a convenient, robust, or theoretically-intriguing formula for characterizing the QI and CR effects, in terms of the parameters of traditional utility and production functions, is, essentially, inconsequential. The objective here is to identify important causal influences on technological change, however inconvenient they may be to model using traditional constructs. On the other hand, the fact that QI and CR *can* be modeled under simplifying assumptions supports their validity as economic concepts. Indeed, at an elementary level, CR is nothing more than a downward shift in supply curves, and QI and upward shift in demand curves when units are not adjusted for quality change.

## NOTES

1. Mueller 1962, p. 324.
2. Freeman 1986, p. 110.
3. Pharmaceuticals were classified in health under the 'Specific Areas of Medicine' to which they applied, in accordance with the notion of identifying the purposes these chemicals served. Many other new chemicals and materials were also associated with the purposes they served in information processing, communications, health, or public concerns and interests; as well as food production and machinery and vehicles, n.e.c. Consequently, the substances remaining in 'chemicals and materials' tended to be experimental, with the chance of being used in the future for a wide variety of purposes. Similarly, 'traditional production' only included machinery and vehicles that were not associated with already-defined purposes. For example, it would not include medical equipment, classified under health, or 'electric cars' whose primary purpose was classified under environmental protection.
4. WWW: http://nemo.ncsl.nist.gov/~sressler/projects/mfg/mfgVRcases.html.
5. Fuchs et. al 1995.
6. One exception could be found in the work by Steenkamp 1989.
7. Another concern was that one would expect the four business journals to be read primarily by business executives, implying that these journals may be inclined to report disproportionately on office equipment, which might bias the overall picture they present on the effects of scientific research. However, office products accounted for approximately 36 percent of the total business-information index for 1994, which does not appear to be distorting given the enormous degree of scientific advancement in such products and the large share of the overall economy that they represent.
8. Maynes 1976, p. 534.
9. Prebisch 1950.
10. Singer 1950.
11. Lewis 1952.
12. The principle of 'unitless quality change' is described in greater detail in Payson 1994a.
13. Yet, as discussed at the end of Chapter 4, we might also imagine a point in time in which CR in information processing and machinery (or robots) has plateaued, and major advances in the exploitation of natural resources again takes center stage as it ventures into space colonization.
14. See , for example, Salton, et al 1994 and *The Economist* 1994b.
15. Misconduct in science, discussed in Chapter 2, could also be more easily identified.

# 9. Capital Input – It Need Not be Metaphysical

## INTRODUCTION

The measurement of physical capital by economists is extremely inadequate, for four basic, interrelated reasons. It is: (1) *ambiguous*, often depending on circumstances unrelated to the object being measured or the purpose of measurement; (2) *metaphysical*, unlike the measurement of labor (in hours) or land (in acres), having no physical interpretation, thereby placing severe constraints on its relevance and usefulness; (3) *underutilized*, confined primarily to the purposes of accounting and productivity estimation, while it could also serve as an extremely valuable tool for understanding evolutionary patterns of technological change; and (4) *anachronistic,* perpetuating a nineteenth-century understanding of economic activity, at a time when many economists are trying to anticipate twenty-first century events. Each of these concerns will be discussed in the next four sections of this chapter, respectively.[1]

This chapter will then propose that all of these problems can be solved through a redefinition of capital measurement, based on concepts that would follow from an interdisciplinary approach to the topic. This approach will borrow ideas and findings from the traditional economic definition of capital, hedonic-price studies of physical capital, and basic concepts in natural science and engineering. The new measurement of capital would entail the quantification of component characteristics, analogous to the 'Lancaster-characteristics approach' (pioneered by Kelvin Lancaster) to consumer goods.[2] However, characteristics of capital will be chosen, not only on the basis of their influence on price, but also on the extent to which they reflect important physical attributes, and the extent to which they may shed light on evolutionary patterns of technological change.

Economists have long known about problems in the measurement of physical capital, and the calculation of variables dependent on such measurement, like productivity. For example, Zvi Griliches remarked:

[M]uch of what passes for productivity change in conventional data is the result of aggregation errors, the wrong measurement of input quantities, and the use of wrong weights to combine them into 'total factor input' indexes. . . . Something more should be said about the rather vague notions of 'explanation' and 'accounting'. National Income and Product accounts and associated index numbers are economic constructs, based on an implicit model of the economy and a variety of more or less persuasive logical and empirical arguments. They are not well adapted to 'hypothesis testing' or debates about causality.[3]

In particular, cost-reducing technological change allows the same physical capital to be sold at lower prices, often making the price of capital, the only proxy available, a poor measure of quantity. Studies of quality change have helped alleviate these measurement problems to some extent, in which prices are adjusted on the basis of previous prices for the same items ('price linking') or on the basis of their association with alternative features, or 'characteristics', of the capital units in question ('hedonic price studies'). However, such measures are often highly dependent on the choice of base year, and on how one interprets new items as either belonging to preexisting categories or to entirely new categories. Thus, even when highly sophisticated, mathematical methods of quality adjustment are employed, such measurement is often greatly influenced by arbitrary decisions regarding meaning and classification.

Another fundamental problem lying underneath the difficulty of measuring capital is the well-known interdependency between the value of capital to the producer and the profitability of the output which that capital is used to produce. This interdependency calls into question the very meaning of the 'quantity of capital', when it is measured in monetary units. This situation, in fact, has changed little since it was elucidated by Joan Robinson[4] and other 'post-Keynesian' economists in the 1950s and 1960s.

## AN ALTERNATIVE MODEL

A model is presented below for the purpose of clarity. It specifies, mathematically, the basic flaw that currently exists in economists' use of standard capital measures when technological change is taking place. Like the product-evolution model presented in Chapter 7, it suffers from four disadvantages in terms of being recognized by other economists. (1) It is mathematically relatively simple (as economic models go these days). Consequently, economists who have come to expect complexity in new models will be unimpressed, especially in subfields where mathematical prowess means a great deal. (2) It has inadequate institutional affiliation – in fact, no institutional affiliation at all – and likewise it is not associated with any research grant. (3) It is interdisciplinary among different subfields within economics itself, and thus the subject matter itself has no preestablished constituency. (4) Finally, it calls into question the usefulness and validity of established methods of measurement, that is, it is critical of some economists' livelihood, which would certainly have negative effects on its popularity. Quite frankly, the only advantage of the model is that it might be useful. (Readers who are not comfortable with mathematical models and/or economic theory should simply skip to the next section.)

Starting with basic principles, consider the standard model pertaining to a particular product within a much larger economy, in which $Y$ is the quantity of the product (produced per year), $p$ its price, $L$ the quantity of labor services (per year) devoted to its production, $w$ the wage rate, $K$ the quantity of capital services devoted to producing the same product, and $r$ the rental price of those capital services. Assume that $K$ is sector specific, that is, capital devoted to producing product $i$ cannot be used to produce any other product. Let $r$, $w$, and $p$, be determined in competitive markets for $K$, $L$, and $Y$ respectively. We know from microeconomic fundamentals that $r$ is rarely exogenous, but must be a function of the other variables, $Y$, $p$, $L$, $w$, $K$ (as well as additional variables pertaining to other sectors of the international economy, especially the financial sector).

Now, suppose $K$ is a well-defined physical quantity (as a flow of services per unit time), but whose quality per measured unit has improved from period 0 to period 1, that is,

$$Y^0 = f^0(L,K^0); \quad Y^1 = f^1(L,K^1) \tag{9.1}$$

where, in terms of *unadjusted* measures, $K^0 = K^1$, but $Y^1 > Y^0$ . This could happen, for example, if $K$ is agricultural land, measured in acres, that is used to the same extent, but is enhanced through better irrigation, giving greater yields per acre, all else being equal. In this case, analogous to the Fisher/Shell (1972) model of quality improvement using utility functions, one could find the effective 'quality improvement' in capital, by simply solving for $\alpha$ in:

$$Y^1 = f^1(L,K^1) = f^0[L,(1+\alpha)K^0] \tag{9.2}$$

Note, the determination of $\alpha$ in the above discussion had absolutely no known relationship with prices, $r$, $w$, or $p$. In fact, the intuition, and often the assumption, that $r$ should also change in proportion to $(1+\alpha)$ is actually not applicable to this framework. For instance, in the case of land, an increase in the productivity of land could easily lead to a fall in $p$ due to an oversupply of

*Y*, and in turn, a *fall in r*, the price of land, as a consequence of the *increased productivity* of land.[5]

Ironically, when the cost of capital, *rK*, is used as a measure of, or proxy for, the true physical quantity of capital, *K*, then the interpretation of quality change, or productivity change, could be completely reversed. Specifically, interpreting a change in the productivity of capital, when capital is measured in dollar costs (*C*), amounts to solving for β in:

$$Y^1 = g^1(L,C) = g^0[L,(1+\beta)C] \tag{9.3}$$

where *g* identifies a new production function for which capital is measured in dollar units. That is, $(1+\beta)C$ dollars worth of physical capital would be needed at time 0 to do the work of *C* dollars of physical capital in time 1, if there is 'productivity improvement' *per dollar* of capital. However, if there are, in fact, measurable, natural units of capital, like acres of land, then $C = K^0r^0$ at *t=0*, and $C = K^1r^1$ at *t=1*, implying:

$$g^1(L,C) = g^0[L,(1+\beta)C] = f^0[L,(1+\beta)C/r^0]; \; and$$

$$g^1(L,C) = f^1(L,C/r^1) \qquad = f^0[L,(1+\alpha)C/r^1] \tag{9.4}$$

$$\rightarrow \; (1+\beta) = \frac{r^0}{r^1}(1+\alpha)$$

Thus, as one might expect, measured productivity increases in capital, when capital is measured in dollars, will differ from measured productivity increases when capital is measured in natural units, with the difference proportional to the ratio of initial to final price per natural unit.

Equation 9.4 illustrates the confusion that is often created by the measurement of capital in dollar terms. For instance, when the productivity of land is said to increase, the impression one might receive is that there is greater production per acre, which one might expect to lead, under normal circumstances, to a rising price of that land per acre. However, when land is measured in dollar amounts, the higher the price rise per acre, the *lower* will be the estimate of productivity change per *dollar* of land. The increase in productive capacity, then, would be explained as resulting from an increase in the 'quantity' of capital, that is, 'capital accumulation' rather than technical change.

In conclusion, the utilization of data on the cost of capital, as a proxy for the quantity of capital, can lead to highly counter-intuitive results in the comparison between different technological capabilities across time. Nevertheless, cost remains an extremely useful tool for assessing quantities of capital when time and technology are held constant. For instance, imagine if all landowners, at the same moment in time, lost all information on how many acres they owned, and could only remember how much they paid for the entire plot, where that payment was based on what their land could actually produce. By controlling for various characteristics of land value, for example, location, environmental quality, and so on, the actual quantities of land owned could be reasonably approximated on the basis of total cost. That is, cost is a much better indicator of actual physical quantity (or productive capacity) in cross-sectional studies in which technologies remain intact, than in time series in which technologies are in flux. It is surely this intuitive utilization of capital costs that formed the basis for using such data to begin with, and it is only fairly recently, when rapid technological change has become more widespread, that the cost-measurement approach to capital has faced its greatest limitations.

## CAPITAL NEED NOT BE METAPHYSICAL

Professor Alfred Eichner maintained 'It is not possible to aggregate . . . capital inputs in physical terms, and thus any argument . . . in which . . . "capital" . . . appears as an explanatory variable cannot be validated empirically. The $K$ term, lacking any empirical counterpart, is metaphysical.'[6] Even those economists whose own work has relied heavily on quantifying capital have often acknowledged this problem in its measurement. As a case in point, Robert Solow's pivotal article of 1957 that gave rise to modern growth theory mentions 'the profound difficulties that stand in the way of giving any precise meaning to the quantity of capital'.[7]

The importance of *natural* rather than *metaphysical* measurement may be easier to recognize when it is already taken for granted, as in the case of labor. Labor is measured in physically-meaningful units of time. If economists discarded this practice, and measured labor in terms of the total wage bill paid by a firm, numbers of employees (or employee hours) would no longer need to be recorded in economic studies of production, because $L$ would simply be a measure of expenditure. Realistically, much would be lost in this form of simplification. For example, if 'labor productivity' is greater in one firm than in another, we would not know if it is because employees of the supposedly-more-productive firm accomplish more per hour of work, or if they simply get paid less per hour.

Thirty-three years ago, Dale Jorgensen and Zvi Griliches, following even earlier work by Murray Foss, explored the measurement of a natural unit of capital.[8] Murray Foss had examined electric motors in manufacturing, in which he measured the quantity of capital services (or 'utilization') in terms of the equipment's level of energy consumption. Professors Jorgensen and Griliches took that idea and 'extrapolated it also to nonequipment components of capital in manufacturing and to all capital outside of manufacturing, including residential structures'. However, this construct was short-lived.

What made it preferable to use energy consumption as a natural unit of capital for manufacturing equipment, and questionable as a natural unit of capital for structures, should be intuitively obvious: from a physical-science perspective, the general purpose served by capital equipment in manufacturing is to manipulate matter. Thus, the extent to which it manipulates matter may be used as a measure of the extent to which it performs its function as capital. One of the best scientific measures of the extent to which anything manipulates matter is the amount of energy it consumes in doing so. Moreover, when technological change occurs, and new equipment can perform the same function by consuming less energy, that equipment has improved in 'efficiency', where the scientific (or engineering) understanding of efficiency (for example, the 'efficiency of an engine') coincides with the economic understanding of the same term. In contrast, structures usually do not manipulate matter as their main function, and can easily change in quality in other ways.

The utilization of land, the provision of space within enclosed structures, and the manipulation of matter are traditional purposes served by physical capital, for which there exist the respective natural units of capital: acres of land, square and cubic feet of space, and energy consumption. Today, of course, there is one other major purpose – the processing of information – which in a general sense may include communication, which broadly-speaking can be interpreted as the movement (or 'transmission') of information. While information processing may first appear as simply another form of energy consumption, the distinction lies in the fact that information, itself, is not tied to physical quantities (see Chapter 7). That is, a certain number of bits of information could be contained in an infinitesimal amount of matter (for example, the placement of nucleotides in DNA) or an infinitesimal flow of energy (for example, minute quantities of light flashing in a specific sequence).

Along these lines, suppose the capital services of information processing equipment were quantified in terms of total calculating capacity, for example, the number of calculations that could potentially be performed per unit time. Such 'hardware' capacity could reflect the existing 'quantity' of capital equipment for information processing, that is, meaningful 'capital accumulation' in information processing, while the development of new software that improves information processing, per unit of that capacity, would reflect 'productivity increases' in the existing capital.

The fact that a 'calculation' is a mathematical idea that, in itself, is neither matter nor energy, suggests that a natural unit of capital could be operationally defined, though still scientific. Once we allow for operational definitions, however, there is no simple distinction between physical and social constructs. Rather, a continuum along this distinction could be identified, in which six levels of natural units of capital could be defined, the last of which is a degenerate form, being nothing more than the way capital has been traditionally measured:

1. *elementary/physical* units of measure; for example, mass, energy, moles, volume, time
2. *elementary/mathematical*: bits of information, number of calculations, surface area[9]
3. *elementary/functional*: calories, floor space, passenger-miles
4. *counts of complex physical objects*: vehicles, rooms, refrigerators
5. *counts of contractual agreements*: software licenses, telephone lines, magazine subscriptions
6. *pecuniary measures regardless of physical properties*: the rental costs of capital services.

## WHY TRADITIONAL CAPITAL MEASUREMENT IS ANACHRONISTIC

No economic resource more easily reflects technological change than physical capital. Consequently, the dissection of capital into descriptive categories, and the tracing of those categories over time, can reveal a great deal about patterns of technological change. Figure 9.1 displays this breakdown for the year 1994. The categories and shares provided in the figure are in reference to net stock values of *capital input*, which the Bureau of Labor Statistics would use in deriving multifactor productivity estimates for industrial groups and for the economy as a whole. This is why land is also included, and measured in pecuniary terms, because, in actual practice, it serves as a component of capital in productivity estimation.

Figure 9.2 displays the evolution of the real value of equipment and real value of structures, per capita, from 1925 to 1994. During this time span, the value of structures rose from $9.5 thousand per capita (in 1987 dollars) to $13.8 thousand, while equipment experienced a much greater increase, from $2.8 thousand to $11.6 thousand. Consequently, the share of physical capital that is equipment had grown consistently over the 70-year period, and had grown exceptionally fast in the last two years of the series, 1993–94, while structures has remained stagnant since 1990.

A further dissection of capital is provided in Figure 9.3, where capital equipment is divided into four major categories, which were constructed from groupings of the equipment categories displayed in Figure 9.1: instruments and office equipment, industrial equipment and machinery, transportation equipment, and other. Industrial equipment and machinery is observed to rise substantially between 1944 and 1981, but remain stagnant thereafter. Transportation equipment and other equipment rose at a much slower pace beginning in 1944 as well, but remained stagnant after 1979. In sharp contrast to these movements, instruments and office equipment grew at a rapid geometric rate (regardless of the data being in per-capita, real-dollar terms), and go from representing a negligible fraction of capital equipment in 1945 to the largest of four categories in 1994. This surge in instruments and office equipment clearly explains the growth of all capital equipment in the 1980s and early 1990s, when quantities of other forms of capital remained virtually unchanged.

Figure 9.4 looks still further into the growth of equipment by dissecting the growth of instruments and office equipment into its component parts: information processing and related equipment; office, computing, and accounting machinery; communication equipment; fixed instruments; and photography and related equipment. As the figure indicates, the rapid growth in instruments and office equipment since 1980 is primarily attributable to the rapid growth of the first three of its subcategories.

By dissecting growth of capital structures, Figure 9.5 clearly demonstrates that growth in structures since 1955 is attributable exclusively to growth in only one of five subcategories: growth in nonresidential, nonfarm buildings. A closer examination of the subcategories of nonresidential, nonfarm buildings (Figure 9.6) reveals that such growth is primarily attributable to growth in commercial buildings, and secondarily attributable to growth in industrial buildings and in hospitals and institutional buildings. As one might suspect, such growth in commercial buildings, hospitals, and institutional buildings reflects the growth that has occurred in the service sector of the economy.

While the above observations do reveal important patterns of technological change, they do not describe those changes accurately, nor do they explain very well the causes of change. As mentioned, a great part of the problem lies in the distinction between true physical changes and changes in economic values – the former being of relevance to the physical process of production, and the latter deriving from reported prices, which, in turn, are functions of a wide range of diverse economic factors (as mentioned, for example, in Chapter 7).

Furthermore, these traditional categories are becoming less meaningful as physical capital evolves from technological change. In particular, one obvious effect of recent technological advances in the information age is the creation

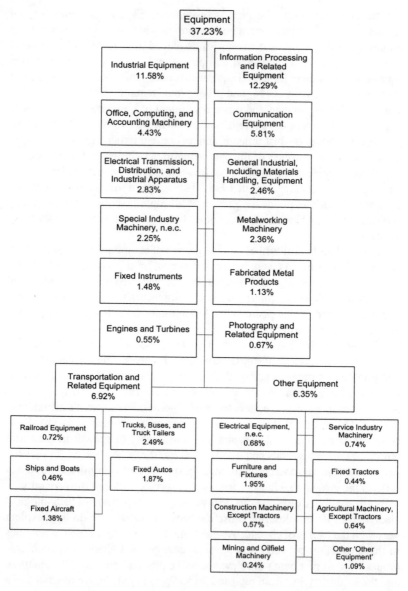

Notes:    Total capital in 1994 was $8.119 trillion in 1987 dollars.
Source:   Payson (1997).

*Figure 9.1    Distribution of capital input (physical capital) in US production
in 1994*

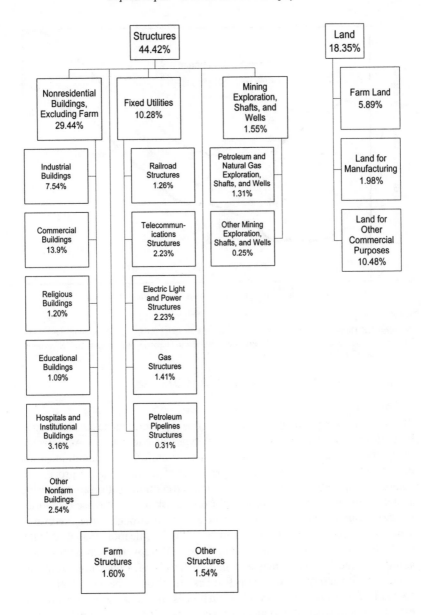

*Figure 9.1   Distribution of capital input (physical capital) in US production in 1994 (concluded)*

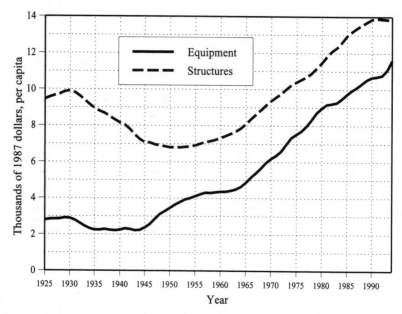

Sources: US Department of Commerce, Bureau of Economic Analysis. Population data were obtained from Economic Report of the President, 1996; and Department of Commerce, *Historical Statistics of the United States, Colonial Times to 1970.*

*Figure 9.2 Evolution of US capital input, 1925–94*

of new forms of equipment that simultaneously perform the tasks that used to be performed by two or more different types of equipment. As personal computers, for example, have become used more often as communication equipment, they may continue to be counted as information-processing equipment. Indeed, information processing and communication are becoming so entwined that it is truly pointless for one to ask which of these categories is largest. Such a question could only be answered through some exercise in semantics or accounting protocol, which would do little more than enable the researcher to rediscover his assumptions. Moreover, because of such ambiguity, the effects of major technological changes over time could be completely misinterpreted by superficial examination of the data. One might conclude, for instance, that 'information processing' is becoming the greatest expanding component of production, when, in fact, it might be communication that is expanding faster, but through Internet connections rather than telephone connections.

One might argue that information processing equipment, communication equipment, and other electronic equipment (for example, equipment for

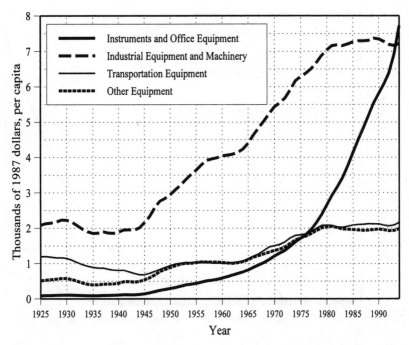

Notes: Instruments and office equipment includes: information processing and related equipment; office, computing, and accounting machinery; communication equipment; fixed instruments; and photocopy and related equipment. Industrial equipment and machinery includes: industrial equipment; fabricated metal products; engines and turbines; metalworking machinery; special industry machinery, not elsewhere classified; general industrial, including materials handling, equipment; and electrical transmission, distribution, and industrial apparatus. Transportation and related equipment includes: trucks, buses and truck trailers; fixed autos; fixed aircraft; ships and boats; and railroad equipment. Other equipment includes: furniture and fixtures, fixed tractors; and machinery for agriculture, construction, mining and oil exploration, service industries, and other equipment, not elsewhere classified.

*Figure 9.3 Capital equipment, 1925–94*

medical diagnosis) are all so heavily integrated in the same technologies that any categorization of capital equipment on the basis of communication devices versus information processing equipment, versus scientific instruments, and so on, would be quite arbitrary, and consequently, would render data that were not very useful. Those economists who would reject this argument in the year 2000 may still be rational for doing so – but they are surely running out of time. All indications of technological change suggest that such distinctions are getting fuzzier and fuzzier by the minute.

One categorical distinction that may continue to be useful for at least a few more years is the distinction between computers (and related equipment) and

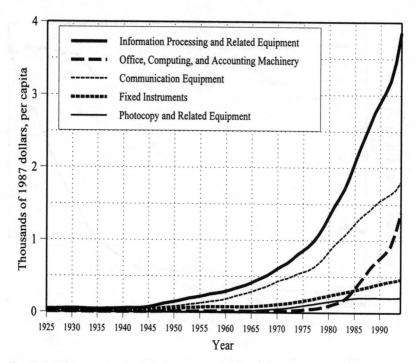

*Figure 9.4  Instruments and office equipment, 1925–94*

industrial machines, which is comparable to the distinction between electronic functions and mechanical functions. If a type of capital equipment actually moves a physical object, in which case it is likely to have a motor, then it can be placed in the categories of machinery or vehicles, which would distinguish it from information-processing devices. However, this distinction is approaching obsolescence as well. The increased usage of computers as components of vehicles, industrial robots, 'smart machine tools', computer-aided design/computer-aided manufacture (CAD/CAM) systems, and modular robotic systems places considerable strain on current methods of classifying physical capital.

## TURNING TO SCIENCE FOR THE ANSWER

The only scientific solution to this seemingly insurmountable problem is to abandon the traditional approach of treating the individual piece of equipment that is purchased as the elementary element of the analysis. As mentioned

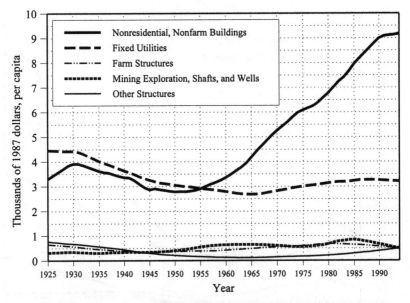

Notes:  Nonresidential, nonfarm buildings include: industrial buildings, commercial buildings, religious buildings, educational buildings, hospital and institutional buildings, and other nonfarm buildings.  Fixed utilities include: railroad structures, telecommunications structures, electric light and power structures, gas structures, and petroleum pipeline structures.

*Figure 9.5  Capital structures, 1925–94*

throughout this book, in *any* scientific discipline, there reaches a point when the traditional element of analysis ceases to facilitate the best explanation of observed phenomena.  Yet, most economists, for no explicitly-stated methodological reason, have stuck to the same basic perspective on physical capital shared by Alfred Marshall in 1890, David Ricardo in 1821, and Adam Smith in 1776.   Rather, a scientific approach toward measuring and understanding the actual changes that are taking place in physical capital must adopt a 'hedonic' or 'characteristics' framework.  In such a framework, an individual item of capital, such as a robot, would not be seen as a single element within a particular category, but as a set of weights attributable to elementary aspects of that item.  As discussed in greater detail below, a robot could be characterized along two dimensions: the amount of mechanical energy it utilizes per unit time (its 'machine' component) and the amount of information it can process per unit time (its 'computer' component).

The most obvious limitation in the natural unit of capital concept is that, as already stated, different natural units of capital would apply for different forms of capital.  How such natural units of capital could be added together to

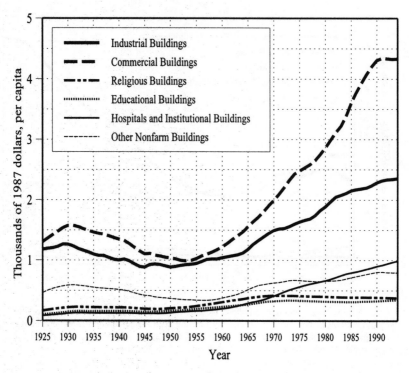

*Figure 9.6  Nonresidential, nonfarm buildings, 1925–94*

construct a total estimate of physical capital would be problematic: how should one combine, for example, energy consumption of manufacturing equipment with total calculations made by information processing equipment? The answer is simple – one shouldn't.  There is no reason for such aggregation, just as there is no reason for land to be interpreted as a form of capital when, in fact, it is not interpreted as such in economics textbooks. Rather, a set of separable natural units of capital could be chosen and tabulated independently, as long as there is no miscounting of features, that is, no incomplete counting or double counting.

Specifically, consider the production function, $Y=F(L,M;K)$, where $L$ is labor, $M$ is materials, and $K$ is capital services.  Now separate capital into measurable characteristics, borrowing from Lancaster's characteristics theory for consumer goods.[10]  However, unlike traditional hedonic characteristics, choose a set of natural units of capital that would apply to all forms of capital. Specifically, choose:

$E$ = *energy capacity of manufacturing equipment*: the amount of energy that would be consumed per unit time (or in physics, the variable 'power', as in the horsepower of a vehicle), if the equipment were operating at full capacity.

$C$ = *calculation capacity*: the potential number of calculations that could be performed per unit time (for example, speed of a computer in megahertz)[11]

$S_1$ = the indoor floor *space* made available by a structure,

$S_2$ = the volume of indoor space made available, not including the volume of space from the floor to eight feet above the floor (which would already be counted in floor space),

$A$ = acres of land,

$R$ = *raw materials* that enhance productive capability of the physical capital, but which have not been already accounted-for as another input into production (for example, the value of the existing trees in an orchard).

These would render the more elaborate production function: $Y=F(L,M;E,C,S_1,S_2,A,R)$, which could be specified as a conceptual end in itself, without any need to reconstruct the aggregate, 'capital'.

In such an accounting of capital services, careful attention would need to be placed on the values of these natural units of capital, and the signs of those values. In particular, the energy capacity of manufacturing equipment would have a positive sign, as it is a measure of the extent to which matter can be manipulated, which is the function served by that equipment. The energy capacity by a computer, in contrast, would not be included, because the service provided by the computer is fully accounted for by $C$. The actual energy consumption (as opposed to capacity) of both the computer and manufacturing equipment should be accounted for in $M$ – the materials used up in the production process. Thus, if there is an industrial robot that performs calculations while engaged in physical production, only the full-capacity energy that would be used in physical production, not calculations, or the provision of space, should be included in $E$. The robot's potential calculation capacity should be included in $C$, and the energy it used up to perform the actual calculations it did make would be a component of $M$. In this way, the accounting would be invariant to whether the robot is defined as a single unit, or as two units: a computer and a mechanical apparatus. Such invariance to methods of aggregation should be a requirement in this methodology, since methods of aggregation are primarily arbitrary, which would otherwise make the results obtained ambiguous.

Invariance to aggregation with regard to $E$ and $C$ would allow comparisons to be made at all conceivable levels of aggregation. For example, an industrial plant could be described in terms of total full-capacity horsepower of manufacturing operations, and total calculation capacity of information processing and 'smart machine'/robotic equipment. Differences across plants could then be made with reference to these variables, as well as differences across industries, or even national economies. Differences across time would be a measure of 'capital accumulation' in a different sense, which might better explain the true causal factors underlying actual production processes and technological change.

Similarly, accounting of $S_1$ and $S_2$ would also have to be done correctly, so as not to double-count natural units of capital. In particular, the space taken up by capital equipment should enter in as *negative* values of space, since such space is an input that is reduced by the presence of the capital equipment. In this suggested method of tabulation, we might better understand how a new piece of machinery that takes up less space, all else being equal, would enter in as a more valuable piece of machinery if it commands a higher sales price, simply by virtue of it taking up less space.

Again, because this discussion deviates from traditional economic approaches to capital measurement, it must be emphasized that one's use of a natural unit of capital does not in any way assume homogeneity of all items measured along that metric. For example, no suggestion is being made that all manufacturing equipment with the same energy capacity is the same, just as no suggestion is ever made in economics that all hours of labor are of equal value, simply because $L$ is measured in hours, or all acres of land are of equal value, because they are all measured in acres. What is being sought in this new method of analysis is a scientifically-meaningful measure of *quantity*, which is uniquely different from *quality*, but might still be useful in efforts to understand the causes of technological change. Economic value is not being ignored here whatsoever – value will simply be treated separately as an aspect of quality – exactly the same way that labor value, which can be measured in terms of the hourly wage, is not ignored when the *quantity* of labor is measured in hours.

In spite of the simplicity of this proposed framework, it challenges mainstream economic thought, because, as economists, we are not accustomed to using measures of quantity that are distinct from economic value. For example, we tend to think there is something wrong with using energy consumption as a measure of quantity, when we know that a precision laser used for neural surgery may use as much energy as a garden 'weedwacker'. We are reluctant to use computer calculations as a measure of quantity, when we know that computer systems used to monitor and control one of NASA's space-shuttle missions may make as many calculations per day as the computer systems operating a major city's telephone lines, but the computers monitoring and controlling the shuttle mission are much more valuable because of the software they contain.

Yet, we do measure labor and land in natural units, when we know the quality or value per unit can vary enormously. We measure labor in hours, rather than dollars, because it enables us, for instance, to better understand how education improves wages. We measure land in acres, rather than dollars, to better understand, for instance, how land development improves land values. Along the same lines, by measuring manufacturing equipment in energy capacity, we may better understand technological change in terms of engineering efficiency. By measuring information processing equipment in terms of calculation capacity, we can study trends in both the 'accumulation' of calculation capacity, and 'programming efficiency' – how well information is processed per unit of calculation capacity. That is, better software increases the value of information processing per unit quantity of calculation capacity, just as employee training can increase the value of human labor per hour of work.

The missing component in this discussion, however, has been the evidence. Why were the above natural units of capital chosen and not others? Support for the choice of these variables can be found among the many hedonic price studies that have been performed on various forms of physical capital. By examining these studies together, it is expected that certain central characteristics of capital, or 'principle components' in regression analyses of capital value (Dhrymes 1970), could be identified that could be broadly used to quantify physical capital in terms of vectors of measurable, physical characteristics.

## FINDINGS OF 'HEDONIC STUDIES' AND THEIR IMPLICATIONS

A great deal of progress has been made in the measurement of quality change through the use of 'hedonic price estimation'. These studies associate prices with the physical characteristics of goods or services, following from Kelvin Lancaster's theory on characteristics.[12] Thus far, three products have dominated the hedonic price literature: automobiles, housing, and computers. Official federal estimates of the producer price index for computers and housing currently employ hedonic techniques,[13] while automobile studies accounted for many of the first, and most influential, papers on hedonic methods.[14] In spite of this domination by a few products, the number and variety of goods and services that have been examined with hedonic methods is remarkable, including, for example, refrigerators,[15] food items[16] and 'the value of quiet'.[17]

Hedonic studies of quality change are feasible when physical characteristics of items can be measured across time, allowing for regression analyses of prices against characteristics. However, their purpose has always been to measure quality change for the sake of proper interpretation of price changes.[18] Moreover, their focus has, almost exclusively, been on finding the most appropriate functional forms for such estimation, based primarily on highly technical, econometric issues. In this sense, the discussion here finds new benefits from hedonic estimation.

The summaries below of the findings of hedonic studies focus only on continuous explanatory variables in hedonic regression analyses. The dependent variable in such analyses is always the price (or rent) of the item in question, and these analyses often contain, as well, discrete variables and dummy variables. The absence of noncontinuous variables in the discussion below reflects only the need for confinement of the discussion, for the sake of feasible exposition, rather than an implicit assumption that such variables are any less important as a general rule. More detailed examinations of the quantity/quality issue in capital measurement would need to take these other variables into account.

The discussion also leaves out any mention of the statistical significance and the value of coefficients for these regression analyses. This kind of information would not be necessary for the issues being addressed, primarily because the values of these coefficients are highly dependent on the particular models and functional forms used, even within the same study (when that study examines alternative specifications). For example, in hedonic analysis of residential housing and commercial buildings, a key natural unit that determines prices in every one of these studies is floor space, as one might expect. However, many of these studies also include the variable, number of rooms, which is not included in our discussion, as it is a discrete variable. Nevertheless, one's interpretation of the numerical coefficient on floor space should depend greatly on the presence or absence of the additional explanatory variable, number of rooms, and would depend, as well, on the coefficient and statistical significance attached to that additional variable. More generally, covariance among the explanatory variables in these analyses usually precludes a simple interpretation of their coefficient values. With this being case for each individual study, the following description of as many as 39 studies would, realistically, not have room for consideration of coefficient values. Finally, it is worth emphasizing that the studies chosen for discussion were simply those that were available with regard to the topics being studied – they were not screened in any sense.

# RESIDENTIAL HOUSING AND COMMERCIAL BUILDINGS

Table 9.1 summarizes the continuous variables used in hedonic analyses in eight studies of either residential housing or commercial buildings. As already noted, they all contained floor space as a variable, $S_1$, and six of the eight contained lot area, $A$. The two that did not include lot area focused on rental units, for which lot area was not a strong determinant of rental price. Some of the other variables included a depreciation factor (the age of the building) and two variables that directly affect economic efficiency: fuel cost per unit of floor space, and distance from city center (which, of course, affects transportation costs). Additional continuous variables included: time of sale, social aspects of the neighborhood, geographical amenities (such as the amount of freely-accessible, open space in the area), and characteristics of housing in the area.

The adoption of a scientific approach to the measurement of residential housing and commercial buildings would first require separate quantification of floor space and land area. Given these well-defined physical quantities, the quality/efficiency of different structures *per unit of floor space* and *per unit of land* could then be calculated on the basis of prices. Separate prices would need to be attributed to floor space and to land, which should not be difficult to obtain, or impute, if empty lots are sold in the vicinity of lots containing structures. Once prices per unit of floor space, and per unit of land, are observed, such prices would reflect the quality of each unit of capital.

# COMPUTERS

Table 9.2 combines hedonic analyses on both mainframe and personal computers. Calculation speed is surely the key natural unit of measure. The two cases involving floor space tend to reflect an earlier age when computers actually occupied significant portions of office space – a factor that is of relatively little importance today. Other physical measures include volume and weight, which is mostly relevant to the distinction between desktop and laptop computers, or the concern over how much desk/table space a computer might occupy. Depreciation is also reported as a factor, which is difficult to interpret for computers, as it is much more a function of operational obsolescence than of wear-and-tear (the traditional reason for capital depreciation). The other variables that continue to be important determinants of computer prices refer to random access memory (RAM) and hard disk capacity.

*Table 9.1 Continuous explanatory variables in hedonic regression analyses of the prices of residential housing and commercial buildings*

| # | Study | Year | Natural units of capital | | Variables directly affecting economic efficiency | | Depreciation factor | | Additional continuous variables | | |
|---|-------|------|-------------|----------|-----------------------------|----------------------|-----------------|--------------|---------------------------------|-------------------------|------------------------------|
| | | | Floor space[1] | Lot area | Fuel cost per floor space[2] | Distance from city center[3] | Age of building | Time of sale | Social aspects of neighborhood[4] | Geographical amenities[5] | Characteristics of housing in area[6] |
| 1 | de Silva and Gruenstein | 1988 | X | X | | | X | X | | | |
| 2 | Cropper, et al. | 1988 | X | X | | | X | | | | |
| 3 | Dinan and Miranowsi | 1989 | X | X | X | X | X | | X | | |
| 4 | Rasmussen and Zuehlke | 1990 | X | X | | X | X | | X | | |
| 5 | Ito and Hirono[7] | 1993 | X | | | X | X | | | | |
| 6 | Cheshire and Sheppard | 1995 | X | X | | X | | | | X | |
| 7 | Gilley and Pace | 1995 | X | X | | | X | | | | |
| 8 | Moulton[7] | 1995 | X | | | | X | | X | | X |

Notes:
[1] Gilley and Pace separate out bedroom area, kitchen area, and other area.
[2] Fuel bills per square-foot of heated floor area (normalized for temperature differences).
[3] Dinan and Miranowski, and Cheshire and Sheppard, measure this factor in miles, while Rasmussen and Zuehlke, and Ito and Hirono measure it in travel time.
[4] These include median income of appropriate census tract (Dinan and Miranowski; and Rasmussen and Zuehlke), percent of families headed by specified ethnic groups (Rasmussen and Zuehlke, Cheshire and Sheppard), and fraction of local population in blue-collar occupations (Cheshire and Sheppard). In addition, Moulton considers percent of families below poverty line, population with three or more years of college, and unemployed population.
[5] Cheshire and Sheppard examine the angle that the property faces (in radians from East), the percentage of land in the area that is in industrial use, and the percentages of land in accessible and inaccessible open space.
[6] Moulton includes percent of housing: (1) in large buildings, (2) which are mobile homes, (3) without indoor plumbing, and (4) with central air conditioning.
[7] Because rental units are considered, the lot area is not used as a variable.

Table 9.2 *Continuous explanatory variables in hedonic regression analyses of the prices of computers (excluding peripherals)*

| # | Study | Year | Natural units of capital | | Other physical measures | | Depreciation (including dummies for age of computer) | Memory size / hard disk capacity | Memory access time | Random access memory (RAM) | Size of online direct-access storage | Cache buffer size |
|---|---|---|---|---|---|---|---|---|---|---|---|---|
| | | | Calculation speed[1] | Floor space occupied | Volume | Weight | | | | | | |
| 1 | Knight | 1966 | X | | | | | | | | | |
| 2 | Chow | 1967 | X | | | | | X | X | | | |
| 3 | Early et al.[2] | 1963 | X | | | | | X | | | | |
| 4 | Jacob[2] | 1969 | X | X | | | X | X | X | | | |
| 5 | Patrick[2] | 1969 | X | | | | X | X | | | | |
| 6 | Schneidewind[2] | 1969 | X | | | | | X | | | | |
| 7 | Skattum[2] | 1969 | X | | | | | X | | | | |
| 8 | Kelejian and Nicoletti[3] | 1971 | X | | | | | X | X | | | |
| 9 | Ratchford and Ford | 1976 | X | | | | X | X | | | | |
| 10 | Stoneman | 1976 | X | X | | | X | X | | | | |
| 11 | Cale, et al. | 1979 | X | | | | | X | | | X | |
| 12 | Stoneman | 1978 | X | | | | X | X | | | | |
| 13 | Archibald and Reece | 1979 | X | | | | | X | X | | | |
| 14 | Michaels | 1979 | X | | | | | X | X | | | |
| 15 | Fisher et al. | 1983 | X | | | | | X | | | | |
| 16 | Cartwright et al. | 1985 | X | | | | | X | | | | |
| 17 | Levy and Welzer[3] | 1985 | X | | | | | X | | | | |

Table 9.2 Continuous explanatory variables in hedonic regression analyses of the prices of computers (excluding peripherals) (concluded)

| # | Study | Year | Natural units of capital | | Other physical measures | | Depreciation (including dummies for age of computer) | Memory size / hard disk capacity | Memory access time | Random access memory (RAM) | Size of online direct-access storage | Cache buffer size |
|---|---|---|---|---|---|---|---|---|---|---|---|---|
| | | | Calculation speed[1] | Floor space occupied | Volume | Weight | | | | | | |
| 18 | Wallace | 1985 | X | | | | | X | | | | |
| 19 | Flamm | 1987 | X | | | | | X | | | | |
| 20 | Gordon | 1987 | X | | | | | X | X | | | X |
| 21 | Dulberger | 1989 | X | | | | | X | | | | |
| 22 | Berndt et al. | 1993 | X | | | | X | X | | X | | |
| 23 | Oliner | 1993 | X | | | | X | X | | | | |
| 24 | Nelson et al.[4] | 1994 | X | | | | | X | | X | | |
| 25 | Berndt et al. | 1995 | X | | X | X | X | X | | X | | |
| 26 | Shiratsuka | 1995 | X | | | | | X | | X | | |
| 27 | Stavins | 1995 | X | | | | X | X | | X | | |

Notes:
[1]Includes memory cycles per second, additions per second, operations per second, multiplications per second, instructions per second, etc.
[2]Unpublished papers summarized by Sharpe (1969) and Triplett (1989).
[3]Unpublished paper summarized by Triplett (1989).
[4]Summarized by Shiratsuka (1995).

The concept used here of 'calculation speed' is admittedly ambiguous, as it all depends on exactly what type of calculation is being carried out. Distinctions between different measures of computer speeds is a very important topic in comparisons among computers at the same point in time. However, given the rapid rate of change in computer technology, if one particular definition of speed is chosen that is representative of consumer preferences for computer speed, then the growth rate of that speed over several years is likely to be quite similar to the growth rates of other definitions of speed. Consequently, if capital is to be measured in a manner designed to shed light on technological change, then the ambiguity in the definitions for speed should not preclude such measurement – a reasonable measurement standard simply needs to be established.

The use of hard disk capacity as a natural unit of capital, in itself, would neither be feasible nor desirable. Since computers can share the same hard disk memory through networks and Internet connections, such memory is not additive – indeed, the Internet makes memory capacity a public good in many respects. The substitutability of hard disk capacity with reading off floppy disks, compact disks, and zip disks confounds the analysis as well. In any case, the importance of hard disk memory as a determinant of a computer's value is not, in any way, being compromised by the use of calculation speed alone to define quantity. The importance of hard disk memory would be captured appropriately as a determinant of computer quality per unit of computer speed (or per number of computer calculations per unit time). That is, as already mentioned in reference to the previous form of capital, once the natural unit of capital is defined (in this case, number of calculations), the quality of each unit is reflected in its price.

## INDUSTRIAL EQUIPMENT

While few hedonic studies have been conducted on industrial equipment, Table 9.3 manages to identify four such studies, with the second one on compact trucks applying to both industrial and consumer purchases of the product. As shown in the table, a key natural unit of measure for industrial equipment would be power usage – a physical measure of the extent to which matter is being manipulated or transported. For an item like a truck, one might be disturbed at the fact that such a measure would not capture the actual number of trucks, or, on a more aggregate level, the total amount of hauling capacity those trucks provide. These considerations would certainly come into play in the determination of quality per unit. However, the existing measure of truck quantity – the aggregate sales value of trucks – probably provides even less information about the number of trucks or their hauling capacity.

Table 9.3 *Continuous explanatory variables in hedonic regression analyses of the prices of industrial equipment*

| # | Type of capital | Study | Year | Natural units of capital, or their determinants | | | | | | Other physical measures | | | |
| | | | | Power usage | Determinants of power generation | | | | | Weight | Length | Wheelbase length of tractor | Aspects of tractor hydraulics |
| | | | | | Boiler rating[1] | Boiler pressure | Boiler efficiency | Turbo-generator capacity | Turbo-generator efficiency | | | | |
| 1 | Tractor | Cooper, et al. | 1993 | X | | | | | | X | | X | X |
| 2 | Compact Truck | Feenstra | 1978 | X | | | | | | X | X | | |
| 3 | Boiler | Ohta | 1975 | | X | X | X | | | | | | |
| 4 | Turbogenerator | Ohta | 1975 | | | | | X | X | | | | |

Notes:
[1]Ohta defines the boiler rating as thousands of pounds of steam per hour.

Because truck horse power is closely tied to hauling capacity, one might be able to derive a rough estimate of total hauling capacity from total horsepower, without knowing the number of trucks or their sizes. An estimate of hauling capacity made from total truck cost might be even rougher. An elaborate sleeping cabin for the truck driver, for example, would increase its value but not change its effective hauling capacity. Similar considerations would apply to all other forms of industrial equipment that consume substantial quantities of energy.

A boiler/turbogenerator complex, which Makoto Otha, in 1975, analysed in terms of hedonic prices (Table 9.3), of course, produces power, rather than consumes it. Consequently, power produced by any generator of power should not be a measure of the quantity of that equipment — it is a measure of the equipment's output. Thus, the quantity of the equipment, itself, in such cases, is not straightforward. It appears that two choices are possible in the quantification of energy-generating equipment: one could evoke industrial engineering theory to calculate a maximum amount of energy that might be siphoned off by the equipment itself from the physical process that generates the energy (for example, the heat absorption capacity of the boiler, or the maximum energy that could be absorbed by a turbine in its rotation). Alternatively, one could adopt a user-cost approach, quantifying the capital in terms of the costs of building it, which utilizes the default unit of measure, $R$. Given the degree of complexity and the theoretical character of the first method, the second method of utilizing cost data would probably be preferable.

## CONCLUSION: WHERE DO WE GO FROM HERE?

Stepping beyond the theory, and into the actual measurement of the proposed characteristics (or natural units) of capital, would, indeed, be a giant step. At present, obtaining such information for the entire economy as a whole would be an insurmountable task. Moreover, the feasibility and logistics of carrying out such an endeavor is a topic that would warrant another book. What may be worth mentioning briefly here is that this problem of estimation could be approached in three ways: (1) derivation of vectors of natural units of capital for several representative pieces of capital equipment, and multiplication of those vectors by the estimated amounts of equipment; (2) indirect estimation, for example, determining $C$ for a certain types of capital based on information about the microprocessors sold to capital producers; and (3) some combinations of these two methods.

Another approach, that is more microeconomic than macroeconomic, would be to build upon the precedent established by hedonic studies, by analyzing natural units of capital as they relate to new forms of capital equipment not yet examined. As an example, an emerging form of capital equipment that has yet to be analyzed in terms of characteristics is a hybrid between two forms of capital that have already been analyzed extensively – the 'autonomous vehicle' – a vehicle driven by a computer, rather than a human being. Autonomous vehicles have enormous potential, and are now being developed for trucks, automobiles, exploratory submarines, warehousing vehicles, heavy construction equipment, heavy agricultural equipment, spacecraft, and military vehicles such as surveillance drones. This example illustrates rather well the dual importance of computer calculations and energy capacity. That is, all else being equal, the greater the number of potential calculations per unit time in a vehicle's computer, the more able the equipment will be to process visual input effectively, and thus, the more capable the vehicle will be to move at higher speeds and with lower chances of accidents. Moreover, the greater the energy capacity of the vehicle, the greater its potential payload, as well as its command over terrain.

Table 9.4 illustrates how measures of natural units of capital could be derived for an autonomous vehicle from data about its design and production costs. The vehicle chosen for illustration is rather small and inexpensive – a 2½ x 4 feet, tracked vehicle that travels up to 4 miles/hour, which could be used for tasks such as carrying a load of bricks to different areas of a construction site. As shown in the table, three measures of natural units would apply in this case: an energy capacity of 3 horsepower, a total calculation speed of 132 Megahertz, and raw material costs of $5,300. Production of the unit would require approximately 2,000 person-hours of labor, or one-person-year, which is quite high, owing to the fact that the mechanism is a prototype developed at a university, not a product of an automated assembly plant. Consequently, if the quantity of capital in this case were based on costs alone, those costs would be highly dependent on the scale of production, which, as argued above, is a factor that is peripheral to physical characteristics of the product itself. Indeed, on the basis of total production cost alone, this small, 4 mile-per-hour, brick-carrying device could be misinterpreted as having the same 'amount' of capital as a cargo truck.

Similarly, at this writing, the microprocessors used in this vehicle are now obsolete, and the designer is planning to build the next vehicle with at least one Pentium processor. Thus, while the vehicle was built in 1996, the $2,000 cost estimate for the computers used is now highly overpriced. A more sophisticated autonomous vehicle would have possessed much greater calculation capacity, suggesting an even greater ambiguity in any cost-based approach to capital measurement. In contrast, the processor speeds reported in Table 9.4 provide precise, and permanent, information about the capital equipment itself.

*Table 9.4 Identification of natural units of capital from design specifics and cost estimates for building an autonomous vehicle*

| (The ANT III Robot developed at West Virginia University[1]) | | |
|---|---|---|
| Cost Component | Estimated Costs ($) | Translation to Natural Units of Capital |
| Drive motors and controllers (purchased reconditioned) (Two motors – 1.5 Hp[2] each) | 1,000 | $E = 1.5 \times 2$ $= 3$ Hp |
| Two 80486 computers, each with 66 MHz processor | 2,000 | $C = 66 \times 2$ $= 132$ MHz |
| Raw Materials: | | |
| Chassis: tracks and bogeys | 1,000 | |
| Drive train components: gear boxes, shafts,    bearings, sprockets, chain, etc. | 500 | |
| Batteries: main and computer, one set each | 450 | $R = $ Total |
| DC Power supply for computer and sensors | 400 | $= \$5,300$ |
| Video camera and frame grabber | 750 | |
| Ultrasonic system (sensors, multiplexer and driver) | 1,000 | |
| Inclinometers, encoders, misc. electronic components | 400 | |
| Materials for superstructure and skin | 500 | |
| Wiring supplies | 300 | |
| Software: compilers and image processing | | |
| This component of cost would not be counted in the *quantity* of capital – it is a factor that improves the efficiency of calculations, and thus the *quality and price* of capital. | 300 | — |
| Labor costs in production of vehicle: approximately 2,000 person-hours (to build prototype) | | |
| This component of cost would not be counted in the *quantity* of capital – it is a factor that affects the overall *quality and price* of capital, given the other measures of capital quantity. The same would apply to other factors used to produce the vehicle, such as energy costs. | (not available) | — |

Notes:
[1]ANT stands for *Autonomous Navigation Testbed*.
[2]Hp = horsepower. One unit of horsepower = 745.7 watts.

Source: Payson (1997b).

In conclusion, measuring physical capital in a useful, unambiguous, manner, that would shed light on the causality of technological change, is surely an extremely difficult endeavor. Natural units of capital, namely, indoor space, land area, number of calculations, and energy consumption, have enormous potential to assist in this endeavor. However, because this approach is so different from traditional methods of capital accounting, and because it has not yet been tried (as far as this author knows), it certainly cannot be looked upon as a substitute for current methods. Rather, it is simply an exploration – a conceptual experiment.

Nevertheless, it is only through such exploration that we may hope to improve economic analysis of technological change. As I have argued in previous chapters, and many others have noted as well, the ultimate limitation in our ability to understand such change may lie with the way we define and acquire data to begin with, before we even attempt to perform an analysis.

The specific variables suggested in this paper, $E$, $C$, $S_1$, $S_2$, $A$ and $R$, are by no means absolute, or sketched in stone – nothing here has been mathematically proven, nor proven in any other sense. The main point is that the definition and classification of capital needs to be addressed as seriously, and as scientifically, as the analyses that use such information. In science in general, how data are classified is neither neutral nor peripheral, but bears directly on how thoughts are organized about the topic being studying. Edward Wisniewski and Douglas Medin, who are cognitive psychologists, have found:

> When categories are meaningfully labeled, people bring intuitive theories to the learning context. Learning then involves a process in which people search for evidence in the data that supports abstract features or hypotheses that have been activated by the intuitive theories. In contrast, when categories are labeled in a neutral manner, people search for simple features that distinguish one category from another.[19]

Looking again at Figure 9.1, it seems evident which of these two cases currently applies to the classification of capital. Hence, in order to observe and understand the real forces that underlie technological change in capital, we need to measure capital scientifically. At first, a scientific effort toward dissecting capital may be as messy as the first dissections were in biology. We can only hope that, eventually, they will be as worthwhile.

## NOTES

1. An earlier version of this chapter had appeared in Payson 1997.
2. See, for example, Lancaster 1991.
3. Griliches 1990.
4. See Robinson 1966.

5. Arguments of this kind could fall under a variety of contexts, such as the notion that hedonic prices 'cannot by themselves identify the structure of consumer preferences and producer technologies that generate them' (Rosen 1974), or the notion of 'immiserizing growth' (Bhagwati and Srinivasan 1984).
6. Eichner 1983.
7. Solow 1957.
8. Jorgensen and Griliches 1967, and Foss 1963.
9. Surface area is more 'mathematical' than 'volume', and 'volume' is more physical, only in the sense that all physical objects exist in three dimensions, while surface area exists more in the context of an 'idea' that one associates with actual physical objects.
10. See, for example, Lancaster 1966.
11. One might also consider the memory features in a computer, such as the memory storage capacity on the hard drive. Reasons for not including it as a natural unit of capital are provided later on in the chapter.
12. See, for example, Lancaster 1971.
13. Siegel 1994.
14. See, for example, Court 1939, Griliches 1961, Cagan 1965, Triplett 1969.
15. Dhrymes 1970.
16. Ladd and Suvannunt 1976.
17. McMillan et al. 1980.
18. Cropper et al. 1988.
19. Wisniewski and Medin 1994.

# 10. Conclusion

In his book, *Why Aren't Economists as Important as Garbagemen?*, David Colander concludes:

> My defense of mainstream economics has been defensive; clearly I don't believe mainstream economics is the only way or even necessarily the best way to study economic reality. But I defend it because, compared to the alternatives, there is no comparison. Critics have simply not established even an outline of a viable alternative. In fact, most critics spend much of their time talking about methodology, leaving them little time to contribute to public knowledge about the economy. Let's assume for the moment that one dissident group took control of the profession. What would change? I just don't know. Thus, for me, at this point in time, mainstream economics is the only game in town.[1]

At the risk of sounding clichéd, I would argue that one of the main thrusts of Professor Colander's synopsis is: those who choose to be critics of economics should realize that, if they are not part of the solution, they are just another part of the problem. In this chapter I will address not only problems but their solutions. In the end, my hope is that mainstream economics may have more difficulty in continuing to be 'the only game in town'.

## CAN ECONOMICS BE MORE SCIENTIFIC?

The bitter truth is that not enough economists today care about whether or not economics is truly a science. If they did, the problems described in Chapters 1 to 3 would not exist to the same extent. Ironically, one of the groups that is most responsible for this apathy may be those of us who have written the most about it, because in our writing we have tended to focus on the philosophy of science, which is an area of inquiry that most economists do not understand very well and have little interest in exploring. Economists specializing in the philosophy of science and/or the history of economic thought, who are, in fact, genuinely concerned about making economics more scientific, must be willing to step outside of their comfortable, scholarly niches and face the profession head-on. If there is too much intellectual baggage associated with the concept of 'science' to allow for a broad-based appeal for better economics, then the concept of 'science' could be set aside in the short term – attention could be given, instead, to the broader, and more universally understood, ideals of legitimacy and usefulness.

As suggested in Chapters 1–3, another step in the right direction would be an organized effort on the part of academic economics departments to require economics students to study natural science. For example, at first, students pursuing graduate-level degrees with specialization in technological change, environmental, agricultural, or health economics, might be required to take certain undergraduate courses in the natural sciences most commensurate with their specialty in economics. In addition, interdisciplinary degrees in economics and natural science could be offered, which could benefit not only the economics profession but the science and engineering professions as well, in which science professionals are often required to be involved in economic decision making. The idea here is that economists could begin to have greater familiarity with, and appreciation for, natural science, which could encourage the economics profession itself to be more scientific.

In addition, the major economic organizations that now control which literature, and which individuals, become prominent in the profession need to adopt a less dictatorial, less paternalistic, less condescending, and more honest relationship with the rest of the economics profession, as well as with the rest of society. For starters, we truly need to drop our discussions about proper ettiquette for new economists, and speak, instead, about proper commitment toward the advancement of useful knowledge. We also need to lower the sociological barriers to entry with regard to having papers published in major journals. In essence, we should try to be less of a social club, and more of a true, scientific body that exists for the purpose of honestly promoting useful knowledge.

Finally, naive fanaticism for prominent economists within the profession needs to somehow be brought under control. Such fanaticism has at least three negative effects on the quality of economic discourse:

1. Individuals become known as heirs apparent of prominent economists, leading to a system based more on entitlement (or 'inheritance' and its adverse effects of 'inbreeding') than on achievement.
2. New economic models receive recognition less for their scientific contribution than for their authors' already-established popularity, reinforcing the game among economists of 'getting yourself known' as opposed to acquiring and disseminating useful knowledge.
3. In association with fanaticism, there is an excessive, unhealthy level of humility among junior economists, which tends to prevent them from aspiring to become important contributors themselves, and tends to turn them into followers rather than scientists.

There is obviously no easy solution to this problem. Perhaps one step that might help is for economists to begin an effort to describe economic ideas according to the ideas themselves, rather than the name of the person(s) who had proposed it. For example, the Cobb–Douglas production function has two names attached to it, while the constant-elasticities-of-production function does not. In the latter case, the popularity of the function has been based less on what people think of Cobb and Douglas, and more on what people think of the function itself. In general, models not named after famous people will face equal scrutiny as those by not-so-famous individuals, with the idea that the *best* model should receive the most recognition, not the one with the most popular author. Nevertheless, this discussion has already extended outside the realm of topics that most economics like to think about, and may even be seen, by some, as evidence that my perspective on such matters is overly idiosyncratic. In any case, I would continue to argue that good science and fanaticism do not mix very well.

## USING ARTIFICIAL INTELLIGENCE TO HELP REDUCE CRONYISM AND EMPTY FORMALISM

As discussed throughout this book, the many subfields of our profession are ridden with empty formalism, a lack of interest in scientific methods, and a lack of interest in understanding technological change from a scientific perspective. Whether we should be paranoid enough to call it a 'conspiracy' is certainly debatable. It is true that power within the profession follows an extremely skewed distribution, but it is probably also true that many of our leading economists genuinely believe in what they, and their colleagues, are doing. Others have admitted that economic discourse is extremely weak in terms of scientific relevance, but they simply do not know how to change it.

As for the issue of cronyism within the profession, many of us are oblivious to it, regarding it as a general problem within all professions, and thus something not worth considering. Others among us might recognize that cronyism is particularly problematic in the economics profession, but see it only as a separate problem, unrelated to the quality or usefulness of economic discourse. Still others might acknowledge that cronyism is both particularly strong in economics and that it adversely affects the profession's output, but they might then argue that it is beyond their ability as individuals to challenge the culture of the economics profession. Individuals in this last group who do oppose cronyism, and the empty formalism and unscientific discourse that often comes with it, may see themselves like the character Schindler in the movie *Schindler's List*: they can only 'do good' within their own purview; if they challenge the culture beyond that, they would lose their status and would be much less able to 'do good' in the future.

Let us face an observable fact: the system of how economics is done, and how we, as economists, are rewarded, is firmly intact. It resists change; it resists criticism; it is a formidable opponent to all critics who would try to attack it. Moreover, because economic subfields do so well at absorbing those of us who would believe in their methods to begin with it, critics who understand the details and complexities of economic models are relatively small in number and not within the subfields that they criticize – those who do exist are often 'exiled' to the history-of-thought subfield.

Although there are many aspects of cronyism in the economics profession, the one that may be most closely associated with the perpetuation of empty formalism is cronyism that exists in the publication process, that is, cronyism in the acceptance or rejection of proposed journal articles, and cronyism in the citations that published articles provide. Without such cronyism, or 'sociologically-based support' empty formalism could not survive as easily, because empty formalism is simply not useful in most cases, and therefore it would not gain the support of a general audience of economists with diverse interests and agendas. Thus, empty formalism is, in some sense, 'allowed to happen', or even encouraged, through sociological support.

Many individual economists who have had good ideas, however, and who have been persistent enough, have been able to get their work published in spite of the fact that they do not belong to a select group of insiders. What is often the case is that those individual economists, or 'outsiders', had to settle for getting their work published in 'secondary' journals – journals that are less prestigious and have lower readerships than the 'top' journals.

Given these circumstances, we may have a means for testing whether empty formalism, on a particular topic, is sociologically supported. I would argue that empty formalism is more likely to be sociologically supported if the following conditions apply with regard to a particular subfield of economics:

1. There are basically two sets of researchers who are writing on the same general topic. One set gets published almost exclusively in top journals, and the other set almost exclusively in secondary journals.
2. The articles in the top journals contain signficantly more formalism (with regard to the topic in question) than those in the secondary journals.
3. The articles in the secondary journals are critical, at times, of the strong assumptions that hold up the empty formalism that exists in top journal articles on the same topic.
4. The articles on the topic in secondary journals cite and acknowledge the articles in the top journals, but not vice versa; articles in the top journals tend to reference themselves only.

If these conditions are met, they should raise suspicions that the insiders are possibly preventing the outsiders from entering the group, and/or preventing them from having their voices heard about their objections to empty formalism. Therefore, if these circumstances can somehow be objectively tested by organizations interested in promoting good, economic science, then those same organizations may be able to identify the worst cases of cronyism and do something about it. However, testing all four of these conditions could be problematic.

Conditions 1 and 4 in the above list are relatively easy to test, using, for example, the *Social Science Citation Index* database and an index of the relative prestigue of economic journals. (See the section in Chapter 2 on 'misconduct versus bad etiquette' and the report by Arora and Gambardella in 1996.) However, conditions 2 and 3 may be difficult for researchers to detect and measure objectively. In fact, many of us might reasonably argue that conditions 2 and 3 simply cannot be feasibly tested, and thus the whole exercise would be an exercise in futility.

I will now argue that conditions 2 and 3 can, in fact, be carried out objectively, through the application of techniques in artificial intelligence. As mentioned at the end of Chapter 8, artificial intelligence programs using 'natural language processing' can identify central and secondary themes in articles and papers and summarize them. At this writing, such programs are now being sold online through the Internet, and can be found, for example, through searches on terms like 'artificial intelligence, text summarization, and natural language processing'. (A search on 'artificial intelligence' alone would render a wide range of other applications of artificial intelligence.) On the topic of 'discourse management, story understanding, and text generation', Bill Manaris writes:

> The objective of discourse management and story understanding systems is to process natural language input to elicit significant facts or extract the essence of what is being said. These systems require access to linguistic knowledge ranging from lexical to, possibly, world knowledge relevant to the domain of discourse. . . . Specific applications range from indexing, . . . to summarization, . . . to retrieval (natural language search engines, data mining), to question and answer dialogs. In order to perform these tasks such systems may incorporate text generation components. These components utilize the collected linguistic knowledge to generate various forms of text, such as news stories . . . and special documents.[2]

He then provides examples of such systems:

> One example of a discourse management application that incorporates a text generation component is the patent authoring system designed by Sheremetyeva and Nirenburg (1996). The system is intended to interactively elicit technical knowledge from inventors, and then use it to automatically generate a patent claim that meets legal requirements. .

. . Examples of other systems in this area (many of which have been marketed) include ATRANS, Battelle's READ, BORIS, Clarit, Conquest, Construe, Freestyle, FRUMP, GROK, J-Space, IPP, Oracle's ConText, Savvy/TRS, SCISOR, Target, Tome, and Westlaw's WIN (Church and Rau, 1995; Obermeier, 1989).

This discussion by Bill Manaris, published in 1998, appears to be based primarily on what existed around 1996. Thus, by the time the discussion here is published and read, the state of the art in the technology of 'discourse management' could quite possibly be further advanced.

The benefits of having an AI program testing conditions 2 and 3 above, as opposed to a panel of human experts, would be fairly straightforward. First, the program would have no human affiliations with any of the authors of the articles in question, whereas a panel of experts certainly would. Secondly, the program would simply carry out its algorithms for each article examined, obtaining objective measures without biases toward particular subfields of economics or with regard to particular topics of discussion.

In order for an AI program to test for condition 2, it would need to be given an encyclopedic background in basic economics, and a repertoire of concepts commonly associated with formal modeling, such as 'steady-state conditions', 'maximization conditional on . . .' 'proposition', 'lemma', and so on. This should not be difficult, given the current state of the art, and of course, every article examined would need to be an electronic file for input into the program. With the proper set-up, which would not be simple, but would certainly be feasible, the program should be able to make a determination quickly as to whether an article is primarily a presentation of a formal model, or is something different. Once the set-up is working, such determinations might be able to be made very quickly for a single article, and perhaps could be done in a matter of hours for hundreds of articles. A simple count, by human or machine, would then illustrate whether articles on certain topics in top journals are more oriented to formalism than articles on the same topics in secondary journals.

Similar techniques could be used in testing condition 3, although more abstract concepts are involved, which would probably make the program more difficult to set up. As an example, concepts such as 'unrealistic assumptions' appearing in the articles could be flagged by the program. If done properly, tests of condition 3 should yield reliable counts of the number of articles that question, or raise concerns about, the strong assumptions made by other authors on the same topic.

It should be emphasized, however, that subfields which meet conditions 1–4 on sociological support for empty formalism, may, in fact, not be subject to empty formalism. Conditions 1–4 are 'indicators' of potential problems, but the final assessment of those problems should continue to be carried out by humans. Unlike AI programs, humans are still the only ones capable of *understanding* the information acquired while testing conditions 1–4. Such techniques, in any case, should tell us much more about whether particular fields or topics in economics suffer from sociological support for empty formalism. If and when those topics do, efforts should be made to eliminate such support, if possible, which might thereby allow for more scientific, and more useful, discourse.


## FOR GOODNESS SAKE, LET'S GET *PHYSICAL!*

In 1970, in his presidential address to the American Economic Association, Wassily Leontief said the following about the economic profession:

> Continued preoccupation with imaginary, hypothetical, rather than with observable reality has gradually led to a distortion of the informal valuation scale used in our academic community to assess and rank the scientific performance of its members. Empirical analysis, according to this scale, gets a lower rating than formal mathematical reasoning. Devising a new statistical procedure, however tenuous, that makes it possible to squeeze out one more unknown parameter from a given set of data, is judged a greater scientific achievement than the successful search for additional information that would permit us to measure the magnitude of the same parameter in a less ingenious, but more reliable way. This despite the fact that in all too many instances sophisticated statistical analysis is performed on a set of data whose exact meaning and validity are unknown to the author or rather so well known to him that at the very end he warns the reader not to take the material conclusions of the entire "exercise" seriously.
>
> A natural Darwinian feedback operating through selection of academic personnel contributes greatly to the perpetuation of this state of affairs.[3]

Clearly, much of the criticism I have put forth in this book is not new to the profession, and it has been recognized as much by prominent economists as by less-than-prominent economists. In short, the general problem with modern economics is empty formalism, that is, highly mathematical theory for its own sake, most of which has little practical value. A corollary to this problem is the lack of progress in the economic study of technological change, in spite of the growing importance of this subfield. Critics have attacked the problem from a wide variety of perspectives – from the philosophy of science, the incentives underlying what economists do, the sociology of the profession, the personality traits of economists, the institutions that fund economic research, etc. What I hope to offer that is new is a more focused analysis on methods of measurement, in which an important distinction is made between physical and metaphysical units of measurement.

Regardless of how the state of economics came to be, what keeps it intact in terms of funding, in spite of its empty formalism, is the supposed application of that formalism *to data*. Academic scholars may admire each other for their mathematical modeling alone, but funding institutions who give those scholars grants want more than systems of equations to come out of their research – they want empirical findings. The game then, is to provide those findings, but by using highly sophisticated methods that entitle the same scholars to similar funds in the future. In essence, empirical work is the job that 'pays the rent'; while sophisticated modeling, combined with cronyism in the peer-review process, is the system that is used to make sure that 'no one else gets the job'. In turn, funding organizations could be:

1. unaware of the game entirely (because, perhaps, they do not have the expertise within their own organizations to observe the game being played – a factor that is probably recognized much more within the economics profession than within those funding organizations themselves);
2. aware of the game but apathetic about changing it (especially if the findings acquired by the research match their own specific agenda); or
3. may be fiercely opposed to the game but powerless to stop it (for example, they may fear that, if they commissioned alternative researchers, those researchers might be discredited by the more prominent researchers who had not been offered the job).

The pillars that hold up 'The Game' are the acquisition, interpretation, and manipulation of data – *again, it is in the guise of supposedly-useful, empirical findings that the vast majority of economic discourse is funded.* Yet, whatever weak relationship those data have with the real world, that relationship is being eroded, with each passing day, by the process of technological change. Economists will never be able to correctly theorize about how the real world works, if they cannot even *observe* how the real world works. The chain is so weak at every link that the only logical solution is to start fresh *from the beginning.* Economists need to have the right kind of data – data that are physically quantifiable and have direct bearing on important economic phenomena.

As discussed in Parts 2 and 3 of this book, and especially in Chapter 6, the economic study of technological change *effectively neglects the physical world* except when extremely specific innovations are being analyzed, or when broad anecdotal observations are being made. That is, there are no physical variables, and for that matter hardly any measurable economic variables that are not tautologically defined. Consider again the list in Chapter 9 of the classification of measures on the basis of their affinity to physical meaning:

1. *elementary/physical* units of measure; for example, mass, energy, moles, volume, time

2. *elementary/mathematical*: bits of information, number of calculations, surface area
3. *elementary/functional*: calories, floor space, passenger-miles
4. *counts of complex physical objects*: vehicles, rooms, refrigerators
5. *counts of contractual agreements*: software licenses, telephone lines, patents, magazine subscriptions
6. *pecuniary measures regardless of physical properties*: the rental costs of capital services.

Nearly all measured economic variables that enter into economic analyses would belong in categories 4–6. Exceptions, like energy consumption levels in natural-resource and industrial-organization studies, physical characteristics in Lancastrian hedonic-price studies, and life-expectancy rates in economic development studies are relatively few and far between. Even when economic concepts have natural physical units, such as land having the physical unit of acres, economists often disregard those units for the sake of convenience in data collection, for example, the 'quantity of land' is often measured in terms of land value – which reveals neither physical quantity, nor inherent economic value per unit, but some obscure, ambiguous combination of both. When questioned about this problem, economists often answer that physical quantity is less meaningful to economics as economic value. That answer is irrelevant – physical quantity is essential for understanding technological change and the value *per physical unit*, because, as argued in Chapter 7, it is true quality change that is most important. As argued repeatedly in Chapter 9, *measurement of physical quantity neither precludes the measurement of economic value, nor suggests that economic value is not relevant.* What is needed is both, just as both current and potential are needed in order to understand electricity.

Economists have been inclined to use only a single parameter to measure a concept, only because that is the way they have been trained to think. This inclination has had a poisoning effect on economic thought. Labor, for example, when it is measured in units of time, *is* physically meaningful, because time is physically meaningful. Yet, the economic relevance of labor is tied to the 'productivity' of labor. Both are essential. The first is useful for understanding employment levels. The second is needed for examining overall productivity in the economy, as well as changes in wages, which in turn has bearing on economic inequality. The pointless quest for a single parameter for labor, such as 'human capital', appears to be rooted in the extremely simplistic and misguided idea that, because hours of labor do not capture labor quality, something 'better' must be developed. This kind of thinking, if one could call it thinking, is ludicrous. Science has proven that useful knowledge is often achievable through a process of dissection. If any progress is going to be made in economics, then economic concepts must be dissected into component, causal elements. Labor is made up of hours, and what is done in those hours. A scientist would not dismiss the hours component for the sake of having a single variable that could emphasize the other component.

In science, water cannot be said to be made out of oxygen only because most of it, in terms of molecular weight, is made out of oxygen. It cannot be said to be made out of hydrogen because most of it, in terms of number of atoms, is made out of hydrogen. Chemists, as scientists, simply know better than to concern themselves with the foolishness of choosing incomplete units of measure, simply for the sake of emphasizing the relative importance of one component of a phenomenon over another component. From a *scientific* – and economic – perspective, labor, capital, raw materials, natural resources, entrepreneurship, and so on, are neither made out of physical characteristics alone, nor economic value alone, but both. Therefore, both quantity, and quality per unit quantity, must be measured separately. Yes, this gives economists more homework to do. That is just too bad – it is required for the course.

## EQUILIBRIUM AS LARGELY AN ANACHRONISTIC PURSUIT

Equilibrium may be defined simply as a tendency for something to remain unchanged, and when it is changed, a tendency for it to go back to its original state. A marble in the center of a concave bowl is a typical example. If the marble is disturbed, it will move around a bit, but eventually wind up in the same resting place. Equilibrium is an essential concept in economics, allowing for the derivation of the equilibrium price and quantity of a market, the equilibrium rate of growth according to a specific model, the equilibrium rate of unemployment, and so on. Equilibrium in biochemistry is largely described by homeostasis, in which the body of an organism works towards maintaining constant concentrations of solvents in bodily fluids. As many know, the concept of equilibrium is essential in all fields of science.

In economics, however, equilibrium may be overrated as an area of research. In particular, considerable attention and resources have been spent on the movements of markets toward or away from equilibrium. Because such movements are difficult to observe directly in the real world, they have often been studied in artifically-created settings. Such studies have included work in experimental economics, in which students have been typically hired to play an auction game in a classroom (as discussed in Chapter 3), where their individual bids are observed. Alternative studies have also recently included work on computer simulations of 'artifical societies' in which a sophisticated computer program generates and aggregates the behaviour of hypothetical 'agents' who act according to preselected parameters, behavioral rules, and changing components of an artificial 'environment'.[4]

These studies are sometimes relevant to policy decision making, especially when they demonstate the effects that alternative trading or auction rules may have, thereby providing useful information for establishing the most efficient and/or most equitable rules. However, as mentioned in Chapter 3, in most cases the problem is that the subjects (in the case of humans) or the agents (in the case of computer simulations) have properties that are distinctly different from the real entities that are supposed to be studied. Students are used in place of genuine stock traders, for example, because they are much cheaper to hire. Likewise, computer-simulated agents in contrast to humans, are endowed with extremely simple rules of behavior, and 'placed' in extremely simple artificial environments. Such studies argue that they are trying to extract general principles of how economic equilibria are established. In truth, they are often generating highly mathematical results, for an audience within their own subfield, and offer little insight into the real world. Yet, ironically, because these new methods of inquiry – experimentation and advanced computer simulation – convey an image of science to a relatively unscientific audience, as such they are heralded as new 'economic science'.

For reasons already provided, these new inquiries into equilibrium are largely unscientific in their own right. However, the continued preoccupaton with equilibrium in economic thought has a worse consequence: it distracts thought away from technological change – the most important force leading to long-run economic growth.

To be more specific, studies of how economies (or individual markets) approach, achieve, and maintain equilibrium, requires a framework in which everything is prearranged: the model, to begin with, is 'specified' so that everything that will happen follows directly from a pre-established information set. It is analogous to dropping a rock from a mountain and observing its path as it rolls down – a path that was predetermined by the rock's shape, its precise position when it was dropped, and the mountain's detailed topography,

In the case of computer simulation, for instance, even if one does not know how agents will behave in the aggregate, their behavior is still predetermined by the initial rules programmed into them, and the programmed environment that was created. The scientific study of technological change, in contrast, requires a completely different framework, in which rules and circumstances are only partially known, and the most relevant rules and circumstances must be discovered as an integral part of the investigative process.

Moreover, when economies undergo technological change, as they surely do, the parameters that are used to determine a unique equilibrium are themselves changing in response to technological change. Demographic factors, for example, are changing as medicine improves life spans; and the relative prices of goods and services are surely changing in response to the cost reduction and quality improvement factors examined in Chapter 7. Preoccupation with equilibrium, when important parameters are constantly (and often rapidly) changing, is generally pointless. What needs to be studied most is how technological change is occurring, and what effects it has on the economy in real time.

## A NEED TO START FROM SCRATCH

As stated at the ends of Chapters 7–9, if economic analysis of technological change is to be at all scientific, and at all useful, it must now start from scratch. Economics must take on new methods of classifying data, new variables, new models, and new orientations. Capital must be partitioned into meaningful physical units. Goods and services must be classified into meaningful categories of functions served. Business interests in scientific advances must studied in multiple dimensions: in what industry does the advancement *occur*; what industry *is served* by that advancement; what functions are served by those industries? In short, what are the specific, real driving forces that account for such changes? Labor should be studied, not only in terms of how technology has affected it, but how labor skills and technology can best evolve together.

Technological change can only be studied properly if there is a sufficient amount of useful data, a clear understanding of what those data actually mean, and an understanding of the causal, physical processes that underlie how the values of those data came to exist. Without this, data are just fodder for econometric theorizing. Such theorizing, at best, simply accentuates common-sense arguments (with perhaps a marginal effect on public policy), and at worse, perpetuates self-serving, wasteful, discourse. Yes, common sense and econometric theory are both potentially useful in their own right, but when it comes to the study of technological change, economists can, and should, do much better – *they can study the difficult, but nonsubstitutable, subject matter of technological change itself.*

Economists, therefore, if they choose to study technological change, should have some knowledge of the science and engineering that underlie it. As discussed above, entirely new, interdisciplinary subfields should be developed – subfields that follow the technology, not the historical economic literature. Unfortunately, the infrastructure of scientific knowledge within the economics profession is not capable of supporting such an effort – economists must therefore learn to collaborate with natural scientists and engineers in their study of technological change. Such collaboration may be hindered by differences in culture – if it is, it is because the culture within the economics profession needs to become more scientific, as discussed at the outset of this book.

In broader, and yet more concrete terms, good science relies not only on scientific knowledge and proper scientific method, but on the trustworthiness of scientists. John Hardwig writes:

> Often . . . a scientific community has no alternative to trust, including trust in the character of its members. . . . Cooperation, not intellectual self-reliance, is the key virtue in any scientific community. But epistemic cooperation is possible only on the basis of reliance on the testimony of others. Scientific propositions often must be accepted on the basis of evidence that only others have. Consequently, much scientific knowledge rests on the moral and epistemic character of scientists. Unavoidably so. Not because "hard data" and logical arguments are not necessary, but because the relevant data and arguments are too extensive and too difficult to be had by any means other than testimony.[5]

However, as has often been said of economics, trustworthiness in economic discourse is difficult to achieve in a world that uses economic discourse to serve the purposes of advocacy. In this sense, it is true that economists are simply behaving as products of their environment. Along these lines, James Galbraith remarks:

> How should economists NOT do economics? Now there's a subject. All of those untenable assumptions, the dense and yet primitive algebra, those cardboard models, the faulty data, the bad writing, the hidden politics, the obsolete episteme, and all this in the best and brightest of what our profession offers! . . . Another reason not to preach lies in the darkling suspicion that the problem does not really lie in deficiencies of intellect, ethics or training common to professional economists as a class; that is to say, in anything for which the remedy of a sermon might be effective. . . . No, the fault dear economists is not in ourselves. It lies in our institutions, in the markets we and our deans and college and university presidents have created for our own services, in their bureaucratic structures and incentive structures and imperfections. . . . The remedy is not moral improvement, a futile quest, but revolution.[6]

Professor Galbraith's argument is well taken, but it is inadequte. *Economists cannot be excused for 'just following orders'.* The institutional revolution that he describes may be a great idea, but it will only be carried out if enough economists are persuaded to support it. Professor Galbraith objects to sermons – and rightfully so, as they are condescending – but the real difference between giving people a sermon and trying to convince them to join a revolution may only be semantic.

Advocates of revolutions in economics tend to have agendas beyond better economic discourse, for example, policies to redistribute wealth. Thus, efforts to improve economics have thus far been divided, and, as a result, thoroughly conquered. Economists who advocate more scientific economics, as an important end in itself, need to be very cautious about making friends with economists who have other ultimate objectives. Those other objectives may be just as important, and just as worthwhile, but if they confuse the debate about making economics more scientific, the debate would be more easily lost.

For those economists who do not know much about actual science, I suggest not thinking too much about what 'science' ultimately means, what 'economics' ultimately means, and so on. (In fact, it is debatable as to whether *anyone* could adequately address such questions.) In the absence of an immediate cure to all the problems I stated in this book, for the moment I suggest we all 'take something for the pain'. The drug that I would prescribe is adrenaline. Adrenaline is a hormone that facilitates intolerance and a strong urge to act quickly and aggressively. As economists, we know we can 'do the math', but as a group we have been much too complacent about whether we, or members of our 'team', are 'doing the *right* math'. Let us start now by being highly intolerant of the wrong math, and, from there, things should eventually fall into place.

## NOTES

1. Colander 1991, p. 163.
2. Maranis 1998.
3. Leontief 1971, p. 3.
4. Epstein and Axtell 1996, pp. 94-137.
5. Hardwig 1991.
6. Galbraith, James 1996.

# References

Acs, Gregory and Danziger, Sheldon (1993) 'Educational Attainment, Industrial Structure, and Male Earnings through the 1980s' *The Journal of Human Resources*, 28, pp. 618–48.

Acs, Z.J. (1996) 'Does Research Create Jobs?' *Challenge*, 39(1), pp. 32–8.

Adams, James D. (1990) 'Fundamental Stocks of Knowledge and Productivity Growth' *Journal of Political Economy*, 98, pp. 673–702.

Agliardi, Elettra (1995) 'Discontinuous Adoption Paths with Dynamic Scale Economies' *Economica*, 62, pp. 541–9.

Alexander, D. L. and Flynn, J.E. (1995) 'Innovation, R&D Productivity, and Global Market Share in the Pharmaceutical Industry' *Review of Industrial Organization*, 10(2), pp. 197–207.

Amirahmadi, H. and Wallace, C. (1995) 'Information Technology, the Organization of Production, and Regional Development' *Environment and Planning*, 27(11), pp. 1745–75.

Andersen, Esben Sloth (1999) 'FAQ of Evolutionary Economics' http://www.business.auc.dk/evolution/evolecon/faq.html; March 10.

Angel, D.P. and Savage, L.A. (1996) 'Global Localization? Japanese Research and Development Laboratories in the USA' *Environment and Planning*, 28(5), pp. 819–33.

Anton, J.J. and Yao, D.A. (1995) 'Start-ups, Spin-offs, and Internal Projects' *Journal of Law and Economics*, 11(2), pp. 362–78.

Archibald, Robert B. and Reece, William S. (1979) 'Partial Subindexes of Input Prices: The Case of Computer Services' *Southern Economic Journal*, 46, pp. 528–40.

Arnott, Richard and Small, Kenneth (1994) 'The Economics of Traffic Congestion' *American Scientist*, 82, pp. 446–55.

Arora, Ashish and Gambardella, Alfonson (1996) 'The Impact of NSF Support for Basic Research in Economics', report to the US National Science Foundation.

Ashcroft, B. et al. (1995) 'UK Innovation Policy: A Critique' *Regional Studies*, 29(30) pp. 307–11.

Athey, S. and Schmutzler, A. (1995) 'Product and Process Flexibility in an Innovative Environment' *Rand Journal of Economics*, 26(4), pp. 557–74.

Atkinson, Robert D. and Court, Randolph H. (1998) *The New Economy Index: Understanding America's Economic Transformation*, Washington, DC: Progressive Policy Institute.

Audretsch, David B. (1995a) 'Firm Profitability, Growth, and Innovation' *Review of Industrial Organization*, 10(5), pp. 579–88.

Audretsch, David B. (1995b) 'Innovation, Growth and Survival' *International Journal of Industrial Organization*, 13(4), pp. 441-57.

Audretsch, David B. (1995c) 'The Propensity to Exit and Innovation' *Review of Industrial Organization*, 10(5), pp. 589–605.

Audretsch, David B. and Feldman, M.P. (1996) 'Innovation Clusters and the Industry Life Cycle' *Review of Industrial Organization*, 11(2), pp. 253–73.

Audretsch, David B. and Feldman, M.P. (1996) 'R&D Spillovers and the Geography of Innovation and Production' *American Economic Review*, 86(3), pp. 630–40.

Bag, P.K. and Dasgupta, S. (1995) 'Strategic R&D Success Announcements' *Economics Letters*, 47(1), pp. 17–26.

Baker, S. and Treece, J. (1994) 'New U.S. Factory Jobs aren't in the Factor' *Business Week*, Special Issue on 21st Century Capitalism (11 November), p. 160.

Baldwin, John R. and Gellatly, Guy (1998) 'Are There High-Tech Industries or Only High-Tech Firms? Evidence from New Technology-Based Firms', Analytical Studies Branch – Research Paper Series, Statistics Canada: Ottawa.

Balk, Roger (1993) 'Public Values and Risk Assessment' in June MacDonald ed, *NABC Report 5, Agricultural Biotechnology: A Public Conversation About Risk*, National Agricultural Biotechnology Council, Ithica, NY.

Balmann, Alfons, et al. (1996) 'Path Dependence Without Increasing Returns to Scale and Network Externalities' *Journal of Economic Behavior and Organization*, 29(1), pp. 159–72.

Baltagi, B.H. et al. (1995) 'The Measurement of Firm-Specific Indexes of Technical Change' *Review of Economics and Statistics*, 77(4), pp. 654–63.

Basant, R. and Fikkert, B. (1996) 'The Effects of R&D, Foreign Technology Purchase, and Domestic and International Spillovers on Productivity in Indian Firms' *Review of Economics and Statistics*, 78(2), pp. 187–99.

Bashin, M. (1995) 'A Necessary Factor for Creating Advanced Technologies' *Problems of Economic Transition*, 38(12), pp. 56–64.

Beach, E. Douglas and Carlson, Gerald A. (1993) 'A Hedonic Analysis of Herbicides: Do User Safety and Water Quality Matter?' *American Journal of Agricultural Economics*, 75, pp. 612–23.

Beed, Clive (1991) 'Philosophy of Science and Contempory Economics: An Overview' *Journal of Post Keynesian Economics* 13(4), pp. 459–94.

Berndt, Ernst et al. (1993) 'Price Indices for Microcomputers: An Exploratory Study' in M. Foss et al. (eds), *Price Measurements and Their Uses, Studies in Income and Wealth* Vol. 57, University of Chicago Press, pp. 63–93.

Berndt, Ernst R. et al. (1995) 'Econometric Estimates of Price Indices for Personal Computers in the 1990s' *Journal of Econometrics*, 68, pp. 243–68.

Bernstein, Jeffrey I. and Yan, Xiaoyi (1996) 'Canadian-Japanese R&D Spillovers and Productivity Growth' *Applied Economics Letters*, 3(12), pp. 763-7.

Bertschek, I. (1995) 'Product and Process Innovation as a Response to Increasing Import and Foreign Direct Investment' *Journal of Industrial Economics*, 43(4), pp. 341–57.

Bhagwati, Jagdish and Srinivasan, T.N. (1984) 'Immiserizing Growth' in *Lectures on International Trade*, Cambridge, Massachusetts: The MIT Press.

Bhattacharjya, A.S. (1996) 'Composition of R&D and Technological Cycles' *Journal of Economic Dynamics and Control*, 20(1–3), pp. 445–70.

Birchenhall, Chris (1995) 'Modular Technical Change and Genetic Algorithms' *Computational Economics*, 8(3), pp. 233–53.

Blank, Rebecca M. (1991) 'The Effects of Double-Blind versus Single-Blind Reviewing: Experimental Evidence from *The American Economic Review*' *American Economic Review*, 81(5), pp. 1041–67.

Blaug, Mark (1992) *The Methodology of Economics or How Economists Explain*, Cambridge: Cambridge University Press.

Bloch, F. and Markowitz, P. (1996) 'Optimal Disclosure Delay in Multistage R&D Competition' *International Journal of Industrial Organization*, 14(2), pp. 159–79.

Bloom, Floyd E. (1995) 'Scientific Conduct: Contrasts on a Gray Scale' *Science*, 268, June 23, p. 1679.

Board on Science, Technology, and Economic Policy (1999) *Securing America's Industrial Strength*, National Research Council of the National Academy of Sciences, Washington, DC: National Academy Press.

Bresnahan, T.F. and Trajtenberg, M. (1995) 'General Purpose Technologies: "Engines of Growth"?' *Journal of Econometrics*, 65, pp. 83–108.

Brown, J.H. (1995) 'Diffusion of a Durable Good Innovation: The Case of High Bypass Turbojet Engines' *Review of Industrial Organization*, 10(10) pp. 33–40.

Brynjolfsson, E. and Hitt, L. (1986) 'Measuring the Spillovers from Technical Advance' *American Economic Review*, 76(4), pp. 741–55.

Caballero, R.J. and Hammour, M.L. (1994) 'The Cleansing Effect of Recessions' *American Economic Review*, 84(5), pp. 1350–68.

Cagan, P. (1965) 'Measuring Quality Change and the Purchasing Power of Money: An Exploratory Study of Automobiles' *National Banking Review*, 3, pp. 217–36.

Callan, Bénédicte et al. (1997) *Exporting U.S. High Tech: Facts and Fiction about the Globalization of Industrial R&D*, New York: Council of Foreign Relations, Inc.

Cale, E.G. et al. (1979) 'Price/Performance Patterns of U.S. Computer Systems' *Communications of the Association for Computing Machinery (ACM)*, 22 (April), pp. 225–33.

Camerer, Colin (1987) 'Do Biases in Probability Judgment Matter in Markets? Experimental Evidence' *American Economic Review*, 77(5), December, pp. 981–97.

Camerer, Colin et al. (1989), 'The Curse of Knowledge in Economic Settings: An Experimental Analysis' *Journal of Political Economy*, 97, pp. 1232–54.

Carlson, Gerald A. and Hubbell, Bryan J. (1993) 'Can Safety, Production and Regulatory Characteristics Explain Use of Pesticides?' prepared for Western Economic Association Meeting, June 24, Lake Tahoe, Nevada.

Carson, C.S., et al. (1994) 'A Satellite Account for Research and Development' *Survey of Current Business*, 74(11), pp. 37–71.

Carson, Rachel (1962) *Silent Spring*, Boston: Houghton Mifflin Company.

Cartwright, David W. et al. (1985) 'Improved Deflations of Computers in the Gross National Product of the United States' Bureau of Economic Analysis Working Paper 4, Washington, DC: US Department of Commerce, December.

Casavola, P. et al. (1996) 'Technical Progress and Wage Dispersion in Italy: Evidence from Firms' Data' *Annales d'economie et de statistique*, (41–42), pp. 387–412.

Casti, John L. (1990) *Searching for Certainty: What Scientists Can Know About the Future*, New York: William Morrow and Company, Inc.

Center for Public Interest Law (1994) 'Privacy Rights Clearinghouse Fact Sheet No. 7' http://manymedia.com/prc/workplace.privacy.html.

Chen, E. Y. (1995) 'Technological Development and Co-operation in Greater China' *Managerial and Decision Economics*, 16(5), pp. 565–79.

Chen, I-Ming (1995), 'Modular Robotics Systems,' http://robby.caltech.edu/~jwb/modular.html.

Chen, Z. (1996) 'New Technology, Subsidies, and Competitive Advantage' *Southern Economic Journal*, 63(1), pp. 124–39.

Cheshire, Paul and Sheppard, Stephen (1995) 'On the Price of Land and the Value of Amenities' *Economica*, 62, pp. 247–67.

Chow, Gregory C. (1967) 'Technological Change and the Demand for Computers' *American Economic Review*, 57 (December), pp. 1117–30.

Church, K.W. and Rau, L.F. (1995) 'Commercial Applications of Natural Language Processing' *Commications of the ACM*, 38(11), 71–9.

Clark, D. et al. (1995) 'Telematics and Rural Businesses: An Evaluation of Uses, Potentials and Policy Implications' *Regional Studies*, 29(2), pp. 171–80.

Clark, Kim B. (1995) 'Notes on Modularity in Designe and Innovation in Advanced Ceramics and Engineering Plastics' Harvard Business School Working Paper, 95–073.

Clower, Robert (1989) 'The State of Economics: Hopeless but not Serious?' in David Colander and A.W. Coats (eds.) *The Spread of Economic Ideas*, New York, NY: Cambridge University Press, pp. 23–29.

Coase, Ronald H. (1992) 'The Lighthouse in Economics,' in Tyler Cowen, ed., *Public Goods and Market Failures: A Critical Examination*, New Brunswick, New Jersey, Transaction Publishers, pp. 255–77.

Cohen, W. M. and Klepper, S. (1996) 'Firm Size and the Nature of Innovation within Industries: The Case of Process and Product R&D' *Review of Economics and Statistics*, 78(2), pp. 232–43.

Colander, David (1989) 'The Invisible Hand of Truth' in David Colander and A.W. Coats (eds) *The Spread of Economic Ideas*, New York: Cambridge University Press, pp. 31–6.

Colander, David (1991) *Why Aren't Economists as Important as Garbagemen?: Essays on the State of Economics*, New York: M.E. Sharpe, Inc.

*Consumer Reports*, all issues, January 1937–December 1991.

Cooper, D. et al. (1993) 'Constant-Quality Price Indices for Agricultural Inputs: Tractors and Fertilizers Revisited' *Journal of Agricultural Economics*, 44(1), pp. 67–81.

Court, A. (1939) 'Hedonic Price Indexes with Automotive Examples' in *The Dynamics of Automobile Demand*, New York: General Motors Corporation.

Cowan, R. and Gunby, P. (1996) 'Sprayed to Death: Path Dependence, Lock-In and Pest Control Strategies' *Economic Journal*, 106(436), pp. 521–42.

Cropper, Maureen L. et al. (1988) 'On the Choice of Functional Form for Hedonic Price Functions' *Review of Economics and Statistics*, 70(4), pp. 668–75.

Cude, Brenda (1992) 'Making Consumer Education "Green": Issues and Approaches' *Proceedings of the 38th Annual Conferences of the American Council on Consumer Interests*, Toronto, Canada.

Curry, M.R. (1996) 'Data Protection and Intellectual Property: Information Systems and the Americanization of the New Europe' *Environment and Planning*, 28(5), pp. 891–908.

Dam, K.W. (1995) 'Some Economic Considerations in the Intellectual Property Protection of Software' *Journal Legal Studies*, 24(2), pp. 321–77.

Daugherty, P.J. et al. (1995) 'Predicting EDI Technology Adoption in Logistics Management: The Influence of Context and Structure' *Logistics and Transportation Review*, 31(4), pp. 309–24.

David, P.A. and Rothwell, P.A. (1996) 'Standardization, Diversity and Learning: Strategies for the Coevolution of Technology and Industrial Capacity' *International Journal of Industrial Organization*, 14(2), pp. 181–201.

De Bijl, Paul. W.J. and Goyal, Sanjeev (1995) 'Technological Change in Markets with Network Externalities' *International Journal of Industrial Organization*, 13(3), pp. 307–25.

De Bondt, R. and Henriques, R. (1995) 'Strategic Investment with Asymmetric Spillovers' *Canadian Journal of Economics*, 28(3), pp. 656–74.

de Silva, Harindra and Gruenstein, John M.L. (1988) 'Hedonic Index Estimation for Commercial Buildings: Assessors and Economists and the Parallel Search for the Optimal Functional Form' University of California, Berkeley; Institute of Business and Economic Research, Center for Real Estate and Urban Economics, Working Paper 88–154.

Deardorff, A.V. (1995) 'The Appropriate Extent of Intellectual Property Rights in Art' *Journal of Cultural Economics*, 19(2), pp. 199–230.

den Butter, F.A.G. and Wollmer, F.J. (1996) 'An Empirical Model for Endogenous Technology in the Netherlands' *Economic Modelling*, 13(1), pp. 15–40.

Dhrymes, P. (1970) 'Price and Quality Changes in Consumer Capital Goods: An Empirical Study' in Z. Griliches (ed.), *Price Indexes and Quality Change: Studies in New Methods of Measurement*, Cambridge, Massachusetts: Harvard University Press.

Diamond, Peter (1993) 'Testing the Internal Consistency of Contingent Valuation Surveys' Working Paper, Department of Economics, Cambridge, Massachusetts: Massachusetts Institute of Technology.

Dinan, Terry M. and Miranowski, John A. (1989) 'Estimating the Implicit Price of Energy Efficiency Improvements in the Residential Housing Market: A Hedonic Approach' *Journal of Urban Economics*, 25, pp. 52–67.

Dixon, A.J. and Seddighi, H.R. (1996) 'An Analysis of R&D Activities in North East England Manufacturing Firms: The Results of a Sample Survey' *Regional Studies*, 30(3), pp. 287–94.

Doi, N. (1996) 'Performance of Japanese Firms in Patented Inventions; an Analysis of Patents Granted in the U.S.' *Review of Industrial Organization*, 11(1), pp. 49–68.

Doms, Mark et al. (1995) 'Workers, Wages, and Technology' paper presented at the National Academy of Science, Washington, DC, Conference on 'The Effects of Technology and Innovation on Firm Performance and Employment', May 1–2.

Dosi, Giovanni (1982) 'Technological Paradignms and Technological Trajectories: A Suggested Interpretation of the Determinants and Directions of Technological Change' *Research Policy*, 11(3), pp. 147–62.

Dosi, Giovanni (1988) 'Sources, Procedures, and Microeconomic Effects of Innovation' *Journal of Economic Literature*, September, pp. 1120–71.

Dufournaud, C.M. et al. (1994) 'A Partial Equilibrium Analysis of the Impact of Introducing More-efficient Wood-Burning Stoves into Households in the Sahelian Region' *Environment and Planning*, 26(3), pp. 407–14.

Dulberger, Ellen R. (1989) 'The Application of a Hedonic Model to a Quality Adjusted Price Index for Computer Processors' in Dale W. Jorgenson and Ralph Landau (eds.), *Technology and Capital Formation*, Cambridge, Massachusetts: The MIT Press.

Duménil, Gerard and Lévy, Dominique (1995) 'A Stochastic Model of Technical Change: An Application to the US Economy (1869–1989)' *Metroeconomica*, 46(3), pp. 213–45.

Dunn, Peter (1994), 'Overview: Workshop on Labeling of Biotechnology Products' in *Labeling of Biotechnology Products*, Occasional Paper of the National Agricultural Biotechnology Council, Cornel University, Ithica, NY.

Eicher, Theo S. (1996) 'Interaction between Endogenous Human Capital and Technological Change' *Review of Economic Studies*, 63(1), pp. 127–44.

Eichner, Alfred S. (1983) 'Why Economics is not yet a Science' in Alfred S. Eichner (ed.), *Why Economics is not yet a Science*, Armonk, New York: M.E. Sharp.

Epstein, Joshua M. and Axtell, Robert (1996) *Growing Artificial Societies*, Washington, DC: The Brookings Institution.

Feenstra, Robert C. (1986) 'Gains from Trade in Differentiated Products: Japanese Compact Trucks' Cambridge, Massachusetts: National Bureau of Economic Research, Working Paper 1978.

Fellner, W. (1970) 'Trends in the Activities Generating Technological Progress' *American Economic Review*, 60(1), pp. 1–29.

Fisher, Franklin M. and Shell, Karl (1972) *The Economic Theory of Price Indices; Two Essays on the Effects of Taste, Quality, and Technological Change*, New York: Academic Press.

Fisher, Franklin M. et al. (1983) *Folded, Spindled and Mutilated: Economic Analysis and U.S. v. IBM*, Cambridge, Massachusetts: The MIT Press.

Flamm, Kenneth (1987) *Targeting the Computer*, Washington, DC: The Brookings Institution.

Foss, Murray (1963) 'The Utilization of Capital Equipment' *Survey of Current Business*, 43(6), pp. 8–16.

Frank, Bjorn (1996) 'On an Art without Copyright' *Kyklos*, 49(1), pp. 3–15.

Freeman, Christopher (1986) *The Economics of Industrial Innovation*, Cambridge, Massachusetts: The MIT Press.

Freeman, Christopher (1987) *Technology Policy and Economic Performance: Lessons from Japan*, London: Pinter.

Freeman, Christopher et al. (1995) 'Diffusion and the Employment Effects of Information and Communication Technology' *International Labor Review*, 134(4–5), pp. 587–603.

Frenkel, A. and Shefer, D. (1996) 'Modeling Regional Innovativeness and Innovation' *Annals of Regional Science*, 30(1), pp. 31–54.

Friedman, Daniel and Sunder, Shyam (1994) *Experimental Methods: A Primer for Economists*, New York: Cambridge University Press.

Friedman, Milton (1953) *Essays in Positive Economics*, Chicago: The University of Chicago Press.

Fuchs, Henry et al. (1995) 'Virtual Space Teleconferencing using a Sea of Cameras' Working Paper, Department of Computer Science, University of North Carolina at Chapel Hill.

Fuchs, Stephan (1992) *The Professional Quest for Truth: A Social Theory of Science and Knowledge*, Albany, NY: State University of New York Press.

Fuchs, Stephan (1993) 'A Sociological Theory of Scientific Change' *Social Forces*, 71(4), pp. 933–53.

Galbraith, James K. (1996) 'What is to be Done (about Economics)?' in S. Medema and W. Samuels (eds), *Foundations of Research in Economics: How Should Economists Do Economics?*, Aldershot, Hants, UK: Edward Elgar Publishing, Ltd.

Galbraith, John Kenneth (1958) *The Affluent Society*, New York, NY: Houghton Mifflin Company.

Gandal, N. and Rockett, K. (1995) 'Licensing a Sequence of Innovations' *Economics Letters*, 47(1), pp. 101–7.

Garrison, W.L. and Souleyrette, R.R. (1996) 'Transportation, Innovation, and Development: The Companion Innovation Hypothesis' *Logistics and Transportation Review*, 32(1), pp. 5–38.

Geroski, P.A. and Walters, C.F. (1995) 'Innovative Activity over the Business Cycle' *Economic Journal*, 105(431), pp. 916–28.

Giere, Ronald (1988) *Explaining Science: A Cognitive Approach*, Chicago: University of Chicago Press.

Gilley, Otis W. and Pace, R. Kelley (1995) 'Improving Hedonic Estimation with an Inequality Restricted Estimator' *Review of Economics and Statistics*, 609–21.

Gloersen, P. (1995) 'Modulation of Hemispheric Sea-Ice Cover by ENSO Events' *Nature*, 373, pp. 503–6.

Goel, R.K. (1995) 'Spillovers, Rivalry and R&D Investment' *Southern Economics Journal*, 62(1), pp. 71–6.

Goldberg, Ken (1995), 'Modular Robotics Lab', http://www.usc.edu/users/goldberg/mrl.html.

Goldin, C. and Katz, L.F. (1996) 'Technology, Skill, and the Wage Structure: Insights from the Past' *American Economic Review*, 86(2), pp. 252–57.

Gordon, Robert J. (1987) 'The Postwar Evolution of Computer Prices' National Bureau of Economic Research, Working Paper 2227 (April).

Gordon, Robert J. (1990) *The Measurement of Durable Goods Prices*, Chicago: University of Chicago Press.

Gould, D.M. and Gruben, W.C. (1996) 'The Role of Intellectual Property Rights in Economic Growth' *Journal of Development Economics*, 48(2), pp. 323–50.

Gowdy, John M. (1991) 'Economic Evolution and Selection: Old Controversies and New Approaches,' *International Journal of Social Economics*, 17(12), pp. 1–13.

Graves, Samuel B. (1989) 'Long Run Patterns of Corporate R&D Expenditure: A Descriptive Analysis of the Period 1965 to 1984,' *Technological Forecasting and Social Change*, 35, pp. 13–27.

Griliches, Zvi (1958) 'Research Costs and Social Returns: Hybrid Corn and Related Innovations' *Journal of Political Economy*, pp. 419–31.

Griliches, Zvi (1961) 'Hedonic Price Indexes for Automobiles: An Econometric Analysis of Quality Change' in *Price Statistics of the Federal Government*, General Series, No. 73, New York: National Bureau of Economic Research.

Griliches, Zvi (1990) 'Hedonic Price Indexes and the Measurement of Capital and Productivity: Some Historical Reflections' in E. Berndt and J. Triplett (eds), *Fifty Years of Economic Measurement: The Jubilee of the Conference on Research in Income and Wealth*, Chicago: University of Chicago Press, p. 197.

Griliches, Zvi (1994) 'Productivity, R&D, and the Data Constraint' *American Economic Review*, 84, pp. 1–23.

Griliches, Zvi (1995) 'Academic Research Underlying Industrial Innovations: Sources, Characteristics, and Financing' *The Review of Economics and Statistics*, 77(1), pp. 55–65.

Gu, Shulin (1996) 'The Emergence of New Technology Enterprises in China: A Study of Endogenous Capability Building via Restructuring' *Journal of Development Studies*, 32(4), pp. 475–505.

Hamermesh, Daniel S. (1992) 'The Young Economist's Guide to Professional Etiquette' *Journal of Economic Perspectives*, 6, Winter, pp. 169–79.

Hamermesh, Daniel S. (1994) 'Facts and Myths about Refereeing' *Journal of Economic Perspectives*, 8, Winter, pp. 153–63.

Hamit, F. (1993) *Virtual Reality and the Exploration of Cyberspace*, Carmel, Indiana: Sams Publishing.

Hardwig, John (1991) 'The Role of Trust in Knowledge' *Journal of Philosophy*, 88, pp. 693–700.

Harris, C. and Vickers, J. (1995) 'Innovation and Natural Resources: A Dynamic Game with Uncertainty' *Rand Journal of Economics*, 26(3), pp. 418–30.

Harris, R.I.D. and Trainor, M. (1995) 'Innovations and R&D in Northern Ireland Manufacturing: A Schumpeterian Approach' *Regional Studies*, 29(7), pp. 593–604.

Hausman, Daniel M. (1992) *The Inexact and Separate Science of Economics*, Cambridge, UK: Cambridge University Press.

Hayek, F.A. (1961) 'The Non Sequitur of the "Dependence Effect",' *Southern Economic Journal*, April.

Heertje, A. (1995) 'Observations on Technical Change and Paretian Welfare Economics' *De Economist*, 143(4), pp. 433–56.

Helpman, Elhanan and Trajtenberg, Manuel (1998), 'A Time to Sow and a Time to Reap: Growth Based on General Purpose Technologies' in Elhanan Helpman (ed.), *General Purpose Technologies and Economic Growth*, Cambridge, Massachusetts: The MIT Press, pp. 55–83.

Henderson, R. and Cockburn, I. (1996) 'Scale, Scope, and Spillovers: The Determinants of Research Productivity in Drug Discovery' *Rand Journal of Economics*, 27(1), pp. 32–59.

Hey, John D. and Loomes, Graham (1993) *Recent Developments in Experimental Economics: Volumes I and II*, Aldershot, Hants, UK: Edward Elgar Publishing, Ltd.

Hodson, Derek (1993) 'Re-thinking Old Ways: Towards a More Critical Approach to Practical Work in School Science' *Studies in Science Education*, 22, pp. 85–142.

Huang, Chung (1991) 'Organic Foods Attract Consumers for the Wrong Reasons' *Choices*, Third Quarter, pp. 18–21.

Huang, J. and Rozelle, S. (1996) 'Technological Change: Rediscovering the Engine of Productivity Growth in China's Rural Economy' *Journal of Development Economics*, 49(2), pp. 337–69.

Hughes, Kirsty (1988) 'The Interpretation and Measurement of R&D Intensity – A Note' *Research Policy*, 17, pp. 301–7.

Huizinga, H. (1995) 'Taxation and the Transfer of Technology by Multinational Firms' *Canadian Journal of Economics*, 28(3), pp. 648–55.

Hutter, Michael (1995) 'On the Construction of Property Rights in Aesthetic Ideas' *Journal of Cultural Economics*, 19(2), pp. 177–85.

Institute for Robotics (1995) 'MODRO, A Modular Robot System,' http://www.ifr.mavt.ethz.ch/projects/robotics/modro/modro.html.

Ionov, V. and Popov, A. (1995) 'Toward Defining the Effectiveness of New Technology' *Problems of Economic Transition*, 38(12), pp. 65–72.

Ito, Takatoshi, and Hirono, Keiko Nosse (1993) 'The Efficiency of the Tokyo Housing Market' *Monetary and Economic Studies*, 11(1), Institute for Monetary and Economic Studies, Bank of Japan.

Jaffe, Adam B. (1989) 'Real Effects of Academic Research' *American Economic Review*, 79(5), pp. 957–70.

Jaffe, Adam B. et al. (1993) 'Geographic Localization of Knowledge Spillovers as Evidenced by Patent Citations' *The Quarterly Journal of Economics*, 108(3), pp. 577–98.

Jensen, R. and Thursby, M. (1996) 'Patent Races, Product Standards, and International Competition' *International Economics Review*, 37(1), pp. 21–49.

Jin, J.Y. (1995) 'Innovation Announcement with Vertical Differentiation' *Journal of Economic Behavior and Organization*, 28(3), pp. 399–408.

Jones, Charles I. (1995) 'R&D-Based Models of Economic Growth' *Journal of Political Economy*, 103(4), pp. 759–84.

Jones, Charles I. and Williams, John C. (1997) 'Measuring the Social Return to R&D' Working paper: Stanford, California, Department of Economics, Stanford University; and Washington, DC: Board of Governors of the Federal Reserve System.

Jorgensen, Dale W. and Griliches, Zvi (1967) 'The Explanation of Productivity Change' *Review of Economic Studies*, 34(3), pp. 249–83.

Joshi, S. and Vonortas, N.S. (1996) 'Two-Stage R&D Competition: An Elasticity Characterization' *Southern Economics Journal*, 62(4), pp. 930–37.

*Journal of Evolutionary Economics* (1999), Springer LINK: 'Journal of Evolutionary Economics – Aims and Scope' http://link.springer.de/link/service/journals/00191/aims.htm, March 10.

Juran, Joseph M. (1992) *Juran on Quality by Design: The New Steps for Planning Quality into Goods and Services*, New York: The Free Press.

Justman, M. and Mehrez, A.A. (1996) 'A Welfare Analysis of Innovation in R&D Markets' *International Journal of Social Economics*, 23(2), pp. 52–65.

Karier, T. (1995) 'The R&D Gap' *Challenge*, 38(4), pp. 60–63.

Karl, D.M. et al. (1995) 'Ecosystem Changes in the North Pacific Subtropical Gyre Attributed to the 1991–92 El Niño' *Nature*, 373, pp. 230–234.

Keeports, David and Morier, Dean (1994) 'Teaching the Scientific Method' *Journal of College Science Teaching*, September/October, pp. 45–50.

Keller, W. (1996) 'Absorptive Capacity: On the Creation and Acquisition of Technology in Development' *Journal of Development Economics*, 49(1), pp. 199–227.

Kenny, S. (1995) 'Defining a National System of Innovation: Implications for Irish Industrial Development Policy' *Regional Studies*, 29(7), pp. 692–7.

Kholdy, S. (1995) 'Causality between Foreign Investment and Spillover Efficiency' *Applied Economics*, 27(8), pp. 745–9.

Khoroshilov, G. (1996) 'Innovation Activity in Machine Building' *Problems of Economic Transition*, 38(12), pp. 43–55.

Knight, Kenneth E. (1966) 'Changes in Computer Performance: A Historical View' *Datamation* (September), pp. 40–54.

Koboldt, C. (1995) 'Intellectual Property and Optimal Copyright Protection' *Journal of Cultural Economics*, 19(2), pp. 131–55.

Koeller, C.T. (1995) 'Innovation, Market Structure and Firm Size: A Simultaneous Equations Model' *Managerial and Decision Economics*, 16(3), pp. 259–69.

Kokko, A. et al. (1996) 'Local Technological Capability and Productivity Spillovers from FDI in the Uruguayan Manufacturing Sector' *Journal of Development Studies*, 32(4), pp. 602–11.

Konan, D. E. et al. (1995) 'Intellectual Property Rights in the Asian-Pacific Region: Problems, Patterns, and Policy' *Asian-Pacific Economics Literature*, 9(2), pp. 13–35.

Koomey, J.G. et al. (1996) 'Energy-Efficient Lighting: Market Data, Market Imperfections, and Policy Success' *Contemporary Economics Policy*, 14(3), pp. 98–111.

Krusell, P. and Ríos-Rull, J.V. (1996) 'Vested Interests in a Positive Theory of Stagnation and Growth' *Review of Economic Studies*, 63(2), pp. 301–29.

Kuchler, Fred et al. (1990) 'Regulatory Experience with Food Safety: Social Choice Implications for Recombinant DNA-Derived Animal Growth Hormones' in David Webber (ed.), *Biotechnology: Assessing Social Impacts and Policy Implications*, New York: Greenwood Press.

Kumar, N. (1996) 'Intellectual Property Protection, Market Orientation and Location of Overseas R&D Activities by Multinational Enterprises' *World Development*, 24(4), pp. 673–88.

Kuri Gaytán, A. (1995) 'Technological Change and Structuralist Analysis' *CEPAL Review*, (55), pp. 191–8.

La Croix, S.J. and Kawaura, A. (1996) 'Product Patent Reform and Its Impact on Korea's Pharmaceutical Industry' *International Economics Journal*, 10(1), pp. 109–24.

Ladd, George W. and Suvannunt, Veraphol (1976) 'A Model of Consumer Goods Characteristics' *American Journal of Agricultural Economics*, August, pp. 504–10.

Lancaster, Kelvin (1966) 'A New Approach to Consumer Theory' *Journal of Political Economy*, 74, pp. 132–56.

Lancaster, Kelvin (1971) *Consumer Demand: A New Approach*. New York: Columbia University Press.

Lancaster, Kelvin (1991) *Modern Consumer Theory*, Aldershot, Hants, UK: Edward Elgar Publishing, Ltd.

Lee, J.Y. and Mansfield, E. (1996) 'Intellectual Property Protection and U.S. Foreign Direct Investment' *Review of Economics and Statistics*, 78(2), pp. 181–6.

Leibenstein, Harvey (1980), *Beyond Economic Man: A New Foundation for Microeconomics*, Cambridge, Massachusetts: Harvard University Press.

Leontief, W. (1971), 'Theoretical Assumptions and Nonobserved Facts' *American Economic Review*, 61, pp. 1–7.

Leontief, W. (1995) 'The Long-Term Effects of Technological Change' *Challenge*, 38(4), pp. 57–9.

Lerner, J. (1995) 'Patenting in the Shadow of Competitors' *Journal of Law and Economics*, 38(2), pp. 463–95.

Leung, C.K. and Wu, C.T. (1995) 'Innovation Environment, R&D Linkages and Technology Development in Hong Kong' *Regional Studies*, 29(6), pp. 533–46.

Levitt, Theodore (1975) 'Marketing Myopia' *Harvard Business Review*, September–October.

Levy, David M. and Terleckyj, Nester E. (1982) 'Effects of Government R&D on Private R&D Investment and Productivity: A Macroeconomic Analysis' paper presented before the Annual Meetings of the Sourthern Economic Association, Atlanta, November 11.

Levy, F. and Murnane, R.J. (1996) 'With What Skills Are Computers a Complement' *American Economic Review*, 86(2), pp. 258–62.

Lewis, A. (1952) 'World Production, Prices and Trade, 1870–1960' *Manchester School of Economic and Social Studies*, 20(2), pp. 105–38.

Leyden, Dennis Patrick and Link, Albert N. (1991) 'Why are governmental R&D and private R&D complements?' *Applied Economics*, 23, pp. 1673–81.

Linstone, Harold A. (1999) *Decision Making for Technology Executives: Using Multiple Perspectives to Improve Performance*, Boston: Artech House.

Loginov, V. and Kulagin, A. (1995) 'Measures to Activate Innovation Policy' *Problems of Economic Transition*, 38(3), pp. 78–89.

MacPherson, A.D. (1994) 'The Impact of Industrial Process Innovation among Small Manufacturing Firms: Empirical Evidence from Western New York' *Environment and Planning*, 26(3), pp. 453–70.

MacQueen, H.L. and Peacock, A. (1995) 'Implementing Performing Rights' *Journal of Cultural Economics*, 19(2), pp. 157–75.

Magnet, M. (1994) 'The Productivity Payoff Arrives' *Fortune*, June 27, pp. 79–84.

Magnusen, Karl O. and Kroeck, K. Galen (1995) 'Videoconferencing Maximizes Recruiting' *HRMagazine* (August), pp. 70–72.

Maillat, D., et al. (1995) 'Technology District and Innovation: The Case of the Swiss Jura Arc' *Regional Studies*, 29(3), pp. 251–63.

Malone, M.S. (1994) 'Perpetual Motion Executives (Call them PMXs)' *Forbes* ASAP Issue, April 11.

Manaris, Bill (1998) 'Natural Language Processing: A Human-Computer Interaction Perspective' in Marvin V. Zelkowitz (ed.), *Advances in Computers, Vol. 47,* Academic Press, Inc., preprinted in http://www. cacs.usl.edu/~manaris/ publications/advances-in-computers-vol-47.html.

Mansfield, E. (1994) 'The Contributions of New Technology to the Economy' Paper presented at a conference on The Contributions of Research to the Economy, held by the American Enterprise Institute for Public Policy and Research, Washington, DC, October 3.

Martin, M.J. and Taylor, T.G. (1995) 'Evaluation of a Multimedia Extension Program in Honduras' *Economics Development Cultural Change*, 43(4), pp. 821–34.

Maskus, K.E. and Penubarti, M. (1995) 'How Trade-Related Are Intellectual Property Rights?' *Journal of International Economics*, 39(3–4), pp. 227–48.

Matsumura, T. and Ueda, M. (1996) 'Endogenous Timing in the Switching of Technology with the Marshallian Externalities' *Journal of Economics (Z. Nationalökon.)*, 63(1), pp. 41–56.

Matutes, C. et al. (1996) 'Optimal Patent Design and the Diffusion of Innovations' *Rand Journal of Economics*, 27(1), pp. 60–83.

Mayer, Thomas (1993) *Truth versus Precision in Economics*, Aldershot, Hants, UK: Edward Elgar Publishing, Ltd.

Maynes, E. Scott (1976) 'The Concept and Measurement of Product Quality' in Nestor E. Terleckyj (ed.), *Household Production and Consumption*, New York: National Bureau of Economic Research.

Mayr, Ernst (1988) *Toward a New Philosophy of Biology: Observations of an Evolutionist*, Cambridge, Massachusetts: The Belknap Press of Harvard University Press.

McCloskey, Donald N. (1985) *The Rhetoric of Economics,* Madison, Wisconsin: University of Wisconsin Press.

McCloskey, Donald N. (1995) 'Once Upon a Time There Was a Theory' *Scientific American*, 272(2), p. 25.

McCulloch, A. et al. (1996) 'Sustainable Development and Innovation: Bringing in the Scottish Voluntary Environmental Sector' *Regional Studies*, 30(3), pp. 305–10.

McCutchen, Charles W. (1991) 'Peer Review: Treacherous Servant, Disastrous Master' *Technology Review*, October, pp. 28–40.

McMillan, M. et al. (1980) 'An Extension of the Hedonic Approach for Estimating the Value of Quiet' *Land Economics*, 56, pp. 315–28.

McPhaden, M.J. (1995) 'The Tropical Atmosphere Ocean (TAO) Array is Completed' National Oceanic and Atmospheric Administration: Tropical Atmosphere Ocean (TAO) Project Overview, http://www.pmel.noaa.gov/toga-tao-overview.html.

Meadows, et al. (1992) *Beyond the Limits: Confronting Global Callapse, Envisioning a Sustainable Future*, Post Mills, Vermont: Chelsea Green Publishing Company.

Meghir, Costas et al. (1996) 'Job Creation, Technological Innovation and Adjustment Costs: Evidence from a Panel of British Firms,' *Annales D'Économie Statistique*, 41–42, pp. 255–74.

Menasse Noble, E.J. and Adler, J. (1996) 'Facilitating Location Independence with Computerized Conversational Systems' *Environment and Planning*, 28(2), pp. 223–35.

Merges, R.P. (1995) 'The Economic Impact of Intellectual Property Rights: An Overview and Guide' *Journal of Cultural Economics*, 19(2), pp. 103–17.

Merrill, Stephen A. and Cooper, Ronald S. (1999) 'Appendix B: Trends in Industrial Research and Development: Evidence from National Data Sources' in Board on Science, Technology, and Economic Policy (1999) *Securing America's Industrial Strength*, National Research Council of the National Academy of Sciences, Washington, D.C.: National Academy Press.

Metcalfe, J. Stan (1995) 'The Design of Order: Notes on Evolutionary Principles and the Dynamics of Innovation' *Revue Économique*, 46(6), pp. 1561–83.

Michaels, Robert (1979) 'Hedonic Prices and the Structure of the Digital Computer Industry' *The Journal of Industrial Economics*, 27 (March): pp. 263–75.

Miller, John and Neff, Gina (1997) 'The Revenge of the Classics: Rational Expectations Wins the Nobel Prize' in Breslow, Marc et al. (eds), *Real World Macro: Fourteenth Edition*, Somerville, Massachusetts: *Dollars and Sense*, Economic Affairs Bureau, Inc.

Mitroff, Ian I. (1974) *The Subjective Side of Science: A Philosophical Inquiry into the Psychology of the Apollo Moon Scientists*, New York: American Elsevier Publishing Company, Inc.

Morasch, K. (1995) 'Moral Hazard and Optimal Contract Form for R&D Cooperation' *Journal of Economic Behavior and Organization*, 28(1), pp. 63–78.

Moulton, Brent R. (1995) 'Interarea Indexes of the Cost of Shelter Using Hedonic Quality Adjustment Techniques' *Journal of Econometrics*, 68, pp. 181–204.

Mowery, David C. (1998) 'The Changing Structure of the US National Innovation System: Implications for International Conflict and Cooperation in R&D Policy' *Research Policy*, 27, pp. 639–54.

Mueller, Willard F. (1962) 'The Origins of the Basic Inventions Underlying Du Pont's Major Product and Process Innovations, 1920 to 1950' in National Bureau of Economic Research, *The Rate and Direction of Inventive Activity: Economic and Social Factors*, pp. 323–46.

Nadiri, M. Ishaq (1980) 'Contributions and Determinants of Research and Development Expenditures in the U.S. Manufacturing Industries' in George M. von Furstenberg (ed.), *Capital, Efficiency and Growth*, Cambridge, Massachusetts: Ballinger Publishing Company.

Nadiri, M. Ishaq (1993) 'Innovations and Technological Spillovers' National Bureau of Economic Research, Cambridge, Massachusetts, Working Paper No. 4423.

National Oceanic and Atmospheric Administration (1994) 'El Niño and Climate Prediction' *Reports to the Nation*, No. 3, Spring, University Corporation for Atmospheric Research, United States Government.

National Research Council (1994) 'Curbing Gridlock: Peak-Period Fees to Relieve Traffic Congestion' National Research Council Committee for Study on Urban Transportation Congestion Pricing, Transportation Research Board Special Report 242, Washington, DC: National Academy Press.

National Science Foundation (1995) 'A Renaissance in Robotics' *Frontiers: Newsletter of the National Science Foundation* (July/August), pp. 4–6.

Nelson, Julie A. (1991) 'Quality Variation and Quantity Aggregation in Consumer Demand for Food' *American Journal of Agricultural Economics*, 73(4), pp. 1204–12.

Nelson, Richard R. (1988) 'Modelling the Connections in the Cross Section Between Technical Progress and R&D Intensity' *RAND Journal of Economics*, 19(3), pp. 478–85.

Nelson, Richard R. (1995) 'Recent Evolutionary Theorizing about Economic Change' *Journal of Economic Literature*, 33 (March), pp. 48–90.

Nelson, Richard R. and Romer, Paul M. (1996) 'Science, Economic Growth, and Public Policy' *Challenge*, 39(2), pp. 9–21.

Nelson, Richard R. and Winter, Sidney (1982) *An Evolutionary Theory of Economic Change*, Cambridge, Massachusetts: The Belknap Press of Harvard University Press.

Niman, N.B. (1995) 'Picking Winners and Losers in the Global Technology Race' *Contemporary Economic Policy*, 13(3), pp. 77–87.

Niosi, J. et al. (1995) 'Technology Transfer to Developing Countries through Engineering Firms: The Canadian Experience' *World Development*, 23(10), pp. 1815–24.

Noland, M. (1996) 'Research and Development Activities and Trade Specialization in Japan' *Journal of Japanese International Economies*, 10(2), pp. 150–68.

Nordhaus, William D. (1994) 'Do Real Output and Real Wage Measures Capture Reality? The History of Lighting Suggests Not' Cowles Foundation Discussion Paper No. 1078, September.

Obermeier, K.K. (1989) *Natural Language Processing Technologies in Artificial Intelligence – The Science and Industry Perspective*, New York: John Wiley & Sons.

Occupational Safety and Health Administration (1995), http://www.osha. gov/newosha/reinvent/reinvent.html.

Office of Management and Budget (1987), Executive Office of the President, US Government, *Standard Industrial Classification Manual 1987*.

Ofori-Amoah, Benjamin (1995) 'Regional Impact on Technological Change: The Evolution and Development of the Twin-Wire Paper Machine from 1950 to 1988' *Environment and Planning*, 27(9), pp. 1503–20.

Oliner, Stephen D. (1993) 'Constant-Quality Price Change, Depreciation, and Retirement of Mainframe Computers,' in Murray F. Foss et al. (eds), *Price Measurements and Their Uses*, Chicago: University of Chicago Press.

Ohta, Makoto (1975) 'Production Technologies of the U.S. Boiler and Turbogenerator Industries and Hedonic Price Indexes for their Products: A Cost-Function Approach' *Journal of Political Economy*, 83(1), pp. 1–26.

Parente, S.L. (1995) 'A Model of Technology Adoption and Growth' *Economic Theory*, 6(3), pp. 405–20.

Park, W.G. (1995) 'International R&D Spillovers and OECD Economic Growth' *Economic Inquiry*, 33(4), pp. 571–91.

Pati, Gopal C. and Bailey, Eline K. (1995) 'Empowering People with Disabilities: Strategy and Human Resource Issues in Implementing the ADA' *Organizational Dynamics*, 23(3), pp. 54–69.

Payson, Steven (1991) *An Analysis of Long-Run Trends in the Prices of Goods and Services, As a Function of Evolutionary Changes in Quality, Production Costs, and Preferences*, PhD Dissertation, Columbia University.

Payson, Steven (1994a) *Quality Measurement in Economics: New Perspectives on the Evolution of Goods and Services*, Aldershot, Hants, UK: Edward Elgar Publishing, Ltd.

Payson, Steven (1994b), *Using Historical Information to Identify Consumer Concerns About Food Safety*, USDA, Economic Research Service, Technical Bulletin Number 1835.

Payson, Steven (1995) 'Product Evolution: What it is and How it can be Measured' *Eastern Economic Journal*, 21(2): pp. 247–62.

Payson, Steven (1996) 'Regardless of Philosophy, Economics Will Not Be a Science Until It Is *Based* on Science,' *Journal of Post Keynesian Economics*, 19(2), pp. 257–74.

Payson, Steven (1997a) 'Product Evolution and the Classification of Business Interest in Scientific Advances' *Knowledge and Policy*, Winter 1996–97, 9(4), pp. 3–26.

Payson, Steven (1997b) 'The Difficulty of Measuring Capital, Revisited; Does *Science* Offer an Alternative' *Technological Forecasting and Social Change*, 56(2), pp. 131–54.

Payson, Steven (1998) 'Quality Improvement versus Cost Reduction: A Broader Perspective on Evolutionary Economic Change' *Technology Analysis and Strategic Management*, 10(1), pp. 69–88.

Payson, Steven (1999) *National Patterns of R&D Resources: 1998*, Arlington, Virginia: National Science Foundation.

Perelman, S. (1995) 'R&D, Technological Progress and Efficiency Change in Industrial Activities' *Review of Income Wealth*, 41(3), pp. 349–66.

Peterson, D. et al. (1995) 'The Role of Climate in Estuarine Variability.' *American Scientist*, 83, pp. 58–67.

Pfirrmann, O. (1995) 'Path Analysis and Regional Development: Factors Affecting R&D in West German Small and Medium Sized Firms' *Regional Studies*, 29(7), pp. 605–18.

Pfouts, R.W. (1995) 'On the Interactions of Economics and Technology' *Atlantic Economic Journal*, 23(4), pp. 248–54.

Pianta, Mario (1995) 'Technology Isn't Working: Review Article' *International Review of Applied Economics*, 9(3), pp. 366–71.

Plein, L. (1990) 'Biotechnology: Issue Development and Evolution' in David Webber (ed.), *Biotechnology: Assessing Social Impacts and Policy Implications*, New York: Greenwood Press.

Prebisch, Raúl (1950) 'The Economic Development of Latin America and Its Principal Problems' presented at the United Nations Economic Conference on Latin America. Reprinted in *Economic Bulletin for Latin America*, (1962) 7, pp. 1–22.

Purohit, Debu (1994) 'What Should You Do When Your Competitors Send in the Clones?' *Marketing Science*, 13(4), pp. 392–411.

Raichle, M.E. (1994) 'Visualizing the Mind' *Scientific American*, 270(4), pp. 58–64.

Rasmussen, David W. and Zuehlke, Thomas W. (1990) 'On the Choice of Functional Form for Hedonic Price Functions' *Applied Economics*, 22, pp. 431–8.

Ratchford, Brian T. and Ford, Gary T. (1976) 'A Study of Prices and Market Shares in the Computer Mainframe Industry' *The Journal of Business*, 49, pp. 194–218.

Rausch, Lawrence and Bond, Jennifer Sue (1999) 'Technology-Knowledge diffusions patterns in the United States' in Inzelt, Annamária and Hilton, Jan (eds), *Technology Transfer: From Invention to Innovation*, Boston: Kluwer Academic Publishers.

Raut, L.K. (1995) 'R&D Spillover and Productivity Growth: Evidence from Indian Private Firms' *Journal of Development Economics*, 48(1), pp. 1–23.

Ravetz, Jerry (1995) 'Economics as an elite folk science: the suppression of uncertainty' *Journal of Post-Keynesian Economics*, Winter 1994–95, 17(2), pp.165–184.

Redding, S. (1996) 'The Low-Skill, Low-Quality Trap: Strategic Complementarities between Human Capital and R&D' *Economic Journal*, 106(435), pp. 458–70.

Reilly, John (1989) 'Consumer Effects of Biotechnology' *Agricultural Information Bulletin Number 581*, United States Department of Agriculture, Economic Research Service.

Richardson, R.S. and Gaisford, J.D. (1996) 'North-South Disputes over the Protection of Intellectual Property' *Canadian Journal of Economics*, 29 Special Issue, pp. S376–81.

Richman, L.S. (1994) 'The New Worker Elite' *Fortune*, August 22, pp. 56–66.

Robinson, Joan (1966) *The Accumulation of Capital*, New York: St. Martin's Press.

Robinson, Joan (1970) *Freedom and Necessity: An Introduction to the Study of Society*, London: George Allen & Unwin Ltd., p. 124.

Rockman, S. (1995) 'In School or Out: Technology, Equity, and the Future of Our Kids' *Communications of the ACM*, 38(6), pp. 25–9.

Romer, Paul M. (1986) 'Increasing Returns and Long-Run Growth' *Journal of Political Economy*, 94(5), pp. 1002–37.

Romer, Paul M. (1993) 'Implementing a National Technology Strategy with Self-Organizing Industry Investment Boards' *Brookings Papers: Microeconomics*, 2, pp. 345–399.

Rosen, Sherwin (1974) 'Hedonic Prices and Implicit Markets: Product Differentiation in Pure Competition' *Journal of Political Economy*, 82, pp. 34–55.

Rosenberg, Nathan (1992) *Inside the Black Box: Technology and Economics,* New York: Cambridge University Press.

Rosenberg, Nathan (1994) *Exploring the Black Box: Technology, Economics, and History*, New York: Cambridge University Press.

Rosenberg, Nathan, and Nelson, Richard R. (1994) 'American Universities and Technical Advance in Industry' *Research Policy,* 23, pp. 323–48.

Roush, W. (1995) 'Arguing over Why Johnny Can't Read' *Science*, 267, pp. 1896–99.

Sahal, Devendra (1981) *Patterns of Technological Innovation*, Reading, Massachusetts: Addison-Wesley Publishing Company, Inc.

Salomon, I. (1996) 'Telecommunications, Cittes and Technological Opportunism' *Annals of Regional Science*, 30(1), pp. 75–90.

Saloner, G. and Shepard, A. (1995) 'Adoption of Technologies with Network Effects: An Empirical Examination of the Adoption of Automated Teller Machines' *Rand Journal of Economics*, 26(3), pp. 479–501.

Salton, Gerard et al. (1994) 'Automatic Analysis, Theme Generation, and Summarization of Machine-Readable Texts' *Science,* 264, pp. 1421–6.

Samuelson, Paul A. (1983) *Foundations of Economic Analysis: Enlarged Edition*, Cambridge, Massachusetts: President and Fellows of Harvard College (first printed in 1947).

Sandman, Peter (1987), 'Risk Communication: Facing Public Outrage,' *EPA Journal*, November, pp. 21–2.

Schnabl, H. (1995) 'The Subsystem-MFA: A Qualitative Method for Analyzing National Innovation Systems-The Case of Germany' *Economic Systems Research*, 7(4), pp. 383–96.

Schumpeter, J. (1934) *The Theory of Economic Development*. Cambridge, Massachusetts: Cambridge University Press.

*Science* (1995) 'Conduct in Science' *Science*, 268 (June 23), pp. 1705–18.

Scotchmer, S. (1996) 'Protecting Early Innovators: Should Second-Generation Products be Patentable?' *Rand Journal of Economics*, 27(2), pp. 322–31.

Scott, J.T. (1995) 'Diversification and Industry Evolution' *Review of Industrial Organization*, 10(5), pp. 607–11.

*Sears Catalog*, Spring/Summer Issues, 1928, 1933, 1938, 1943, 1948, 1953, 1958, 1963, 1968, 1973, 1978, 1983, 1988, 1993.

Sen, Amartya (1985) *Commodities and Capabilities*, New York: Oxford University Press.

Sen, Amartya (1993) 'The Economics of Life and Death' *Scientific American*, May.

Senior, Nassau William (1827) 'Introductory Lecture on Political Economy' in *Collected Works of Nassau William Senior*, Bristol: Thoemmes Press, January 1999.

Sharpe, William F. (1969) *The Economics of the Computer*, New York and London: Columbia University Press.

Shepherd, Carl and Payson, Steven (1999a) *U.S. Corporate R&D – Volume 1: Top 500 Firms in R&D by Industry Category*, Washington, DC: US Department of Commerce and the National Science Foundation.

Shepherd, Carl and Payson, Steven (1999b) *U.S. Corporate R&D – Volume 2: Company Information on Top 500 Firms in R&D*, Washington, DC: National Science Foundation.

Sheremetyeva, S. and Nirenburg, S. (1996) *Designing the User Interface: Strategies for Effective Human-Computer Interaction,* 2nd edn, Reading, Massachusetts: Addison-Wesley.

Shiratsuka, Shigenori (1995) 'Effects of Quality Changes on the Price Index: A Hedonic Approach to the Estimation of a Quality Adjusted Price Index for Personal Computers in Japan' *Bank of Japan Monetary and Economic Studies*, 13(1), pp. 17–52.

Siegel, Donald (1994) 'Errors in Output Deflators Revisited: Unit Values and the Producer Price Index' *Economic Inquiry*, 1994 (January), pp. 11–32.

Siegel, Donald (1995) 'The Impact of Technological Change on Employment: Evidence from a Firm-Level Survey of Long Island Manufacturers.' Paper presented at the National Academy of Sciences Conference on *The Effects of Technology and Innovation on Firm Performance and Employment*, Washington, DC, May 1–2.

Simon, Herbert (1959) 'Theories of Decision-Making in Economics and Behavioral Science' *American Economic Review*, reprinted in Edwin Mansfield (ed.), *Microeconomics: Selected Readings*, 3rd edn, W.W. Norton & Company, New York, 1979, pp. 85–98.

Singer, Hans W. (1950) 'The Distribution of Gains Between Investing and Borrowing Countries' *American Economic Review, Papers and Proceedings*, 40 (May), pp. 473–85.

Sivitanidou, Rena and Sivitanides, P. (1995) 'The Intra-metropolitan Distribution of R&D Activities: Theory and Empirical Evidence' *Journal of Regional Science*, 35(3), pp. 391–415.

Sjöholm, F. (1996) 'International Transfer of Knowledge: The Role of International Trade and Geographic Proximity' *Weltwirtschaftliches Archiv*, 132(1), pp. 97–115.

Smallwood, David and Blaylock, James (1991), 'Consumer Demand for Food and Food Safety: Models and Applications' in Julie Caswell (ed.), *Economics of Food Safety*, New York: Elsevier Science Publishing Co., Inc.

Smith, Vernon (1982) 'Microeconomic Systems as an Experimental Science' *American Economic Review*, 72, pp. 923–55.

Solow, Robert M. (1957) 'Technological Change and the Aggregate Production Function' *Review of Economics and Statistics*, 39 (August), pp. 312–20.

Solow, Robert M. (1993) 'Faith, Hope, and Clarity' in David Colander and A.W. Coats (eds) *The Spread of Economic Ideas*, New York, NY: Cambridge University Press, pp. 37–41.

Spence, M. (1973) 'Job Market Signaling' *Quarterly Journal of Economics* (August).

Stadler, M. (1995) 'Geographical Transaction Costs and Regional Quality Ladders' *Journal of Institutional and Theoretical Economics*, 151(3), pp. 490–504.

Stavins, Joanna (1995) 'Model Entry and Exit in an Differentiated-Product Industry: The Personal Computer Market' *Review of Economics and Statistics*, 77(4), pp. 571–84.

Steenkamp, J.E.M. (1989) *Product Quality: An Investigation into the Concept and how it is Perceived by Others*, Assen, The Netherlands: Van Gorcum.

Stein, J.R. (1995) 'Towards a Socio-economic Framework on Technological Change' *International Journal of Social Economics*, 22(6), pp. 38–52.

Stephan, Paula E. (1996) 'The Economic of Science' *Journal of Economic Literature*, 34, pp. 1199–1235.

Stigum, Bernt (1990) *Toward a Formal Science of Economics: The Axiomatic Method in Economics and Econometrics*, Cambridge, Massachusetts: MIT Press.

Stokey, N.L. (1995) 'R&D and Economic Growth' *Review of Economic Studies*, 62(3), pp. 469–89.

Stone, R. (1995) 'Global Warming: If the Mercury Soars, So May Health Hazards' *Science*, 267, pp. 957–8.

Stoneman, Paul (1976) *Technological Diffusion and the Computer Revolution: The U.K. Experience*, Cambridge, UK: Cambridge University Press.

Stoneman, Paul (1978) 'Merger and Technological Progressiveness: The Case of the British Computer Industry' *Applied Economics*, 10, pp. 125–40.

Suarez-Villa, L. and Karlsson, C. (1996) 'The Development of Sweden's R&D-Intensive Electronics Industries: Exports, Outsourcing, and Territorial Distribution' *Environment and Planning*, 28(5), pp. 783–817.

Sullivan, R.L. (1994a) 'The Office that Never Closes' *Forbes*, May 23, pp. 212–13.

Sullivan, R.L. (1994b) 'Fast Lane' *Forbes*, July 4, pp. 112–16.

Tassey, Gregory (1999) *R&D Trends in the U.S. Economy: Strategies and Policy Implications*, US Government, National Institute of Standards and Technology, April.

Taylor, C.R. (1995) 'Digging for Golden Carrots: An Analysis of Research Tournaments' *American Economic Review*, 85(4), pp. 872–90.

Taylor, M.Z. (1995) 'Dominance through Technology: Is Japan Creating a Yen Bloc in Southeast Asia?' *Foreign Affairs*, 74(6), pp. 14–20.

Terleckyj, Nestor (1980) 'Direct and Indirect Effects of Industrial Research and Development on the Productivity Growth of Industries' in *New Developments in Productivity Measurement and Analysis*, Chicago: University of Chicago Press.

Teubal, M. (1996) 'R&D and Technology Policy in NICs as Learning Processes' *World Development*, 24(3), pp. 449–60.

Thach, Liz and Woodman, Richard W. (1994) 'Organizational Change and Information Technology: Managing on the Edge of Cyberspace' *Organizational Dynamics* (Summer), pp. 30–46.

*The Economist* (1994a) 'Evo-economics: Biology Meets the Dismal Science' January 7, pp. 93–5.

*The Economist* (1994b) 'Short Cuts' December 17, pp. 85–6.

Tisdell, Clem (1995) 'Transaction Costs and Markets for Science' *Technology and Know-How*, Australian Economic Papers, 34(64), pp. 136–51.

Trajtenberg, Manuel (1990) *Economic Analysis of Product Innovation: The Case of CT Scanners*, Cambridge, Massachusetts: Harvard University Press.

Triplett, Jack E. (1969) 'Automobiles and Hedonic Quality Measurement' *Journal of Political Economy*, 77, pp. 408–17.

Triplett, Jack E. (1989) 'Price and Technological Change in a Capital Good: A Survey of Research on Computers' in Jorgenson, Dale W. and Landau, Ralph (eds), *Technology and Capital Formation*, Cambridge, Massachusetts: The MIT Press.

Triplett, Jack (1993) 'Economic Concepts for Economic Classifications' *Survey of Current Business*, November, pp. 45–49.

Tushman, Michael and Anderson, Philip (1986) 'Technological Discontinuities and Organizational Environments' *Administrative Science Quarterly*, 31, pp. 439–65.

Tversky, A. et al. (1990) 'The Causes of Preference Reversal' *American Economic Review*, 80(1), pp. 204–17.

Uno, Kimio and Bartelmus, Peter (1998) 'Identifying Research Priority' in Uno, Kimio and Bartelmus, Peter (eds), *Environmental Accounting in Theory and Practice*, London: Kluwer Academic Publishers.

van den Bergh, J.C.J.M. et al. (1997) *Meta-Analysis in Environmental Economics*, London: Kluwer Academic Publishers.

van Dijk, T. (1995) 'Innovation Incentives through Third-Degree Price Discrimination in a Model of Patent Breadth' *Economics Letters*, 47(3–4), pp. 431–5.

van Dijk, T. (1996) 'Patent Height and Competition in Product Improvements'

*Journal of Industrial Economics*, 44(2), pp. 151–67.

van Ravenswaay, Eileen (1992) 'Public Perceptions of Food Safety: Implications for Emerging Agricultural Technologies' Staff Paper No. 92–71, Department of Agricultural Economics, Michigan State University, East Lansing, Michigan.

van Reenen, J. (1996) 'The Creation and Capture of Rents: Wages and Innovation in a Panel of U.K. Companies' *Quarterly Journal of Economics*, 111(1), pp. 195–226.

Varian, Hal R. (1984), *Microeconomic Analysis: Second Edition*, New York: W.W. Norton & Company.

Veblen, Thorstein (1898), 'Why is Economics Not an Evolutionary Science?' *Quarterly Journal of Economics*, May.

Vega-Redondo, F. (1996) 'Technological Change and Market Structure: An Evolutionary Approach' *International Journal of Industrial Organization*, 14(2), pp. 203–26.

Visser, Margaret (1993) 'Thinking About Food' in Burke, W. (ed.), *The Societal Issues of Food Biotechnology: Conference Proceedings*, North Carolina Biotechnology Center, Research Triangle Park, NC, pp. 5–21.

Wallace, William E. (1985) 'Industrial Policies and the Computer Industry' The Futures Group Working Paper 007, Glastonbury, CT: The Futures Group (March).

White, Robert W. and Watt, Norman F. (1973) *The Abnormal Personality*, New York: The Ronald Press Company.

Wiegand, J.P. (1996) 'Competitive Effects of Cable Copyright Law' *Antitrust Bulletin*, 41(1), pp. 61–78.

Wilde, Oscar (1891) *The Picture of Dorian Gray*, reprinted in Richard Ellmann (ed.), *The Picture of Dorian Gray and Other Writings by Oscar Wilde*, Bantam Books, New York.

Wisniewski, Edward J. and Medin, Douglas L. (1994) 'On the interaction of theory and data in concept learning, *Cognitive Science*, 18, pp. 221–81.

# Index

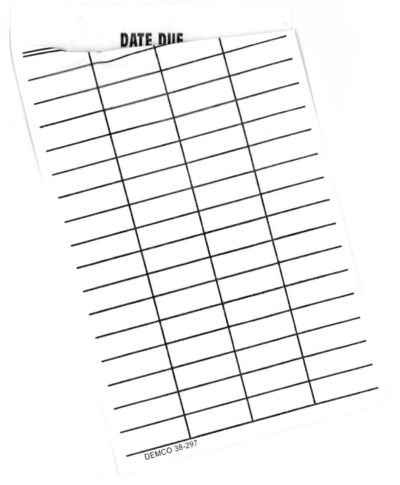

DATE DUE

DEMCO 38-297